SOLO
DOWN
THE
GANGES

SOLO DOWN
THE
GANGES

MANYA NORRIS

COPYRIGHT

ACKNOWLEDGEMENTS

My sincere thanks to my friends and their acquaintances who welcomed me into their homes. To Judge Basu who arranged my Christmas stay at Siuri Tourist Bungla and the Bank Manager who found me accommodation at the bidi factory. Thanks also to the nuns in Baktiapur, and to the Chandak family in Calcutta.

A sincere thankyou to the named and unnamed individuals in India, who were kind and hospitable on my way, and to all who donated to Lepra on my behalf.

My thanks to Sarah for her drawing of me on a bike and to Sainath for help with some of my sketches.

DEDICATION

To my Children

To Lepra

CONTENTS

MAPS and ILLUSTRATIONS

THE RIVER GANGES

Hindus consider the Ganges to be the most sacred river.

They revere her as the goddess Ganga, along the length of her 2525-kilometre course, from the Gangotri glacier in the Himalayas, to the mouth in the Bay of Bengal.

To bathe in the river is the lifetime aspiration of many Hindus.

Millions of people immerse themselves totally in its waters, confident that their sins will be forgiven and their release from the eternal cycle of rebirth will assure them a place in heaven.

To bathe at Hardwar and the confluences of the Ganga with other rivers, is regarded as particularly auspicious

Ironically the Ganges is also one of the most polluted rivers.
All varieties of aquatic species, not only people, are in peril.

The Ganges valley has been the epicentre of man and society in India since prehistoric times.

The river features in the myths, dreams, hopes and aspirations of the people.

***

*'The Ganges especially, is the river of India, a symbol
of India's age-long culture and civilisation, ever
-changing, ever-flowing and yet ever the same"*
J Nehru

i

Manya Norris

THE GANGES RIVER SYSTEM

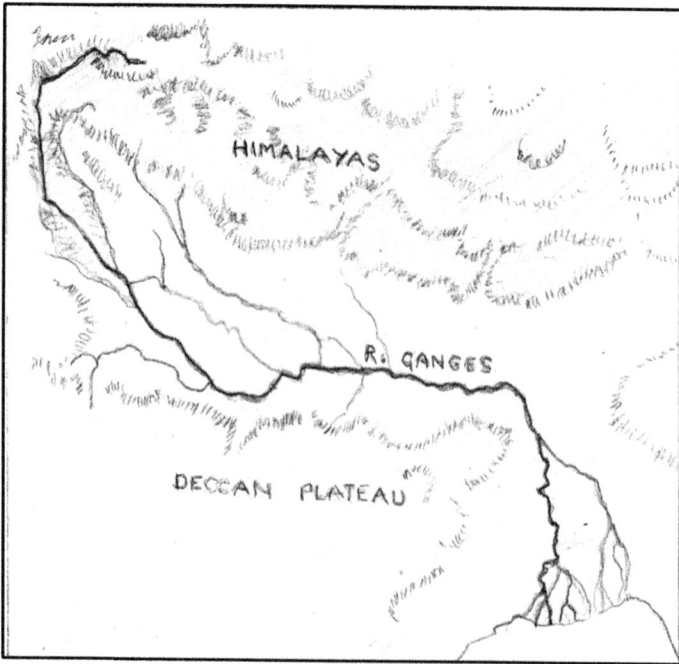

The Ganges, its tributaries
and delta.

Introduction

My Morris Minor failed yet another MOT and, on moving to Cambridge in 1986, where everybody seemed to have a bike, I decided it was time to take up cycling again. I heard that, now and again, the police held auctions of the bikes they had pulled out of the river Cam, those left hanging from railings around the market square, or found abandoned with wheels missing. I went to one such auction in a multi-story car park. I didn't know much about bikes, or their current prices. The auction began with normal-looking bikes but as it progressed there were cheaper offerings - incomplete bikes. If I didn't make a bid soon the sale would be over. I plucked up the courage and bid for half a Puch bike and a few minutes later for another half bike of the same make, hoping it would complement the first one.

Not knowing the make, I discovered that it had a three-speed hub gear, like the Sturmey-Archer I had on my Raleigh-Lenton bike when I was a teenager. My emerald-green, drop-handlebar "racing" bike was bought with the proceeds of a year's babysitting money, at five shillings a time. I was fifteen and used it to cycle regularly to school, to Girl Guides meetings, and to visit school friends around northwest London. In those days the North Circular Road around London had a cycle track, and I would go further afield and visit my brothers at their boarding school 20 miles away in Epping Forest. I only remember having one accident; when cycling uphill in a snowstorm, bent over my drop handlebars, I went into the back of a snow-covered stationary

1

lorry! I also remember being chased by a man on a bike in the forest, but I could ride faster than him and escaped. I didn't tell my mother or my brothers.

In 1952 we were still recovering from wartime austerity and, in common with many people, going away for a holiday hadn't become fashionable. I suppose I had an adventurous spirit and then, as now, felt that if I wanted something badly enough, I must do it myself. I had learned independence at an early age. My father died when I was seven. My mother went to work at a telephone exchange, and I looked after my brothers for several months, learning to cook dinner for them, change the baby, and do the clothes washing in the kitchen sink, with a 'scrubbing' board, and a block of 'Sunlight' soap. Telephonists had to work nights in those days. After several months the boys were found places in an orphanage, and I lived at home, going to the local convent school as a 'charity' student. I have a vivid memory of being frightened one night, alone in the house, by my own shadow, on the wall behind me, as I was going up stairs.

My widowed mother trusted me, aged fifteen, to take my thirteen-year-old brother on a cycle tour, staying at Youth Hostels which included Cheddar Gorge, Corfe Castle, and Swanage. In those days The Youth Hostel Association provided basic dormitory accommodation, but only for walkers and cyclists. We were required to work for our suppers, peeling potatoes or doing other allotted jobs. Years later, when two fellow university students were in a TB sanatorium in Berkshire, I would cycle 40 miles to see them and for the return journey, I begged for a lift on a bus that ran to London from the adjacent HM Prison. My youngest brother dismantled and sold bits of my beloved bike while I was at university.

Various parts of the Puch bikes were joined together, and feeling very pleased with myself, I re-learned what the gears did, as the bike was suspended by a rope, from the garage ceiling. The next step was to use the gears to help me ride to and from work. I had done a lot of gardening and DIY work over the previous ten years, renovating a derelict farmhouse, but nothing requiring leg or lung power. Going to work in Cambridge involved a nice downhill stretch and the rest was town riding. Coming home each day I made a note of how far I had been able to cycle up the hill before getting off the bike and walking to the top. Up to a certain drain cover, or some telegraph pole, and eventually I was able to manage all of the hilly section. Of course, I was a fair-weather cyclist and avoided strong winds, rain, ice, and snow.

My husband died on Christmas day 1988, only three months after his cancer was diagnosed. The girls had married, and the boys were at boarding school. I moved house but continued to work at the local council offices in the centre of Cambridge. I got to know more people and heard about 'Sunday bike rides' raising funds for various charities. I decided to have a go and after a few weeks of practising riding around the villages near me, and going further afield to find a hill or two, I enrolled for a thirty-mile ride to Long Melford, and back again.

I now needed to persuade colleagues to sponsor me and as two hundred people were working in my building, it was not very difficult to find some kind soul to promise a few shillings. I would buy the charity's tee shirt and that helped the fundraising too! Despite a history of back injuries, I found that cycling was the easiest form of exercise for me. Stanley, a colleague's husband, was a bike mechanic, in his spare time he sold second-hand bikes. He offered to make a more suitable bike for me, using an old frame with new components as necessary. A purple, man's, ex-Raleigh bike, was delivered to me with shifters, gear ratios, new cables, double-butted spokes, derailleur gears, and things I didn't know existed! Among these were ways to lessen the vibration of the road through the bike into my bones! There was a headset gizmo that dampened the vibration through the handlebars and another in the tube under my brand-new Brooke's leather saddle. I treated the leather every evening, after my practice runs, with an oil designed for horse saddles.

By the time I had ridden five hundred miles, it was moulded into the shape of my rear end, the unevenness reflecting my spinal curvature, with one side higher than the other. These two suspension gadgets were a godsend and a great help in reducing vibration-induced neck pain and later enabled me to ride on rough terrain in India. I bought a repair manual and treated myself to a monthly cycling magazine and slowly began to learn about my bike. An hour-long detour, with a hill, was included, on my way to work. I bought cycling shorts lined with chamois leather, a rainproof jacket, and a cycle computer. Having studied Geography, I could read an Ordnance Survey map, these were pre-'sat nav' days of course, so I was able to find my way around Cambridgeshire villages I had only heard the names of and not get lost! After work and at weekends, I went further afield to find steeper hills.

One evening while cycling in a very rural place, I could hear a 'sh-sh' noise. I listened, trying to find out what it was. It varied with my speed. I stopped to look for a puncture or a faulty valve. Whenever I got back on the bike the air-sucking noise came again. Eventually, I discovered that the chamois leather lining of my new cycling shorts had little holes in it, and they were causing the noise! The thing I dreaded most on my solitary training runs was getting a puncture. I didn't know anybody with a car who might come and rescue me so I decided to put some puncture-proof tape between the inner tubes and the rims. It was made of the same material used to make police jackets bulletproof. It took me a whole day to put the tyre back on the wheel, after inserting the tape, as I had no strength to stretch the tyres over the rims. A few plastic tyre levers got broken and I resorted to using forks from the kitchen drawer, as we had done as children. I also learned how to repair the chain and adjust the gears, everything taking, I was sure, twice as long as normal.

By the end of the summer 1992, my four 'Sunday rides' for Help the Aged, the World Wildlife Fund, Oxfam, and the Spastic Society had raised over £400.

It was on the annual 'London to Cambridge' bike ride that, as I cycled, I mused about the possibility of cycling day after day, for a week perhaps, raising money for a particular charity. I thought about places I'd like to discover. I was interested in the geography and history of the great river-valley civilizations and my mind ranged over them. I'd like to visit the Amazon but there were no roads, the USA would be too expensive for me, and I had already been to China. Remembering my recently discovered leprosy-treating charity, Lepra. I decided the Ganges valley in India would be an ideal choice. The British Leprosy Relief Association, now renamed Lepra, was started in 1924. It returned to India in 1989 providing equipment and training, while the Indian government paid salaries and the Japanese government provided the drugs.

I made it back to Cambridge in good time, finishing in thunder and lightning, wondering if I'd be electrocuted and unable to see a thing through the raindrops on my glasses, on what was reported the next day as having been the hottest day of the year. I was pleased with my first long-distance, 66 miles, with Lycra-clad cycle club cyclists, and many people younger than my 54 years. It was a professionally organised ride with marshals at road junctions, pointing out the route to be taken. I didn't stop at pubs, as many seemed to, fearing that I might not make it to Cambridge, so I stuck to my bottled water, bananas, and sandwiches. It was only in the last five miles, in the rain, that I began to feel tired, but the thought that my friends had sponsored me, spurred me on to the finishing line. This first 'event' raised £146 for research into children's diseases, thanks to the generosity of my family and friends.

I began to think an Indian bike ride was quite possible. Why leprosy? My husband, Tony, had TB, a microbiological cousin of leprosy, when he was seventeen, and was in the hospital with fellow Leeds University student, Ramesh. They both had operations and a year of medicine, returning to university to complete their degrees. Ramesh went back to India, and I married Tony. I had become re-acquainted with Ramesh in 1991 when I finally fulfilled my childhood

5

dream of visiting India. It had taken me 41 years to be able to take a seven-day package tour of the 'Golden Triangle'. Ramesh was now a businessman who could arrange to rescue me if I got into trouble, plus he had connections who might be persuaded to contribute to Lepra.

I read a few cycling books, bought German maps of North India, from a famous bookstore in London, as there were no Google Maps then, learned some more Hindi, and made plans. Working from the maps and various tourist manuals, I had to decide from the size of the town, whether there might be a 'tourist hostel' or Indian hotel of the kind that I could afford to stay at, bearing in mind that I was financing the fare, accommodation, and living costs myself. I set a limit of 80 km or 50 miles a day but this had to be exceeded when towns were far apart. From the start, built into the itinerary, were breaks of two days every week or so, for a rest and to do some sightseeing. My objective, my mission, was to see village India and spend time looking at their way of life, talking to as many people as possible, visiting sights of religious and historical interest on the way, and taking every opportunity to increase awareness about leprosy and that it could be cured.

When I told my Indian friends that I was going to cycle in Bihar they were horrified, as Bihar had the reputation of being one of the most lawless states in India. They regaled me with stories of women being beheaded on trains to steal their gold necklaces and I met a nun whose neck was severely cut when someone forcibly tugged her stainless-steel chain, thinking it was silver, and would break easily. There were often newspaper reports of kidnappings in Bihar and despite ransom money being paid, a dead body would be recovered. My Bihar friends never went out alone at night, even in a vehicle, there were always two of them. However, I was plainly not rich as I was riding a bike. I did, however, wear a gold cross and chain under my tee-shirt, so that in the event of a fatality I would be given a Christian burial!

My daughters were now married, and the boys were at university. I told them about my plans for Christmas 1994. I needed to take more than my allotted four weeks' annual leave. We were able to accrue extra days by working what was called 'flexitime', and if I joined two years' leave, on either side of the week-long Christmas-New Year holiday, plus some 'flexi-days' I could take twelve weeks' leave. South Cambridgeshire District Council agreed, and it was time to make more detailed plans

Working for South Cambridgeshire District Council I had a security pass with photo, position, various crests, and signatures on it. My office was next to the one in which these cards were produced, so one morning I went to see Tim. "Tim, you sponsored me for my Lepra ride down the Ganges, well...". I explained that I wanted a new photocard that described me as a Government Officer, leaving out the word 'local'. The word was changed on the computer and my pass was printed, a back-up form of identification, which proved useful when encountering Indian government officialdom. Apart from training rides after work I included lunch-time sessions at the YWCA gym just around the corner from my office. Being new to a gym I followed the recommended exercises and routines from posters on the walls. I liked the rowing machine best!

I had to find supporters, before the days when sponsoring was a common form of fundraising. It was 1994. There were no mobile phones and computers were expensive luxuries that most people couldn't afford. The internet was only just getting going. There were no internet fundraising sites, and no smartphones. My parish priest allowed me to speak from the pulpit. That was another learning curve, how much I could fit into three minutes, what to say about leprosy and I prepared sheets of paper with a space for name, address, and telephone number, and armed with a few clipboards and pencils, I stood at the back of the church, with my bike, wearing my helmet to be obvious, hoping to catch people as they left. My other source of support was my office, using my lunch breaks and the in-house magazine which I edited, to explain what I was going to do. The next target group was my village, Grantchester, going house to house, telling the residents about leprosy and my 2000-mile cycle ride to raise funds for its treatment. Handbills bearing my photo were made, entitled "Granny down the Ganges", and put through letter boxes. Radio Cambridge interviewed me and my picture was in the local paper.

Stanley offered to service the bike before I left but I had to arrange all the other things like clothes, equipment, injections, medicines, and not least a ticket for me and, if possible, a concession fare for my bike. I would need to reach Gangotri, the Himalayan town nearest the source of the Ganges before it was engulfed in winter snow, which I gathered was usually before the festival of Diwali. I booked my flight for October 22nd. I used a Cambridge travel centre to have a host of recommended immunizations and vaccinations, among them ones to prevent, or lessen, the effect of rabies, encephalitis, polio, meningitis, typhoid, and hepatitis. I was cheeky enough to ask for, and receive, a ten percent discount as they were expensive, some of them cost seventy pounds. I bought a portable mosquito net from them too.

For the bike I needed pannier bags, and frames to clip them to. I fixed two large panniers over the rear wheel, two small ones on the front wheel, and a bag on my handlebars. I had a mirror, a bell, and water bottles, clipped to the frame. I printed instructions on how to service and mend the bike in tiny script, carried spare cables, nuts and bolts, brake blocks, chain breaker and compact versions of the usual tools, degreaser and oil. All the nuts to secure the frames were special ones that would not shake undone with prolonged vibration. I wrote to some companies and received two tyres from Nokia and two chains from Sachs.

A self-inflating mattress, a fleece jacket, and a sleeping bag would be strapped to the rear luggage rack. I chose long cotton tights and oversized tee shirts to cycle in, as shorts and tight tops on a woman would offend Indian ideas of decorum. I packed one 'best' dress for sightseeing, and a skirt that could be screwed into a ball but would be useful if I had to resort to squatting to wee in the open. Surprisingly, I didn't feel the urge to pass urine, something that I was dreading as village women must go secretly before dawn or after dark. Men pee quite openly, anywhere. I lost water by sweating and every evening my clothes had a white tide mark of salt around the waist. For early morning starts, I had a woollen jumper with a cowl neck, which could be pulled over my head to cover my hair for temple visits. Three sets of underwear, plus skiing long-johns and ski top layer, three tee shirts, an anorak, and needle-cord trousers for the trekking part of my two-thousand-mile journey. I took some sandals for the evening and wore socks and trainers to cycle in. For the end and beginning photos, I had a new white t-shirt with the Lepra logo and a Lepra baseball cap. A purple cycle helmet completed my clothes list.

Bottled water was only available in large towns, and I would be in remote places, using irrigation ditches, natural streams, and village wells, to get water. Many villages had only 'open wells', large circular wells where the water was accessed by lowering a bucket into it. Newer wells would be a cement circle with a tube well and have a pump handle to bring water up into the spout. A company that supplied water filters to the British army kindly gifted me a filter bottle with an extra filter to remove the iodine taste. The unit was said to enable the most contaminated water to be drunk safely.

My reading of 'India Weekly' informed me that some areas of Bengal had water contaminated by arsenic, from their underground rocks. I asked if my unit could remove arsenic and was told "No!" I would have to use bottled water instead! Drinking water was necessary to avoid dehydration and I set my new watch's alarm to remind me to drink every hour. Besides my usual heart and blood pressure medicines (no recommended statins in those days),

I had a first-aid kit that included the usual things plus, sunscreen, and a cream that alleviated the itching of mosquito bites, which always seemed worse on the second or third day! I wasn't afraid of cockroaches which often appear in bathrooms. Rats, snakes, and scorpions were another matter, and I hoped that I wouldn't come into close contact with them. Once, when eating an apple, a monkey swung down from a tree and snatched it out of my hand. Monkeys, as well as dogs, may carry rabies and are to be guarded against, usually with a stick. A scratch could have led to being infected with rabies. I was given a high-pitched whistle device, to stop dogs from getting too near, but it works best at a distance of five feet, so I will have to put my bike between me and the dog.

While planning my route I discovered that the Ganges was approximately 2000 miles long so I set myself the target of raising £2000 for Lepra, the British Non-Government Organisation, who were hoping that it might be possible to eradicate the disease of leprosy by the year 2000. Two thousand, two thousand, two thousand! Lepra gave me a dedicated bank account to ensure all donations that were eligible, received charitable status and agreed to allocate my sponsorship specifically to their work in India, where in 1991 there were 75% of the world's leprosy cases, an estimated 3 million cases of the disease. I asked Lepra if there were any of their projects in the Ganges valley that I could visit. They told me about their new project at Bhabua in Bihar state

I planned to cycle an average of fifty miles a day, but this depended on the terrain, obviously much less in the mountains, and on the distances between places where I might find accommodation. I had been learning Hindi, on and off, since my first tourist visit to the Golden Triangle in 1991 and knew about a thousand words. The trouble was that my grammar was virtually non-existent and I'm sure my accent will be bewildering, however, at least I try! This northern part of India has many local languages and not more than one or two people in a village are likely to speak pure Hindi. Officials and government employees do and sometimes know English too. There is always sign language!

Photos of my family and Cambridge will be used to break the ice. A woman travelling alone is always a curiosity, and you get used to being stared at and asked all sorts of personal questions. Translation made for some funny responses. I was once told that I would be accosted when it was time to leave! He meant he would call me when the taxi arrived! On another occasion, an old man asked me, when surrounded by photographers, if I was in any moral danger! Generally, however, it was the bike that attracted the most attention.

I hoped to stay at cheap hotels or in a government 'tourist bungla' whenever possible and to take advantage of the government 'pilgrim' or 'rest houses' near my route through some of the poorest and most heavily populated rural areas of Uttar Pradesh, Bihar, and Bengal. My pilgrimage down the Ganges, including visits to some leprosy treatment centres, should take about ten weeks, but there was always the possibility of delay due to breakdowns - of me or the bike, so I had to factor in some leeway.

Three thousand kilometres of cycling for anything up to a hundred kilometres a day, requires about seven or eight hours of peddling, with stops for chai, bananas, and the occasional omelette. My average speed was 15 km per hour but it varied with the road surface and inclination. Following the Ganges from source to mouth fitted in with the religious explanation of its creation as the Goddess Ganga. King Bhagirathi prayed for a thousand years for the souls of his ancestors and was rewarded with the creation of river goddess Ganga. My visit to the new Lepra-funded leprosy centre at Bhabua in Bihar, was to be the focal point of my journey, my mission, my yatra.

Chapter 1

Getting to Gangotri

October 23, 1994

Delhi to Hardwar approx.150 miles

My plane arrived in Delhi on time. I was quickly through passport control, in the new building, making my way to the 'facilitation counter'. I asked for Air India and was shown my bike in its blue homemade, zipped bag, all ready for me on a trolley. I collected my pannier bags from the conveyor belt and wheeled the trolley to the exit with my cabin luggage of rucksack and bar bag. My bike tools, maps, water filter, and clothes were in the pannier bags and weighed 17 kilograms. The rucksack I used as cabin baggage held heavier paraphernalia and my bar bag had cameras, a dog alarm, two tins of tonic water saved from the plane, plus the usual personal items, tickets, money, and passport.

Indrasingh, Ramesh's driver, was waiting outside to meet me. The bike was bundled over the back seat into the very small boot of the Sierra Tata estate car. I had to take the back wheel off, as well as the front, to get it into the car and was fearful of upsetting the gears. Ramesh had arranged, without telling me, to bring Gopal, a security guard from his Rajasthan factory, to go with us to the Garhwal district, saying there had recently been political unrest and some deaths. I wasn't too pleased when I found out that Gopal was armed but all I saw was his long wooden stick, which proved useful in helping us get up the steep mountain paths. I sat in front and the security guard, Gopal, was cramped up in the boot with my bike.

Ramesh was booked into the Centaur hotel near the airport. After picking Ramesh up, we went to get Prem from her mother's house, and had breakfast there. Prem had a fair amount of luggage, including two heavy stainless-steel thermos flasks which were carried all week.

We set off about midday and arrived at Haridwar, 'the gateway to the gods' just before it got dark. At 10,000 feet above sea level, it lies at the foot of the Shivalik hills, where the Ganges comes down from the high Himalayas, passes through a gorge, and starts its slow descent across the plains of northern India to the Bay of Bengal. We checked in at the first five-star hotel we came across, on the outskirts of the town just before it got dark.

Prem and I went at once to the most important religious bathing ghat – flights of steps into the river. We had to hold onto the provided chains to avoid being swept downstream by the strong current. Prem said we were to immerse ourselves completely. I didn't want any water above my head, despite assurances from Prem that it was clean. The water temperature was like an outside swimming pool temperature in the UK. The bathing is done fully clothed, and while Prem was changing into dry clothes in a walled-off section, I saw a rat scurrying towards the water. Ramesh and Prem then took part in their religious ceremonies, led by a priest, a Pujari, reciting the names of their gods, the holy Ganges, and sipping 'holy water', plus putting it on their heads and praying for their ancestor's souls. At dusk, a conch shell was blown to mark the beginning of the 'Aarti' ceremony. There was much banging of gongs, chanting, and the waving of Christmas tree-shaped brass candelabra. The flames were burning cotton wicks soaked in ghee. Little boats of various sizes, made of laced together leaves, filled with marigold flower heads and roses,

13

with oiled cotton wicks, were lighted and launched onto the river. Prem set her leaf boat afloat on the water. It travelled quite a way, joining the hundreds of boats, large and small, which drowned in whirlpools, hit steps or crashed into the chains suspended from a bridge. There were about 2000 people gathered on both sides of this fast-flowing canalised part of the Ganges. It was a very pretty and quite moving ceremony.

We returned to the hotel, had dinner, and sorted out things for the trek, and things that I might like to be brought to me later. I shared a room with Prem and Ramesh had the adjoining room. I discovered that my camera had stopped working after taking some pictures on the plane. We tried unsuccessfully to find a photography shop in the market. Prem had the same camera, as she had admired mine on an earlier visit, and she very kindly offered me the use of it for the duration of my adventure.

October 24, 1994

Hardwar to Gangotri

We were up early to cover the twenty miles to Rishikesh, a less noisy and less commercialised town. We visited some temples, seeing a lovely white marble Shiva Lingam decorated with roses and other flowers. We visited another temple, showing all the stories of the Ramayana and Bhagavad Gita in pictures. Ramesh met a textile magnate friend from Calcutta and, having told him about my cycle pilgrimage, or yatra, Mr. Chandak invited me to stay with him and his family in Calcutta. We had a breakfast of 'dosa', dry wafer-thin pancakes, and sweet Indian masala spiced tea. Prem and I took a boat ride to the other bank of the river. Ramesh brought me a crucifix and chain, but sadly I lost it, probably when I washed my hair. Ramesh took a taxi back to Delhi. It cost 800 rupees. Prem and I went in the car with Gopal and Indrasingh.

We drove all day, reaching the very basic Gangotri Tourist Hostel at 11 pm. There was no electricity, no hot water, not even by the bucketful, a squat toilet and it was freezing cold. The only food available was cold by the time it arrived. We were given an oil lamp and shown our room. I was OK with my thermals, cord trousers, fleece jacket, and sleeping bag plus the provided cotton quilt. Prem wasn't very well-equipped clothes-wise, her thin sleeping bag was only supplemented by their thin quilt and her woollen shawl.

The river could be heard roaring outside!

Chapter 2

The Trek to Gau Mawk

October 25, 1994

Gangotri to Bhojbasa.

We woke at six o'clock. Prem discovered that our room led onto a veranda overlooking the turbulent Ganges – here called the Bhagirathi – swirling through white stone boulders, sculpted into sensuous curves by the force of the water, its suspended silt, and stones. The sun shone, the huge boulders glistened, and the river roared and foamed at our feet, as the Himalayas towered overhead.

After a potato pancake and sweet, 'boil everything together' Indian tea for breakfast, we set off up the dirt road to the 18th-century temple of Gangotri. King Bhagirathi is reputed to have meditated here, praying for his ancestors, and was rewarded by God sending the river Ganges to earth, its power being modified by passing the water through Shiva's hair. Prem said her prayers and received blessings from the temple pujari. River Ganges worship chiefly is about prayers for departed relatives.

Ramesh had, unbeknown to me, instructed his driver, Indrasingh, to hire donkeys to take us up to the source. I wanted to walk. Prem and I agreed to use the donkeys 'just to carry the luggage'. We set out on the pilgrim way with red powder 'tilak' marks on our foreheads, we trudged up some very high-treaded concrete steps, to meet the donkey men with two fillies, Ruby and Diamond, mother and daughter. Indrasingh stayed behind to rest after his three days of driving and to mind the car, my bike, and non-trekking luggage.

At first, the path was well-graded. Rough white stones bedded in silver sand, crossing small valleys on raised causeways of dry-stone walling, filled with rubble. Soon the going got rougher and steeper, and we were clambering up and down, over large boulders left by the retreating glacier, and steeper areas where areas of small sliding stones, scree slopes, crossed our way.

Prem found it difficult to breathe and, although she walks 5 km. a day in Bombay, she had to keep resting as the altitude made the going tough for her. The first three-and-a-half kilometres took two hours. At that rate we'd take eight hours, instead of five, to reach our night stop at Bhojbasa. Prem agreed to ride one of the donkeys, Gopal carried my rucksack, and I walked the eight kilometres to the tea stop at Chirbasa.

We had tea, munched biscuits, and ate bananas for breakfast in the three-sided tent arrangement, which had real tables and chairs, either inside, the smoke-blackened tent or outside, in the sunshine. There was a sleeping platform at the back of the tent, piled high with quilts. The owner squatted at a wood-burning fire, made in the cleft of a rock, so that the kettles and pans rested on top of the boulder, and the burning wood was poked in underneath. I lay down for half an hour. I too was feeling breathless, and my legs were tired. There were signs all over his place saying 'Don't spoil our Himalayas'. The tent owner made Gopal put the banana skins in a special box for rubbish.

We carried on trekking. The only graffiti we saw higher up the trek was 'No Dam' – a reference to the planned building of the Tehri Dam. When I became breathless again, I reckoned I'd done my bit, and it was time for me to give in, and ride on the second donkey. The donkey seemed very small to my five-foot 9 inches height but, with a few shoves, I was sitting on its back, and the donkey man was trying to get my long legs into the stirrups, that were designed for smaller Indian people's legs. Every time the donkey stopped to eat some vegetation, I felt I was in danger of sliding to the ground over her head! Gopal followed on foot with just his stick to help him.

The vegetation changed as we got higher. The golden birch trees were interspersed with autumn red rhus, (the smoke tree or the sumac tree), cotoneasters, and berberis – reminding me that so many of our garden shrubs were brought from this part of the Himalayas by Victorian botanist-explorers. The birch trees gave way to pine and cedar until the altitude left the hillsides clad only with a shrub, which when rubbed, smelt of vinegar. The weathered rocks and this vegetation provided a brown backdrop as we rode on the sure-footed donkeys across sparkling white, rounded boulders.

Recent landslides of rock had left white gashes in the hillside -a scree of white stones above and below us. Above, at 21,000 feet and before us, were the Bhagirathi triple peaks. The Matterhorn-shaped Shivling at 21,460 feet, sparkled in the sun, the deep corrie, like a slice out of its side, emphasising its needle shape.

Just as the sun was setting, and I was beginning to feel the cold, we rounded a cliff, and there at our feet, some 100 ft below us, were two buildings, a whitewashed Ashram, and the concrete Tourist Hostel. We reached Bhojbasa an hour or so before Gopal, who had walked all the way alone. Prem chose the government tourist place to stay in, as being more 'private' and where the toilets were likely to be less smelly. The toilets were of the squat variety!

We settled in and were given oil lamps. I noticed that electricity was fitted, but was not connected to the generator that stood on the porch! I borrowed some extra quilts from an empty room, knowing that it would be minus 4 degrees. After ordering food and hot water, boiled in the yard in a tall metal cylinder with a wood fire underneath, we paid a visit to the Ashram. We were greeted with a huge stainless-steel beaker of hot tea. We chatted to Swami Lal Baba who runs the Ashram, and I managed to make some joke in Hindi about Prem being my little friend – at 5 ft. 2 inches, I towered over her!

On returning to our hostel, I chatted with the manager and two escapees from the Ashram who were partaking of cannabis, or ganga, huddled over a log set alight by throwing kerosine over it. They asked me if I had a cigarette and I said I didn't smoke but that I had one somewhere. They took it to bits and filled the tube with a cannabis-bhang-tobacco mix. Prem came out to warm herself by the fire. The wall behind the log threw the heat back at us and we were provided with chairs. It got dark at 6 pm so we retired to our room, with the oil lamp, and ate some dinner but we weren't very hungry for the lentils and chapattis offered – we were too tired and both of us had altitude headaches. We were now at 14,800 ft. We slept with everything on again. I had my ski thermals under my jumper, cords, and fleece jacket, and was inside my sleeping bag, with two quilts each this time. I slept reasonably well, after a couple of painkillers and more tea from the stainless-steel flask, which we kept topped up with boiled water.

We woke as daylight streamed through our windows and the sun shone on the snow-covered mountains.

19

October 26, 1994

Bhojbasa to Gau Mawk approx. 4 km

Prem rose at 6 am. I waited in bed for tea. We breakfasted on potato pancakes again, sitting in the sunshine in the open-sided corridor leading to the kitchen, metal plates balanced on our laps and a view of the Bhagirathi peaks before us. These were the snow-covered triple peaks that had greeted us from our bedroom window. The donkey men were late arriving; they'd gone back to Chirbasa for the night. I remembered the sleeping platform and quilts!

We were on our way to the source of the Ganges by 9 am. It was slow going, crossing tributaries and piles of mud and boulders. Some places were very narrow for the donkeys, and we had to walk across plank bridges. The valley floor was crossed by lines of this clay and stones, looking every bit like the work of a giant excavator on a construction site, but really the debris deposited by the Gangotri glacier as it has retreated up the valley over the years.

The main view on our way up was dominated by the beautiful Shivling peak, a Matterhorn-shaped mountain. As the sun reached it, it shone majestically at 21,000 feet. The Bhagirathi triple peaks were beside us. The stones in the river and along its banks were white and gleaming with mica. There were occasionally rocks of red ironstone and chunks of black basalt, a metamorphosed limestone. The valley sides had numerous white scree slopes interspersed with patches of sparse vegetation, which may have been dried grass. We saw deer near Bhojbasa – five small beige coloured ones. The river was an aquamarine colour, with white foaming rapids all along its course. It is called the Bhagirathi here, not the Ganges, to honour the sage who prayed for his thousands of ancestors and was rewarded with the river's creation. I decided the best description of the colour was 'pale jade'.

After an hour or so we left the donkeys at another tent, of black plastic this time. It was a 'temple' with a sadhu, a holy man, almost naked! I helped Prem over the boulders until a young man appeared

20

and offered to help her. He turned out to be a pujari from Gangotri Temple. He held her arm and they proceeded slowly, step by step, across large boulders and rocks. I went ahead in case they didn't make it!

At last, the face of the glacier came into view. The dark opening in its left side was the cave under the glacier, from where the creamy jade-coloured river Ganges emerged. It is known as 'Gau Mawk' or 'the mouth of the cow'. The face of the glacier was a dirty white with many brown crevasses. New falls of ice crashed down from the 'mouth' and deposited fresh chunks of ice in the river. The top of the glacier was dark brown with the accumulation of debris falling on it from the surrounding mountains.

It was impossible to get close to the cave because of the continual rain of small stones from the surrounding mountainsides, caused by the alternate freezing and thawing action of frost and sun, shattering the rocks. I should have worn my cycle helmet! The river water was icy cold, yet it is customary to perform a Ganga puja.

I helped Prem perform a modified version of the bathing. She sat on a large boulder, and I poured water, which I collected from the river in my plastic water bottle, over her feet and hands, and she washed her face and eyes. I had remembered to bring a towel! After the puja, I filled the bottle again with the 'holy' water, known in Hindi as 'Ganga Jal', to be taken back to Bombay.

And Back to Gangotri approx. 18 km

There had been a change in the weather.

The snow would soon arrive and everybody from Gangotri would move down to Uttarkashi for six months.

21

On the way up we had been hot in the sunshine, wearing tee shirts, but on our return journey, we wore jackets, hats, and gloves and felt quite chilled. We were now more acclimatised, and the altitude was getting lower all the way back to Gangotri, from 14,800 ft to 10,000 ft, so we were able to complete the journey in one day.

The Birla Ashram, which Prem had chosen for our return stay in Gangotri, was across a suspension footbridge. The road was too narrow for the car to be brought nearer than half a mile from the ashram, along an unlit, rock and rubbish strewn 'road'. The dormitory room was so huge, and Prem was so cold, that she got into bed while we were waiting for our dinner.

I went to get my bike from the car to reassemble it. Indrasingh had chosen to park the car on a hill (because the diesel froze at night), outside a tea shop with electric light. Foam rubber and masking tape were removed, and I started to re-assemble the bike there and then, with Indrasingh's help. Two French men, Laurant and Yves, who'd been in the teashop, came to watch, and I, ladylike, let them take over the fitting of the pedals and the front pannier carrier. They were very patient and kept adjusting until it was exactly horizontal. The gears worked very sweetly, the wheels and brakes were checked, and it was on with the panniers, mattress, and sleeping bag and up to the ashram. It was dark by the time I had loaded it and wheeled it up the muddy street and over the bridge to the ashram. Indrasingh and Gopal lifted the bike up the ashram steps for me. I found Prem in bed with a little iron brazier of glowing charcoal under the bed, to give her some heat. Some cool water and a cold dinner of rice and dahl arrived, but we didn't eat much. I started to sort out my trekking and cycling things as some could go back to Bombay with Prem. I couldn't work for long however, as the generator stopped and the lights went out.

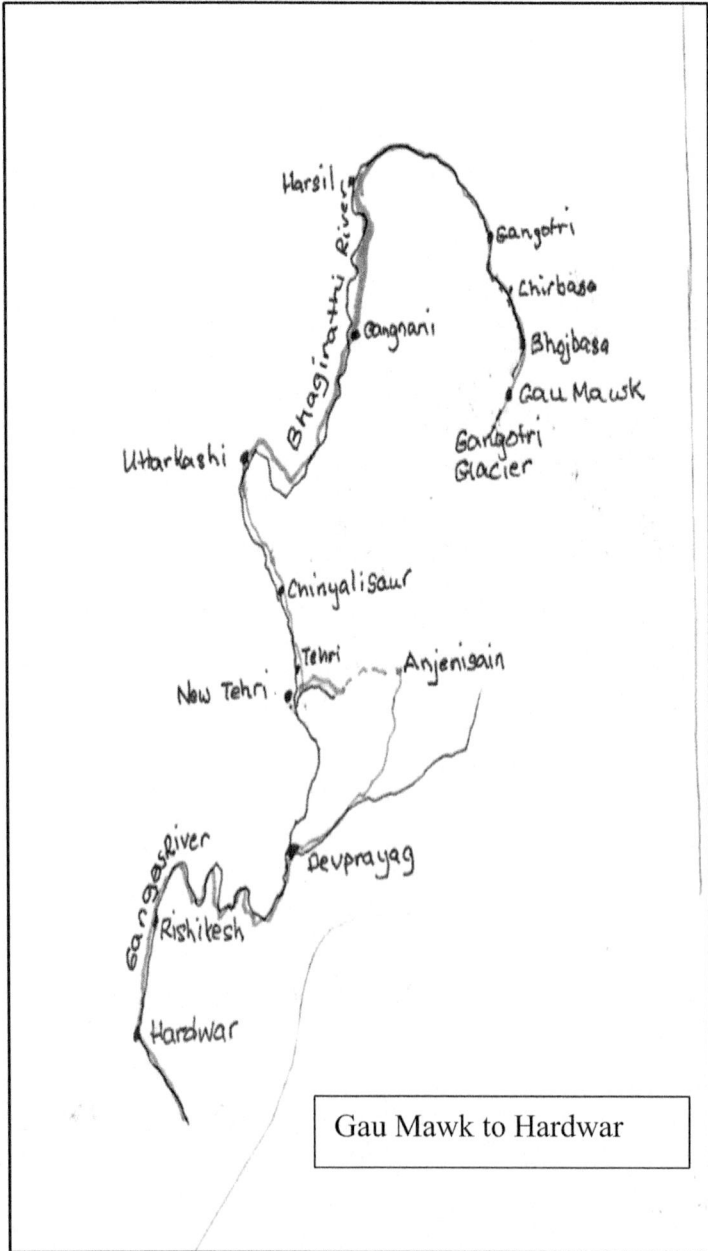

Gau Mawk to Hardwar

Chapter 3

Riding the Himalayas

October 27, 1994

Gangotri to Gangnani 52 km/ 33 miles

I slept well and carried on sorting my luggage out. Prem wanted to start early and get to Delhi and civilization (hot water, warmth, and beauty parlours) in one day. She left the ashram with Indrasingh and Gopal and I thought they had gone without saying goodbye.

However, I caught up with her, huddled over a fire, drinking tea. She was in the dhaba where I had assembled my bike, seated on an upturned ghee tin, covered with sacking. We drank tea and ate aloo paratha. The temple priest was in the dhaba, hovering to get more donations, and he put the Toshniwal family names in his red book. As per custom if he was ever in Bombay, he would come calling their house.

Prem admitted to not being well prepared for the trek. Ramesh had not shown her my fax about what to wear. The heavy stainless-steel flasks we hauled everywhere were not necessary, and her handbag had everything but the kitchen sink in it. Prem wore denim jeans with diamond earrings and ruby and diamond bracelets – rather a giveaway

25

of her wealth for the temple priests! Gangotri hostel accommodation cost 160 Rs, Bhojbasa 260 Rs, and the Birla Ashram 200 Rs. Prem paid for everything, and the donkey man asked for more than their agreed 1000 rupees, despite a 100 Rs. tip!

Indrasingh had set fire to some sacking under the car to defrost it but it didn't start until he had a shunt from a jeep. Before 9.30 am. I said goodbye, walked to the top of the hill, and gingerly mounted my bike, well laden with 18 kilos of luggage. It was downhill, thank goodness, and I soon got used to the steering. My friend's present of shock absorbing headset was very good in tempering the vibration of the patched and potholed tarmac. The pine trees cast shadows across the road, and it was difficult to spot the potholes. Soon, however, I was doing 18 mph. downhill. Not long after 10 am. Prem passed me in the car, hidden from sight by dark glass windows, but I waved until they were out of sight, around the next of many hairpin bends.

I was now alone and on my way to the mouth of the Ganges!

I stopped for a rest at 11.40 am. and started writing in an old exercise book from my teaching days. 'Hello, Hugh Crossley wherever you are!' Hugh's name was on the front of the old Geography exercise book I used as a diary. I wondered if he was still interested in Human Geography. My love of Geography had certainly brought me to this remote corner of India.

At eleven years of age, I became interested in things Indian, thanks to the arrival of new next-door neighbours, who had left India at the partition of the Indian subcontinent, into India and Pakistan. This painful birth of a nation was vividly relayed to me by these Anglo-Indians who had what I thought was a lovely name, Mr. and Mrs. Dear! Mr. Dear had been 'in charge' of Bombay Telephone service and he realised that with the newfound independence it was time for him to retire. They took a succession of lodgers into their north London home, many of whom I found most helpful when I was stuck with my homework, especially maths! The smells emanating from

Mrs. Dear's kitchen and the whispers in the street of 'goings-on' with a weiga board added the sense of the mysterious orient and no doubt whetted my appetite for travel.

I sat on a drystone wall, the sun shining on my back through the thin tree cover, overlooking the Bhagirathi River as it meandered across a stony floodplain, amid huge, folded limestone peaks. Some were snow-covered, others thinly clothed in cedar and pine trees. Lower down the valleys the trees changed to birch which were, as winter approached, beginning to lose their golden leaves. Two villages hugged the terraced hillside and there were still some apricot and apple trees, which were first introduced by a Mr. Wilson, in Harsil. The houses were made of wood and most had corrugated tin roofs. The noise of rain beating on them in the monsoon season must have been quite deafening.

I was six miles past the tented army post at Harsil. It was mostly downhill; my average speed was 18 mph. I had my brakes on, to avoid being catapulted into the gorge 1000 ft below if I hit a pothole, or one of the rocks which littered the road. These were not missiles thrown by local vandals, but the result of the constant exfoliation of the rocks on the mountains above, 'raining' down the shattered pieces. The mountainsides and valleys are strewn with these sharp cornered pieces of rock, only the pieces which end up in the river are worn into smooth rounded pebbles. According to my cycle computer, the few relatively flat parts of the road were done at 10 kmph. Walking uphill was the worst – my heart beat fast, and I was panting and doing only 2 or 3 km per hour, the bike being so heavy and the hills so steep.

Gangnani was 25 miles ahead, with an ashram to stay at and with a 'tourist place', according to the monk at Bhojbasa. I think this must have been where Indrasingh, our driver, had found people smoking cannabis on our way up, and reported that it was not a suitable place for the memsahibs to stop. I could see a mile of the uphill road ahead of me. Only God knew what was around the hairpin bend. I had to get over this ridge, which was part of the Karakoram range, and down the other side. The pujari from Gangotri temple passed me as a passenger on a scooter and gave me a wave. Being India there were three men on the scooter! Illegal of course!

I once missed a splendid photo opportunity in Rajasthan when I encountered three burly policemen on one pedal cycle! Fathers, with one child on the crossbar and one or more on the rear carrier, are a common sight in the early morning as they ferry the children to school. Wives can be seen sitting side-saddle on bikes and scooters, sometimes holding babies too. Considering the state of the roads and the absence of helmets I wondered what the accident rate was for these poor people. I wore my new purple (to match my bike) helmet while I was in the mountains and on busy roads – and felt that it was merely the modern equivalent of the solar topi of the old colonials.

I walked uphill for five kilometres; it was very hard going! (This was to be the longest uphill stretch of my route through the Himalayan parallel ranges, but I didn't know it at the time). I was beginning to wonder just how much walking I would be doing, and how long it would take me to get to my potential 'night-halt' places, as overnight accommodation stops are called in India. I saw a little, white-painted temple with the trident emblem on its roof, showing that it was dedicated to the god Shiva and thought that it was probably sited on the top of the hill. My spirit revived, and I pushed with renewed energy, only to be disappointed when I found that the road was still going up. Eventually, I reached the top of the mountain and was face to face with a wooden sign that informed me that I was now at 11,000 feet. I stopped to watch a group of children who were at a little school, alongside a few houses perched up here on the ridge. Rewarding myself with a snack of dried apricots and a rest, I looked forward to a long freewheel in the sunshine, the south-facing slopes being scrub-covered, rather than wooded. There were many temporary patches of road where a landslide had carried the road surface, and part of the surrounding hillside, into the gorge.

The eleven miles downhill were countered, once I crossed a swaying girder bridge, with its loose metal sheet planks, by the usual uphill stretch. At half-past-two I was pushing the bike on the shadier inside of the road, cutting corners to save a few yards at a time. I would count my steps and try to go fifty paces before pausing for a couple of minutes to get my breath. After another bridge, the uphill, through woodland, was about three miles.

It was there that I met my first two dogs. They were mangy, and about the size of Eskimo dogs, with a curled-over tail, one brown and the other black, typical mountain dogs I was told later. They seemed scared of me. I was pushing the bike uphill at the time, and I froze while they sniffed around me. Of course, I did not have my dog frightening device handy, but made sure it would be just inside my handlebar bag from the next day onward, because I had not gone far when I had my second encounter with a dog. This time I was much more frightened of being bitten by a rabid dog. This canine specimen belonged to a man who was sitting at the side of the road in a makeshift shelter. He may have been a shepherd, but the hillsides were quite heavily forested, and I hadn't seen any sheep or goats recently. The dog started barking and snarling at me. The owner threw a stone at it and called it back, but it still came towards me, so in desperation, I called out to him in English. A few more words from him and the dog circled me, sniffing at the bike while I moved gingerly upwards and onwards, hoping it wouldn't follow.

Near the top of the mountain, I met a boy, aged about 12, who was thirty miles from his home village of Harsil. He volunteered to push my bike for me, and we chatted as far as my Hindi could be understood by him, for he would have spoken in the Garhwal language. We shook hands when we parted at the top of the hill, and I regret not having taken a polaroid photo of him for his kindness to me. I hadn't gotten into the swing of things yet-a-while, or perhaps my brain was too tired to think properly! Then it was downhill, all the way to Gangnani. The yellow Uttar Pradesh tourist sign said, 'hot springs and restaurant'. I called up to ask if there was a tourist rest house.

"No!" came the reply, "did I want a night halt? Two rooms, one big and one small".

I agreed to take the small room for 30 rupees. The room was nine feet square, and a rickety charpoy (a wood and string bed) was the only piece of furniture in the room. There was a little, green shuttered, barred, glassless, window overlooking the Ganges in its gorge. The quilt was dirty, of course, but I would put my sleeping bag on the bed, and it had a hood to protect my hair. I was helped up the steps and slopes with my luggage and went down to carry the bike up on my shoulder, as I'd seen in the advert for Giant bikes. My room was about

40 feet above the road and the watching men were calling out, highly amused at a woman carrying what they must have thought was a bike as heavy as their Indian iron monsters!

Locking my door, which led onto a small terrace, and faced the Ganges-Bhagirathi, and the majestic mountains above it, I went in search of the restaurant. This turned out to be closed until evening, but there were several little roofed, but otherwise, open to the air, tea shops that would serve meals at the appropriate time. I had tea for 2 Rs and talked to a Scottish girl in hippy-style clothes, smoking pot and reading some esoteric book. She was staying with a tea shop owner for 20 Rs. a night.

I was taken in tow by the resident pandit, for there was a shrine to Shiva here, and he showed me the sulphur springs and said I could bathe in the separate lady's pool. This was behind an eight-foot wall but the entrance was an opening nearly filled with a sheet of corrugated iron, and a piece of sacking. I ducked and squeezed through, only to get a tirade from a woman who was washing clothes in a side basin. I tried to get her to understand that the pandit had said it would be alright for me to bathe.

She returned to minding her children and to her clothes washing, but only after I had gone to ask for his help, and he had put his head around the 'door'. I climbed down the steps into the hot water, which was just bearable, but I like a hot bath, and so deep that I had to stand on tiptoe to keep my head above the water. The water was quite buoyant and not at all sulphur smelling. I tottered around the pool enjoying the warmth on my aching muscles, despite the soggy feeling, though being fully clothed for decorum's sake.

There was an altar in front of the far wall, which separated the ladies from the men's open-plan pool. It looked like an open four-poster bed, its top festooned with tinsel, and the mattress area adorned with pictures of gods, flowers, and shiny pieces of material. The hot water entered the pool directly from the hillside into which this pool area had been cut. Limestone deposits and other chemicals had created a painted waterfall effect, rather like a giant steaming curtain of stalactites. I dressed in dry clothes, hiding behind my towel, as quickly as possible, because it was getting cold as night began to fall. I put my washing, which I had returned to the side of the pool to do, on a line of wire outside my room but the sun had gone down and I didn't expect it would dry – more weight to carry! I went in search of food.

The Government Tourist Restaurant has a large banner on it saying,

'VEGETARIAN BREAK FAST LUNCH & DINNER

PREPARED INHYGENIC CONDITIONS

SERVED INDECENT MANNERS'

There were not many people around, it was too early, but I met the almost toothless friend of the Scottish lass. He had been wandering about India for many years, and was thin and haggard looking. I was not surprised to be told that he did not sleep because he was too cold, and that he went into the hot pool in the middle of the night to warm up, before squatting with several others, where the underground water source warmed the paving stones of the circular tunnel around the temple. I found them all sleeping there when the pundit showed me around the next morning, and he had to wake them so that I could get by as part of the religious ceremony.

The tea shops were still not open, so I decided to explore because I wanted to go to the loo. I could see a dilapidated canvas loo tent, stamped with the words 'Government Tourist Company'. The path to it was littered with faeces and it was a case of stepping between! I decided the sagging and translucent tent wouldn't afford much privacy, so I went further along the steep hillside until I found a large enough bush. I washed standing on a rock at a hot spring that gushed from the hillside.

The temple pujari came to talk to me, and invited me to see the temple, but I was not going to be hassled and told him I would come later. I had had enough of begging for donations which is second nature to these temple guardians.

I found an Italian hippy having his supper at one of the dhabas and seated myself at the next table. I talked to him in the only language we had in common, German! The waiter brought a jug of water to fill my beaker, and the Italian said it was alright to drink the local water because it came straight out of the mountain. I didn't risk any then, but afterward, whenever I was high up in the mountains, far away from a village, I drank the water without filtering it.

I ordered one paratha, vegetables, and tea. The potatoes and cauliflower were too spicy for me and I had to soothe my mouth with sweet tea. The Italian told me that there were snakes in the undergrowth, and that I should be careful when going to the toilet. He said there were snakes here because the shrine was dedicated to Shiva, who is associated with the cobra, but I thought it was more likely that he was seeing things under the influence of marijuana.

It was dark when I returned to my room and lit the mini brass oil lamp, about the size of a bottle of ink, the chowkidar had given me, and a candle I had bought from the pujari. I checked the thermometer in my bar bag, and it was 15 degrees C when I went to bed. It was the same in the morning - not surprising as the room was built into the side of the mountain and I had closed the little window and door. I wrote my diary, but soon felt tired and, placing the candle and matches near to me on the floor, I made sure the door was bolted and blew out the lamp.

On one of my toilet forays in the night I noticed how myriad the stars were, how close they seemed, almost touchable, I'd never seen so many constellations. I was warm enough with just my ski- thermals on and soon fell asleep again, after all I had walked miles pushing the bike with its heavy luggage.

October 28, 1994

Gangnani to Uttarkashi 45 km/ 28 miles

I woke to my watch's alarm which was set for 6.10 am.

The temperature of the room was still 15 degrees. I hurried outside to find an 'open toilet' before anyone else was up and washed under the hot spring. There was a plastic pipe carrying cold water down the hillside, so I filled my bottle, via the filter, and took my anti-malaria tablets with the rest of the water. I find them very bitter. Why can't they be sugar coated? They completely ruin any nice-tasting breakfast one may have had.

I decided to visit the temple, and I found the pujari sitting on the steps. He had a little white beard and a thin black moustache. His brown eyes twinkled as he spoke. Being winter he wore a brown balaclava helmet, a vee-necked jumper, and a brown patterned woollen dressing gown, with a satin-piped edge to the collar, just like the ones worn by boys at boarding schools in the 1950's. Around his shoulders, he had what looked like a glass drying cloth, but it was fringed and may have been his badge of office because it didn't serve any obvious function.

He wore a necklace of brown beads which looked like the fruits of an alder tree, only they were round, and a silver amulet with two large stones, one yellow and the other green. He carried a brass pot of holy water, decorated with a garland of marigolds The outside of the shrine was festooned with swathes of tinsel - embroidered red cloth, dead and dying marigold flower garlands, plastic flowers, and glossy pictures of various deities.

Entering the shrine, he lit some joss sticks and sprinkled water around the idol, intoned some prayers, and invited me to follow him on a walk around the statue and make a donation.

After this religious puja, we talked on the little terrace, surrounded by marigold plants, and I asked him whether the Uttarkashi earthquake of 1991 had had any effect on the area. He seemed pleased that I knew about the event and went on to describe how the spring ceased to flow, leaving the hot springs without any tourists. He told me to follow him to the back of the temple. The hippies were still sleeping on the warm pavement, and they had to be awakened and moved so that we could get around the circular tunnel-like walkway to the place where the water came bubbling out of the earth. I had performed a circumambulation!

I carried my luggage and my bike down to the road and decided to wash the bike in a stream of hot spring water that flowed in a ditch at the side of the road. I was starting on this when a young man came and invited me to use a hose that was snaking across the road. He connected it to the spring supply and when I had de-greased the gears, he had fun spraying the bike with hot water. I loaded up the bike, lubricated and silicone-sprayed the gear mechanisms and chain, and waited for the chowkidar to arrive with my change. I asked various onlookers to find him, reminding them that I still had the padlock, but he was either stoned like most of the inhabitants, or missing, with my 20 rupees. I waited down on the road.

I was waiting for something to happen, showing the small group around me that I still had the key, when a white Ambassador Tourist Taxi pulled up in front of me. Four people got out, including an elderly lady. They looked up the steps and decided that they would be too much for the old lady, so the younger couple went up to the 'holy spring' and the lady contented herself with washing in the warm water which flowed down the face of the hill. Her guardian came over to speak to me and introduced himself as Justice Dilip Kumar Basu of the Calcutta High Court. He asked me what was detaining me so I told him about the change. He spoke quietly to some bystanders, and someone was dispatched to get my money. He gave me his phone numbers and addresses and told me to look him up when I arrived in Calcutta. He told me that one of his colleagues was connected to a group that helped leprosy patients and would be pleased to take me to their centre near Calcutta.

I set off on the road to Bhatwari, stopping to take photos whenever I was forced to dismount by the many landslides which had washed the road away. The scenery was changing; there were more fields now. The road was mostly downhill. When the surface was good my computer registered 18 mph but most of the time I had to go slowly, at 10 mph, because of the potholes and the need to be prepared for landslide sections. I drank my first 'neat' water from a waterfall. Tourist cars passed me frequently on their way up to Gangotri with their Indian passengers. People from Calcutta are very attached to the Ganges and have a reputation for being fond of travelling. The judge and the families I had met on the way to Gau Mawk were all from

Calcutta, so perhaps it was true. Lorries belched black smoke, grinding the way through their gears, as they climbed up the hills. Fine mica dust blew off the road and I was filthy. I was continually on the lookout for a telephone but the first time I found a telegraph office in a little village, the lines didn't go through to Bombay, only as far as Uttarkashi.

The fields were terraced behind dry stone walls wherever the valleys were wide enough. Neat earthen farmhouses with stone slab roofs dotted the hillsides. The harvest was being gathered from the Garhwali terraced hillsides and valley-bottom rice-paddy fields. Women and children were busy collecting fodder and firewood and transporting it on their heads. Their heads were completely invisible, and I was worried that my bell wouldn't be heard by them, so I called out 'hello' and greetings. They rarely saw westerners and certainly not females on bikes! I would hear them remark "it's a girl!", or "lady!" as I went by. Sometimes the women were carrying long baskets on their backs, their weight being taken by a band across their foreheads. In between villages men were busy ploughing while in the untidy main-road streets of the villages they stood around in groups, reading the newspapers at tea stalls or going about their daily business in little shops or wooden stalls. Clouds scudded across the blue sky, but there was no discernible wind at road level. I would start the morning wearing my fleece, for the air felt cold, especially when gathering speed on the downhill stretches, but I was soon warm enough to take it off and ride in just a tee shirt and cotton leggings. Now and then a tributary joined the Bhagirathi-Ganges, tumbling over boulders to enter the mainstream of swirling and foaming jade-green water. The river looked so small at the foot of the massive mountains which were alternatively clothed in pines or scruffy golden grass where the sides were very steep the scars of old, and not so old, landslides were evident in the valley. Where the road repairing teams of men and women had been removing recent landslides, my road was frequently just a soft mixture of soil and jagged rocks. The advantage to me of cycling in these border regions is that they are politically sensitive, internationally, and as such, the roads are maintained by the army so that they are always passable. The labour used is local and, therefore, an additional source of income for these farming people, whose winter lasts six months. Roads have been blasted through huge overhanging rocks, but I found out that most of the excavation has been done by hand. In one place I saw a yellow JCB road digger lying at the bottom of the 1000 ft. gorge. Two men were trying to split a huge rock, which had blocked the road, with a simple bolster chisel. Now and again, there were government notices at the side of the road extolling drivers to drive slowly, 'Don't be in hurry, enjoy the splendour of the Himalayas.

In the mountains there were numerous natural springs, issuing as tiny waterfalls by the side of the road and I used these to fill my bike water bottles. Where they were miles from habitation I didn't bother to use my portable water filter, which was given to me by a company in England. It was developed for the army and was supposed to remove bacteria from even the muddiest water. The main filter unit leaves the water with a slight iodine taste, but I had another small pump that I could use to remove the antiseptic taste if I wanted to. Actually, by the end of my journey in the hills, I was quite lazy and didn't bother to use the pump. Besides, I was travelling in an area where iodine is deficient in the water.

When I reached the plains after Haridwar, I put salt in my water bottles to compensate for that which I lost through perspiring. I carried the salt in an old film canister and filled it whenever I could, courtesy of various chefs. Once, when I had to buy some, I couldn't get a small enough amount and the shop assistant prodded a little hole in a large packet and filled my container for me and refused payment too! I wondered how he would explain the whole thing to his employer. Would it be blamed on rats?

I always aimed to reach my night halt by four o'clock, before it got dark. I got into the routine of making my water for the following day, putting some aside for teeth cleaning and for taking my anti-malarial tablets, filling the bottle which fitted onto the holder in the frame of my bike, and washing my tomatoes for lunchtime. If I had the luxury of a geyser, I would wash my clothes after I'd washed myself in the usual large bucket with a jug substituting for a shower head, then, where I was able to take my bike into the normally concreted attached bathroom, I would clean the bike – true water conservation! Usually, though, I only had cold water which was bearable in the evening but always a penance for me in the morning. Luckily, the water is soft in the Ganges valley, and it is very easy to work up a good lather to wash off the black coating of lorry and other vehicle exhausts, which cover every inch of exposed skin. I used moistened baby wipes, which I brought from England, during the day, and I discovered that they were useful for cleaning the bike.

Behind me the highest ranges were snow-covered, we had been told that the snow would soon force the people of Gangotri to leave the village for Uttarkashi, 159 km to the south. I was heading for Uttarkashi myself, but it would take me another day or two to get there. I passed 'haystacks' in trees - roadside trees that had been festooned with grass to dry for winter feed. Where the valleys opened out the fields were larger, but still separated by raised earthen banks, which served the dual purpose of fence and walkway. I even saw pigs using these embankments to cross fields.

The little towns were just a collection of flat-roofed houses, usually with balconies, along unpaved dusty streets. The traditional stone-roofed houses had presumably been destroyed in the 1991 earthquake and these reinforced concrete boxes were the recipe for seismic safety. Men sat on charpoys and read newspapers in the early morning sunshine, or stood about in groups talking. Shopkeepers were in their open-fronted shops or wooden stalls. The Garhwali people are very friendly, smiling people with, I learned later, a reputation for honesty, which means that they are often employed in other areas of India as chowkidars (caretakers).

39

Children were making their way to school. The 'private' school children wore uniforms of skirts and blouses, trouser shirts, and ties. Older girls wore salwar-kameez suits or sarees. The times at which school began seemed variable. I would pass children walking in groups, clutching books wrapped in paper, or bags with logos in English, up to 10 am. and pass them returning home from midday onwards. I met a nice unemployed man 5 km. before Uttarkashi who spoke English and was very impressed with my Lepra journey. He bought me a little glass of tea. The café had a telephone which could reach Mumbai. It cost 50 rupees to phone Ramesh's office, however, he was in Rajasthan, so I left a message with his PA, Krishnan, to tell him I was still alive and had reached Uttarkashi. I asked him to forward the information to my family in the UK as there were no international lines up here in the mountains. It would have been the first time they had news of me since I reached Haridwar on the 23rd, on the way up to Gangotri.

I reached Uttarkashi and checked in at the Tourist Bungalow. My room had a balcony, so I hung out my wet washing from Gangnani, and washed my hair in a bucket. The sun went in, so I brought the washing in and draped it around the room. I rearranged my belongings and tried to contact Bombay again, using a phone that required winding a handle. I wore my black jumper and polo neck for my evening walk with my, no-need-to-iron, crinkled fabric skirt, ankle socks, and trainers. I found the fruit and vegetable night market and bought 2 juicy, and not too sweet, green oranges called 'musumbie', 2 tomatoes, and 2 bananas for 7 rupees, plus 2 boxes of apple and mango juice, to be a change from water. I visited the bazaar looking for a cycle shop, as I wanted a pressure gauge to measure the air pressure in my tyres, but couldn't find one. I met a boy on a bike who wanted to practise his English, and he told me to visit the Vaisa Mandir temple. The Ganges was past the market, and some people were bathing in the dark, for religious reasons or for cleanliness I couldn't tell. They may have been early or late arrivals for an Aarti ceremony. The electricity here in Uttarkashi is hydroelectric, using water from Manali Dam, brought by a pipe through the mountains. Uttarkashi was a big town with lots of modern, reinforced concrete apartment blocks and houses built after the 1991 earthquake. Its 1991 census gave the population as 17.000 whereas Gangotri was 605.

I was now in mosquito country, as they don't like altitude. My room had an electric anti-mosquito device, but there were no curtains. I put some paper up at the windows with sticky tape, but the fan removed it. The temperature was 25 degrees C. with the windows open. I used my sheet sleeping bag, but the bedding was very thick, and I thought I might be too hot. The left side of my neck and left shoulder were hurting and I blamed it on travelling in the Tata Sierra car! I woke up sweating after an hour or two and took some Brufen for the aches in my shoulders and legs. I also put in some earplugs to not hear a tap running, somewhere! I'd not taken any Brufen since Gangotri.

October 29, 1994

Uttarkashi to Chinyalisaur 58 km/ 23 miles

I tried phoning Ramesh in Rajasthan at 7 am. but there was 'no line'! I went to the office to collect some hot water, washed myself and the bike, and sprayed it with oil after breakfast. I was on my way by 8.30 am. The front tyre had been pumped up to 35 lbs and the back to 30 lbs per square inch in Uttarkashi, but I stopped in Dharhasu to top up both tyres to 40 lb – it made riding easier. I pedalled downhill and got to 18 mph. I rode up some small hills but had to keep stopping for buses and lorries, losing my momentum and then having to walk.

I got to Chinyalisaur at about noon – a short day, with only two big hills of about four miles. I drank water from mountain streams and waterfalls. The valley widened out allowing terraced plots on the old flood plain and I could see rice being cultivated. My lunch was two

41

tomatoes with salt, on stale buns from the previous day. The temperature was 40 degrees C. while I was cycling but only 30 degrees in the shade. I talked to a Sadhu who said he was going to Sarnath, a Buddhist place of pilgrimage near Bodh Gaya in Bihar. There were many more buses and lorries today – was it because it was Saturday? Justice Basu stopped his car to say hello again, and wanted to know if I was in trouble as I was pushing the bike!

I stayed in a motel outside the village and gave the receptionist a note written by Ramesh, with the result that my bike and half the luggage was carried up to my room for me. I was given a bucket of hot water and a mug of tea. I did my washing and wrote my diary with my head in the shade and my legs in the sun. I'd noticed one or two spots on my thighs, so I was airing them. By 2.20 pm. the sun was losing its heat, and the wind was getting up. I saw neem trees for the first time near Uttarkashi. They have medicinal properties. Their leaves are made into a paste for treating skin infections. Neem oil is supposed to be good against mosquito bites, but I found the bad cabbage-like smell very off-putting when I tried some. Near Dharasu they line the roads – young ones grown with irrigation. Cactus plants formed hedges after Uttarkashi.

At Gangotri and Dharhasu there were orange butterflies about the size of our small tortoiseshells. There were 'little blues' and white butterflies with horizontal black stripes across their wings. The artemisias; cotoneasters, and rhus were left behind at Gangotri. I saw my first bougainvillaea after Uttarkashi and a few 'green' banana trees. I found a stick insect and a furry green caterpillar crossing my road. Lizards were bigger, I saw two about one foot long and one and a half inches wide

Most fields were now being ploughed for the winter, using a wooden plough, with a boy sitting on it for extra weight, pulled by two oxen. Women used mattocks to break the soil to a fine tilth. Girls collected baskets of straw and manure and dumped them by the roadside for women to pick up and put in the baskets worn on their backs, supported by a headband to distribute the weight. The women wearing these baskets would take rest by backing onto a wall or stone boulder for support. Eagles soared about ten feet above my head. Pigs in villages were beige with black spots. There were lots of donkeys and I saw my first three horses today, on the road between Uttarkashi and Dharhasu.

The next morning, I would have to start early for Tehri, as it may be my longest ride! I'd done my washing and written my diary, with my head in the shade and my legs exposed to the sun! Luckily there was no one around! I was getting conflicting information about the road to Devprayag and was told there was ashram accommodation but definitely no tourist night halts. I would ask again in Tehri. Tehri is 58 kms - a long ride so I packed my bike and hoped to get an early start. From my room I could hear the noise of the river as it tumbled over rapids - it sounded like a distant motorway at home! It was very dark by 6.40 pm. There were four men in the motel playing rummy by the light of an oil lamp. I was starving, dinner was supposed to be at 8 pm but the cook was one of the card players! He kindly agreed to make my dinner sooner. I was feeling very hungry. Mosquitoes were buzzing around the open doors where I sat on the restaurant steps until it was too dark to write. I went in and sat at the vacated card table with the oil lamp, hoping the food would not be too spicy for me. I asked if there were any English books or papers, "No!" I'm the only guest. I ordered a bucket of hot water for 6 am and 'oubla pani', boiling water, for tea at the same time, hoping to get away early. After dinner, I asked for hot water to wash myself and the bike. At this rate I'm going to run out of PTFE spray soon, it was only day 3 of riding! I wished I had a book to read but at least I was catching up with my journal.

I was ahead of schedule - I had missed out the Harsil stop because I was able to cover more than the planned 20 kms a day after leaving Gangotri. Bhatwari should have been a stop between Gangnani and

Uttarkashi, so I had gained two days over the planned route. The problem is finding places with accommodation. I'd been told there was a Swami, a Hindu religious teacher, and hence the possibility of somewhere to stay, en route to Devprayag' but I had conflicting advice regarding the route to take.

October 30, 1994

Chinyalisaur to Tehri 96 km/ 60 miles

The hot water in a mug for my tea, and in the bucket, were almost boiling. I washed myself and the bike and left at 7.35 am. I breakfasted on nuts, and apricots, and drank slightly salted water overlooking a charming neat and clean village. Men were ploughing, women hoeing, children were being washed and goats wandered around. There were stacks of hay on roofs and conical haystacks in the fields. I could hear a radio playing music and I enjoyed the rural scene, bathed in the sunshine. My route was mostly uphill. When I reached the top of the hill, I could see the road going down and up to the same height as I presently was, and calculated that it should take me two hours to climb the hill and 2 minutes to go down the other side! I covered the last 12.2 miles in three hours.

A large market occupied Tehri's centre, with fruit and vegetable stalls, spice, clothes, and hardware shops. A religious meeting was taking place in a curtained-off enclosure. Makeshift shops set up on the street were selling fireworks, sweets and coloured powders. Itinerant vendors held poles of paper lanterns aloft, selling them for the coming Diwali Festival. Buses were blocking the streets near the bus station called a 'bus stand'. There was much hooting and shouting as their attendants called out destinations, trying to attract passengers. Generally, buses don't keep to a timetable, they wait until they are full and then go.

I was told that there was a government PWD (Public Works Department) bungalow outside the town. I found it with the help of Ivaya, whom I met in the market. It cost 150 Rps. for the night, but with no sheets, pillows, or towels. That was not a problem because I had my own. However, inside the building the walls and mirrors had been daubed with huge anti-Dam slogans. There was no resident caretaker and there was no geyser either. It looked as if the rooms were recently vandalised. Some of the local people were obviously very upset by the flooding of their town to make a reservoir and hydro-electric power station. It was too late to go and look for somewhere else so I decided I would have to manage.

Ivaya, worked at the girls' convent school, (with 200 children) teaching maths and science. He was a 25-year-old science graduate with a master's degree in literature as well. He invited me to his place opposite the convent. He lived in a wooden shack, one room with a kitchen annexe. He had electricity and gas. There were pictures and calendars all over his walls. He showed me photos of his students on festivals and school trips, for example to Rishikesh. He probably thought I was younger than my 57 years, or maybe, like many Indians I met, he wanted help to get a visa to go to the UK or USA. I showed him pictures of Cambridge and asked him about Mass, with the vague hope that there might be a Sunday evening service at the convent. He called the convent and invited the sisters over. They were a Franciscan order from Kerala. Sister Alfred, who taught physical geography, came over. There were five nuns in all but only two were in Tehri as the others were on a retreat. The next week was the Diwali holiday, but the school had been closed for the last two months because of the 'Uttarakhand Separatist Movement' creating problems. They wanted independence from Uttar Pradesh, but couldn't survive economically. Sister Alfred told me that although their 'new school' was ready for the children, the parents did not want to move to the new town. 'New Tehri' was fifteen miles away.

The Tehri Dam project was part private and part government, but the private element (the USSR) withdrew from the project. The Indian government didn't have enough money to complete the project and had to revise the plans many times. The Tehri Dam is a huge 265-metre-high dam in an area with considerable past, and recent, volcanic activity. The local people are worried about rehabilitation. They wondered where they would find good agricultural land. There was no industry here in the Garhwal hills, it is all agriculture and shops. They said the new lake will cover the best land up to the Dharasu bridge. The government of Garhwal wouldn't fund the project because it was anti-environmental. The national government has spent most of its money in New Terhi building houses to rent. There had been many revisions of the plans, fewer kilowatts of power to be produced, ecological surveys not done but must be completed, and roads to be built. There were 'No Dam!' signs everywhere.

The nuns have been in Tehri for 16 years and have built their own place in New Tehri, but the local tradespeople don't want to go, and people want the school to stay here in 'old Tehri'. I was invited to stay at the convent but as I had paid 150 Rs for the PWD, I said no! Sister Alfred recommended that I go and see a social service project in the hills at Anjenisain. Ivaya offered to call for me in the morning and help me put my bike on a bus which leaves for Anjenisain at 7.30 am.

A servant came and changed my room as, being recently vandalised, there were no locks on the door. Ivaya took me down to the market on his motorbike. I called Bombay and spoke to Dinu, Ramesh's son-in-law, who was home for Diwali. Ramesh was still in Banswara. My supper was bread, tomatoes, apples, bananas and an orange bought for 30 Rs. in the market. The phone call was 27 Rs. Back at the PWD, I was asked for 30 Rs. by the man who had moved me to the new room, but I only gave him about seven rupees, saying it was all I had because I needed 21 Rs. for the next day's bus fare. It was 20 km. and all uphill to the ashram and I could have just about walked it in a day, but the bike was heavy, and I'd have to save my arm and neck, as I was still having pain there the previous night. I think the solid rubber pillows at last night's hotel were too high for me

I was locked in, but could hear someone moving around in the next room. I held my breath and listened carefully, but all became quiet. For safety, I put my bike against the inter-communicating door. There were curtains and electricity but only cold water. As there was no bedding I slept in my sleeping bag with my jacket as a pillow. Crickets were making a lot of noise outside. We were on top of a hill near Rani's Palace, she had moved to Delhi! The Raja's Palace was a government office! I took two Brufen Retard for my aches and pains. There was mosquito netting on the windows, but it had some holes, however, I may have already been bitten in the market as it was getting dark as we arrived back at the PWD.

Despite not usually smoking in India, I had brought a packet of cigarettes with me. My colleague Rajni had told me that if I was seen smoking I would 'lose face'. I was not a heavy smoker, up to 5 a day in England. I associated smoking with relaxing and would enjoy one when having a cup of tea after I got home from work, or on social occasions which were few and far between. Cigarettes were, however, useful for their laxative effect. I think that is how I got started on them. Anyway, in Tehri, I found my cigarettes, and as I hadn't been to the loo properly since Uttarkashi, I had one. I was feeling vulnerable. Sister Alfred had told me that two bus-loads of women went to Delhi to demonstrate against the dam, and they were raped by policemen. Rioting followed, in which fifty people died, but the numbers were kept quiet. They said 'some' people went to prison.

I could hear noises in the building. I was the only occupant, and people were talking outside in the compound. The boss man had been very off-hand, he lived in a separate house. The chowkidar had a corrugated iron roofed shed in one corner of the compound. The chap

47

who moved me lived somewhere else on the site – there were so many outbuildings in the compound. The lights keep flickering, so I put my lighter and a candle near me. I had washed in cold water when I arrived and washed my leggings, so I didn't bother to wash again. I had just enough water left to do my teeth in the morning. It was 7.45 pm. and I was ready for bed. I wondered whether to wear earplugs to deaden the sound of the hundreds of crickets, as well as the background music from Tehri town centre. However, I wanted to hear if there was an intruder! I slept in my thermals for decency, just in case!

In my mind, I went through the schedule for the next day. Ivaya was calling for me at 6.45 am. and I reckoned it would take me a quarter of an hour to get down to the bus station, where I would have to load the bike on the bus roof, by climbing up the narrow metal ladder attached to the back of the bus. I would have to find somewhere for my 4 + 2 bags, handlebar bag, and helmet. I would have to be careful with the gears and lay the bike on its left side.

Still worried, I picked up a large stone that was in the room and put it next to my bed, with my torch. I had a terrible night, sure that someone was trying to get in, and was glad when morning came and that the bike was already loaded up.

October 31, 1994

Old Tehri to Anjenisain - by bus

Ivaya didn't come, so at a quarter to seven, I cycled to the bus stand, bought a 21-rupee ticket, and hoped he'd turn up. He didn't! I nearly killed myself carrying the bike up to the bus roof. Everyone was watching but no one helped. The bus journey was wonderful, up and up, round and round hairpin bends, higher and higher for two hours to Anjenisain at 7000 feet and 22 km from 'Old Tehri'. I had some help getting the bike down from the roof of the bus, but I had to climb up to unstrap it.

From the bus stop, I was directed to the Ashram by an old man living at the roadside. I'd cycled about 1 km. from the bus stop when another man said, in English, that he'd make sure no one touched the bike luggage, while I was escorted to the principal's office by a young girl, who turned out to be in charge of the crafts and toy production. She also taught home science and singing. She was carrying homemade Diwali cards, and I bought 6 for 24 Rs. She read through a list of things they make here, which included honey.

I sat on the edge of a dirt playground in front of cream and blue concrete roofed buildings, with netted doors and closing metal shutters. I watched as children stood in lines and spaced themselves with arms on the shoulders of the person in front of them. They said prayers and sang the national anthem. Then a couple of children came forward and recited something to the 400 or so children. Their uniform was a blue shirt with green trousers or skirts, with red ties. Older girls wore blue kameezzes with green pants and dupattas and red hair ribbons. Some children wore trainers, others had flip-flops. In class, they sat at double desks with sloping tops and said 'good morning, ma'am' as the teacher entered. It was lovely to hear the babble of children's voices chattering between lessons.

The ashram was founded by an Indian man who has since died. I spoke with Cyril, the Principal, he was half Canadian and half Indian.

He wanted the ashram to be a resource centre for the surrounding villages, with an emphasis on the beauty of nature. There were forty permanent staff, including some members of the Chipko environmental movement. (They hugged trees to save them from being cut down and they cared about nature).

Children pay 10 or 12 rupees a month for their education, and some live-in, either because there are problems at home, or because they are too poor.

There was a craft centre providing women's employment and Cyril would like to see metal and woodworking established, especially carving. There were several varnished wood sculptures and pots of flowers about the ashram. He also wanted to start TV and auto-mobile repairing and provide a surgery dispensary-cum-hospital.

Most of the village houses had electricity, were roofed with slabs of stone, and painted the traditional red and white. Newer earthquake-proof houses were all white and had flat reinforced concrete roofs. It was the weight of those stones that caused so many injuries and deaths in earthquakes.

Local crops included pulses, wheat, rice, and some maize Donkeys, buffaloes, cows, and sheep were reared. Lunch was brought to me at 2 pm, dal, sabzi, and red rice, all local and high in protein. I sat on the veranda and talked with Dev Swami, a lawyer, about England, divorce, education, and jobs He photocopied a map of UP for me. The Haridwar to Kotdwara road was not quite as on my maps. He said I should find tourist accommodation at Dugadda.

Before supper I talked with the two born and bred English girls of Indian origin, from University College London. They were on their sixth-year, two-month foreign assignment, a part of their course to give them experience in another country. They had heard about Anjenisain from the records of a previous student, who was here in the early days of the Ashram, when the founder was alive. There were only 16 children in the school then!

November 1,1994

Anjenisain to Devprayag 44 km/ 27.21 miles

Breakfast was at 8.30 am and I planned to leave at 9 am. I donated 250 rupees (The ashram is funded by Canadians and the Save the Children Fund). I had been given free accommodation and food and appreciated the opportunity to wash my clothes, rest and find my appetite too!

It was eleven o 'clock by the time I got away. I arrived in Devprayag after 10 miles of almost level road and a glorious freewheeling of 17 miles downhill. There was no need for walking that day.

I found the recommended hostel about 1 km from the centre of town. "The first place you come to on the Tehri side of town". Devprayag is the largest town in the Garhwal district. It was a linear town, hemmed into its valley by the beautiful blue river Alaknanda. I was given a de-luxe room with attached bathroom and toilet. My bike was put in a three-bed dormitory next door, and I was handed the key. My luggage was carried up for me and I was offered coffee. The first thing

I did after settling in my room was to go and see the confluence, the 'Sangam', of the Alaknanda and the Bhagirathi.

It was 34 degrees in the shade when I stopped for my first breathtaking view of the river Alaknanda. A temple on the hillside has been playing the same record all day, maybe because it is the main part of the Diwali festival on Wednesday and Thursday. The cook's little boy has been setting off crackers outside and I encountered more of them, with startling, echoing bangs, on my wanderings around the town.

The turquoise and jade colours of the water of the two rivers flowed alongside one another, until they mingled downstream, on the way to Hardwar. The usual pujari was there, trying to get me to do the Ganga Puja, I said I'd wait. I sat and photographed the rivers and when some Calcutta people arrived, I spoke to them and their teenage daughter. I told their guide that I didn't want to do puja and I was very embarrassed when he told the pujari! I bathed my feet at the foot of the steps which led into the river and contemplated the power and beauty of the river and its surroundings.

There were 1 ft 6-inch-long fish swimming by me, upstream against a tremendous current. The Bhagirathi carries a lot of silt – hence the jade colour. The Alaknanda has algae that give it the blue colour, according to a man I talked to.

The confluence, of the Bhagirathi and the Alaknanda, gives the town its name, Dev means 'god' and 'prayag' means confluence or 'sangam'. It is only downstream of Devprayag sangam that the river loses the name Bhagirathi and becomes known as the Ganges, personified as the goddess Ganga. People come here to worship the river and receive blessings from its holy waters. Where there are small beaches on the opposite west bank of the Ganges, people can perform pujas, immerse themselves three times in the waters.

The town's older houses are rather decayed but once had lovely carved doorways. There were shops at road level whose upper storeys, supported on carved pillars, were open on one side, like a large veranda and had closed rooms at the back. The streets are just narrow concrete pathways about four to six feet wide, and the roofs had large overhangs above them. There is no space for vehicular traffic like cars, often referred to in India as 'four wheelers'. A suspension bridge connects the two halves of Devprayag, the confluence side, and the south side. It is only for walking, moving unnervingly as you cross it. I chatted to an old man who had a little vegetable garden growing spinach, coriander, potatoes, paw-paws and a baby banana tree, as well as some other greens I couldn't recognise.

There were still no telephones, Devprayag only had local lines as far as Rishikesh, but all Garhwali Government Tourist hostels and municipal centres have private radio contact with Delhi. I bought four bananas and three tomatoes – the first I've seen since Tehri. I photographed some 10,000 to 14,000 ft. snow-covered mountains, the first I'd seen since the Bhagirathi Parhat and the Shivling near Gangotri.

November 2, 1994 - Diwali Festival

Devprayag to Rishikesh 91 km/ 57 miles

There was a small downhill on leaving Devprayag and then it was almost three hours of walking uphill for 11.58 miles to about 10.000 ft. I would cut corners while pushing my bike on the deserted road. Up and up round hairpin bends, hoping each blind corner would be the last.

After a lovely freewheel down to 480 ft. above sea level, I stopped and sat in the sunshine for an hour at Kanyala, a rafting centre. My bike computer recorded my average speed as 3.5 miles, in 2.55 hours, with a maximum speed of 23 mph. My computer decided to pack up at this delightful spot which was where intrusive seams of slate rocks crossed the Ganges causing the rapids. The newly established camping site supervisor showed me a double tent. Did he think I'd be persuaded to stay or tell my friends? I must say they looked very comfortable. They were lined with colourful block-printed material, had a real double bed, electric light, and a fan. As a hobby he collected driftwood, to serve as sculptures. However, I had to press on toward Rishikesh.

I saw a man cutting up goat meat for the festival Hindus are generally vegetarian, but some eat goat meat and poultry. They do not eat beef as the cow is regarded as a sacred animal. The road was up and down now to Shivpuri or Brampuri where, according to Dev Swami, there was a leprosy colony. Rishikesh was signposted as 57 miles.

There were blue campanulas, white heather, and what I think were mango trees. I missed the leprosy colony, there were no signs or English words, and not a soul around to ask. I later met an English cyclist who was on a 'day cycling' holiday, staying near the Laxman-Jhula, just before Rishikesh. I decided that I would go there too, as it was already 4.30 pm. and I didn't want to get bitten by mosquitoes or be out in the dark. The turn-off was downhill – I'd have to walk uphill in the morning!

My cell in the ashram was very basic. There was no bed, or any covers, – just a concrete floor. My bike was with me, and fitted into the space under the window. I took off the bags and arranged them neatly on the floor and on some shelves built into the wall, so that they were easily accessible, and I could wipe the day's grime off my bike, with a 'wet wipe'. I laid my mattrass on the floor and put the rolled sleeping bag at the end near the wall, to act as a pillow. Strangely I felt proud of myself for being so neat and tidy. I took a photo!

I had a padlock, so I could safely leave my possessions and go out to look for a phone. I spoke to both Prem and Ramesh. Ramesh agreed to phone my daughter, Sarah, who could pass on news of me to the rest of the family, relatives, Lepra and some of my sponsors. Ramesh wanted to know when I would reach Lucknow and Prem invited me to stay in Bombay after my ride.

I'd decided I couldn't bear to wash in cold water, so I just used a wet wipe. It was 22 degrees C. in my cell.

washing and maintenance jobs on the bike I decided I would go to Hardwar the next day. I could hear Diwali fireworks and crackers being let off outside, but I slept quite well and woke at 5 am for the usual call of nature. I'd borrowed a rusty tin to save myself the trip to the loo! I washed in cold water – it wasn't too bad.

November 3, 1994

Rishikesh to Hardwar 39 km/24 miles

I left the ashram near the Laxman-Jhula, another pedestrian only suspension bridge, at about 8 am. It was an uphill start to get to the main road, and my left shoulder was painful – I may have been sleeping with my arm above my head, and pushing the bike didn't help. I passed an obelisk at the roadside engraved with instructions for good living by Swami Vivekananda, a Hindu monk, and philosopher of the 19th century, who is credited with having brought Hinduism to the status of a major world religion. His 'Twenty Instructions' for a good life, included

'Give up smoking, narcotics, intoxicants and rajasic

(non- vegetarian) foods'

'Simple living and high thinking',

'Speak the truth at all cost, speak little and sweetly'.

He encouraged the practice of yoga and searching for God in ourselves and in others. He said every Indian should be treated as a brother, irrespective of whether he was born poor or low caste. Swami Vivekananda based his thinking on the ancient Indian scriptures known as the Vedas. The Vedas were hymns from about 900 BC to 1500 BC.

Vivekananda was admired and followed by many influential people including Rabindranath Tagore, Mahatma Gandhi, and Barack Obama. His instructions about smoking, eating and abstinence are current today!

Nearer to Hardwar I found a Telegraph Office, where I wrote out a fax, in capital letters for legibility, as Krishnan, Ramesh's personal assistant, would have to read it and retype it, for sending by fax machine to my daughter Karen, in her office in Nottingham. Karen would re-type the fax on to normal paper, and send it by post, to her sister in Bury St Edmunds. The fax couldn't be sent for some reason, so I sent it later from a large General Post Office in Hardwar for 30 Rs

I passed roundabouts and streets decorated with tinsel and shops selling sweets and fireworks for Diwali. The Ganges has been canalised at Hardwar to provide a permanent stream of water for religious bathing, for the Aarti ceremony, and for a hostels and hotels are situated.

The Tourist hostel at Haridwar was huge, and on several floors. My room was on the second floor and relatively mosquito free. It overlooked the canalised Ganga, downstream of the Aarti ceremony area. I booked in for two nights, asked for a bucket of hot water, and ordered a tray of tea. The water was brought up to me. I had a lovely hot bucket shower and washed my hair. The ordered pot tea was 'adrak chai' – tea with ginger. It stretched to three cups and had no sugar either!

I dried my towel through a broken window facing the sunrise and in the wind. I washed my black wool jumper and socks and left them to dry outside my door, over the veranda railings. I noticed that there was a dhobi facility, a laundry service, so I sent some more things. Apart from a yellow stain on my tee shirt, they came back very quickly, clean and pressed.

I decided to go to visit Daksha Mahadev temple, several kilometres south of Hardwar, on an unladen bike – sheer pleasure! I refused a pujari's attention and just sat beside the river on the ghats - steps leading into the water, said some silent prayers and dabbled my feet. I looked around the temple and was given tea by Om Dutt Sharma. He had a stall selling religious souvenirs. I showed him pictures of Cambridge and my family photos. I took pictures of an old-style, decaying townhouse, opposite the temple, with intricate mosaic work and pillared windows.

Returning to Hardwar I went into the town, still looking for a cycle pump with a pressure gauge, but no luck. One young man, who spoke English, gave me tea at his shop and suggested I try a place that sold scooters. A good idea but I didn't find one. I bought two strips of Diazepam mg. for 860 rupees, without the need of a prescription, for my neck pain. I phoned Ramesh and he said he couldn't get to Lucknow until the 13th or 14th of November because Prem's sister, Mala, was visiting them from America.

Back at the Tourist Hotel I cleaned and oiled the bike. There were no loose screws – a tribute to the Nylox ones I had fitted before leaving my home on the edge of Cambridge. I pumped the back tyre up to 45 lbs but I'd have liked to have had it checked! I lunched on bananas and biscuits and drank 'nimbu pani', lemon-flavoured water. I spent the afternoon writing an article 'To the source of the Ganges' for Lepra magazine. It was eight pages long and I calculated it would cost £10 to fax, so I will give it to Ramesh in Lucknow, to send by courier with some photos, to Lepra in Colchester. My thermometer read 28 degrees.

On my second day, I explored Hardwar. I walked up the main street and went up to Mansa Devi temple on a chairlift up the Shivalik Hills, the most southern mountain chain of the Himalayas. This temple goddess is noted for granting wishes. People tie threads to the branches of a tree in the temple grounds. Once the wishes are fulfilled the person is supposed to come back and untie the thread! I didn't go inside as I had forgotten my 'temple socks', which saved me from going around temples bare-footed. They kept my feet clean and safe from burning, on the hot marble or concrete floors.

In the evening, I went to take photos of the aarti ceremony and later I was invited to sit with a family from Delhi having snacks at 7.30 pm – they had ordered them at 5.30 pm! The waiter had the cheek to ask them if they wanted dinner! They mentioned that there were mosquitoes on the first floor so I was thankful to be on the second floor. I slept well and when my washing water didn't arrive, I went down to the kitchen to ask for it. I took some luggage down with me at the same time. At breakfast, I shared a table with a government chemist from Delhi.

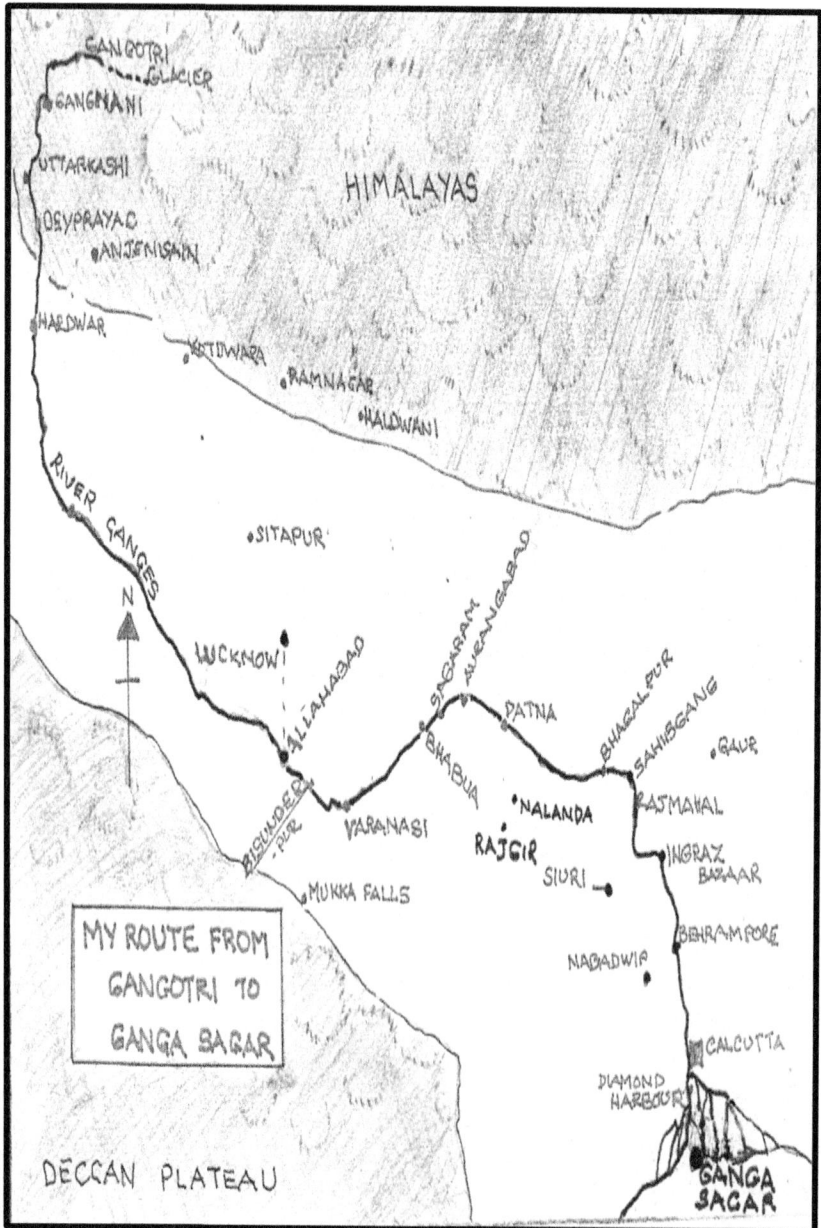

My Route from Gangotri to Ganga Sagar

Chapter 4

Foothills and Plains

November 5, 1994

Hardwar to Kotdwara 73 km/ 45 miles

The Kotdwara road is National Highway 49, and it appeared to be heading in the wrong direction for me, but signs insisted it was going to Kotdwara and Najibabad. It was going due south and although it was tarmac, there was a bone-shaking patchwork of piece-meal repaired tarmac over bricks. It was not dusty and was wide enough for two vehicles to pass one another. I cycled through stands of eucalyptus forest – man-made and being harvested. Men were cycling with large bundles of split wood on the backs of their bikes. I found out that they were taking the wood to fuel a brick making concern further along the road. Most of the lorries passing me were conveying wood or stone. There were fields of rice and sugarcane, the cane was being transported on bicycles. I saw plenty of cattle, in quite large herds. One field was being rolled with stone rollers behind oxen. I had lunch at a 'posh' restaurant where there were bamboo-shaded gazebo-like structures, with brick-paved floors. I didn't mention in my diary what I ate, but it only cost 8 rupees!

While I was getting air for my tyres a doctor came to meet me. I wasn't charged for air. I explained that I wanted to buy an air-pressure gauge, but he didn't know where I could get one. I was just starting off when he asked me to "please have some tea or coffee". He took me up to his house – of two storeys, and the best in the village, above a chemist's shop. He introduced his wife and two children, and we both took photos. He asked for my address and gave me 50 Rs. "For Cancer Research!". I had told him all about my ride for the treatment of leprosy, but as my address was pre-printed on a label by a cancer charity I had previously supported, he gave his donation "for Cancer Research". Hard luck Lepra! He gave me tea, savoury snacks called namkeen, and singara – water chestnuts. He was a local doctor and said his workload was mostly dysentery and malaria.

Later that day I was knocked off my bike by three young men racing me and cutting in front of me with tractors. They were young men from the Punjab, who were part of the many teams that took harvesters and tractors from the Punjab, down the Ganges valley, getting contracts to cut fields of wheat, as the harvest ripened successively as they progressed from west to east. The big machines cut the grain, and the smaller tractors transport it to the government grain storage centres, called 'go-downs' or warehouses. They probably thought it might be fun to race the rarity of a lone woman on a bicycle. The bike was OK, but my knee was bruised, and I was angry.

I stopped at a garage to see if they had drinks for sale. I was given sweet tea – it was still the Diwali festival, and my water bottle was filled for me. Not knowing the source of the water, I stopped when out of sight, and purified the water with my iodine filter. I was quite tired when I arrived at Kotdwara, at about 4.30 pm. My urine was scalding me, I hadn't had salt that day as I thought it wasn't going to be very hot, as there was shade from trees and a light breeze. However, when I stopped for my banana lunch, it was hot.

Last night's receptionist had said the best hotel was 'Ambey' which charged 60 to 80 Rs. – three girls had pointed it out to me but they had obviously considered it expensive and recommended the Tourist Hostel, which turned out to charge 118 Rs. For that princely sum, I had a fitted carpet, a geyser, and a fan. A very welcome and huge pot of very strong tea cost only 4 Rs.

November 6, 1994

Kotdwara to Ramnagar Dam 54 km/ 33 miles

Men at the tourist hostel in Kotdwara told me that there were robbers on the road to Kalaghar, which was 30 miles or 50 km ahead. The Kalagarh road was a forest road, metalled in places, dirt in others, up and downhill. What to do? There was a bus, or the alternative was to go back for 26 km. to Najibabad, and then take the road to Moradabad, Bareilly, and Kanpur.

I decided to get the bus from Nagina to Aligarh, after cycling 54 km. I climbed onto the bus roof by the narrow ladder attached to the rear of the bus and secured the bags and the bike with my elasticated bungee straps. The bus took me 35 km to Aligarh, which was 10 km from Kalagarh Tiger Project. The project was closed but I went to see the Security Officer who directed me to the Forest Ranger.

My planned night halt at the Public Works Department bungalow had no water, so I went back to the Forest Ranger, and he suggested the peon, servant, take me to the Irrigation Department Bungalow near Ramnagar Dam, who were charging 150 Rs. plus 50 Rs. for dinner. The chowkidar served my dinner and stood at attention while I ate, his children watching me intently. He had prepared boiled cauliflower, roast potato, rice, paratha, and a thick dahl. A slice of lemon was put in my water bottle. I can remember him serving me with white gloves on his hands - very old-fashioned! He told me proudly how he had worked for the British. He offered to bring me tea at 4.30 am and my washing water at 5.00 am as I wanted to be on my way by 5.30 am.

The Forest Road through the Buffer Zone would be 50 km of which the last 17 km., at the Ramnagar end, was a metalled road. (32 miles plus 11 miles) It had taken ages to get permission to use the road, but the Ranger drew me a sketch map with names, in Hindi script, on it.

November 7, 1994

Through the Buffer Zone

<u>Ramnagar Dam to Ramnagar</u> 67 km/42 miles

Tea without milk arrived at 5.50 am but I had some dried milk Prem had given me. Water arrived later but I was all packed and, on the road, reaching Corbett Park by 6.30 am and entered the Park Buffer Zone at 6.45 am. The Buffer Zone was an area of land that surrounded the Tiger Reserve in which villagers and tigers coexist, and where nature is conserved, alongside compatible human uses of land and water.

The first kilometre was fine, cycle tracks were visible, winding in and out along the unmetalled road. Later this deteriorated to stony gravel with many dry streams crossing my path, and patches of thick sand when it felt as if I was pushing my bike through a Saharan sand dune. Sometimes it was up and downhill. I saw peacocks and heard buzzards, vultures, and monkeys. I saw creatures with bushy tails spread out flat behind them. There were footprints of large cats, leopards, or tigers, I wondered! I saw deer and elephant footprints and a three-toed bird print as large as my hand. I could hear noises of animals in the trees and wondered if at that early hour I would see tigers having a morning drink at the various shallow streams. It took me nearly three hours, hardly daring to stop, to get through the 32 miles of the buffer zone. I reached a tall wire netting fenced-off area in which several men were sitting around a water pump drinking tea.

I was invited to join them and drank my own filtered water and the tea they offered me. I took a polaroid photo and gave it to them. The headman arrived later and was disappointed that he was not in the photo. They told me the metalled road began 15 km from Ramnagar town. I carried on, stopped for tea again. The first 'night halt' I came across was closed but I found a government one next door. It was Ramnagar Tourist Hotel charging 100 Rs. for a room with a geyser. I showered, washed my hair and some clothes.

Needing to stock up on food I went for a little walk and bought 12 bananas for 10 rupees and two Citra drinks for mixing with my water for 14 Rs. They can be opened by jamming them against the door handle. My bike is in my room so it can be showered. However, the luggage was very dusty, and I couldn't find a suitable brush with which to clean it. The Indian way of dusting is to hit something with a stick so that the dust bounces up and settles down again, in the same place or in a slightly different place! I've watched so many shop-keepers dust like that!

I went out a second time, looking for a railway station, but ended up in a police station! I did my best 'namaskar', said my name, and asked for help. I was referred to the Station Officer, Mrs. Krishna Thapa, who spoke good English. She offered me water, which I refused, in case it wasn't boiled or filtered, but accepted tea and little Deepavali (Diwali) cakes and sweets. I told her that I wanted to send some of my excess luggage, cold weather clothes, and sleeping bag, to Lucknow with the idea that Ramesh could take it back to Bombay. I said that I thought I had better buy a case, as my panniers had no locks. She arranged for someone to phone the railway station and ask how long it would take to send a case to Lucknow. The reply was "two days to 2 months – no guarantee!"

I was taken by a senior policeman, on a motorbike, to buy a case. The cheapest was 687 Rs. I was driven back to the tourist hostel to pack it and then taken to the train station, where the policeman explained that I wanted to send the case to be collected by me at Lucknow Station. The Ramnagar Station Commercial Manager did all the paperwork, and I paid 37 Rs. I was given a receipt to produce at Lucknow station when collecting the case.

Returning to the Tourist Hostel I washed my bike with the provided hot water and oiled it. I was given clean sheets and a towel. The pillow looked horrid so I used my jacket instead. I popped out again, phoned the Bombay residence and got Ramesh's daughter, Kavita. I later managed to speak with Ramesh in his office. He gave me news of my family, "Sarah is OK, Steven has found a job and my house is OK," It was a bad line but he rang me back. I will try to fax Ramesh when I reach Haldwan to let him know when I might arrive in Lucknow, if I get there before the Post Office closes, as he is off to Delhi on Thursday 10th.

November 8, 1994

Ramnagar to Haldwani 52 km/ 33 miles

I met a lady called Kamlesh. I was walking, because the road was uphill and cobbled, through the village of Bel Parau. She was carrying a tray on her head holding little pots of yoghurt, covered with a crocheted cloth. She thought my bike had broken down and told me her husband had a cycle shop. He tested my tyres with a gauge; the pressure was still 45 lb! Kamlesh invited me to tea and I met her daughter, who made the tea. When I went to take her photograph, she declared that she looked a mess, and put a shawl on her head. They were delighted with the Polaroid photo I gave them. They had posed in front of their prize possessions, a fridge, and a TV, covered with cloth to protect them from dust. Another daughter, or maybe a daughter-in-law, arrived and wanted a photo but I said I only had eight possible pictures left, which was true. She worked in a family planning unit. The son has a workshop in the next village. I was given namkeen snacks and rice pudding for breakfast.

I had been recommended to visit the Jim Cobbett Museum by a chap who wanted to take me on a half-day trip in Cobbett Park. It was his house during the summer months, unfortunately, it was closed. I must read Cobbett's life history. Apparently, he worked for the railways, was a hunter-turned-conservationist and knew animal calls. He killed many man-eating tigers and had written four books about India. He left for Kenya at Partition. It was Jim Cobbett who was Princess Elizabeth's bodyguard at Treetops when King George VI died, and she became queen.

Jim Cobbett wrote in the hotel's register,

"For the first time in the history of the world, a young girl climbed into a tree one day as a Princess, and after having what she described as her most thrilling experience, she climbed down from the tree the next day a Queen – God bless her."

Riding until about 4 pm, through the hottest part of the day, when it was 32 C. degrees in the shade, I needed a water refill and stopped at an irrigation ditch where water gushed out of a pipe. I filled my bottles and wet my tee shirt and face to try and cool myself down. My legs felt tired when I stopped so I ate two more bananas. I'd had ten so far, including two for breakfast! I bought sliced bread from a nice man and his friend, five kilometres outside Haldwani. I was asked if I'd like butter but explained that it would melt on a bike! We got on quite well in my Hindi and their bit of English. I also chatted with some army people when I changed direction at a T-junction. I carried on, stopped for tea again, and was pestered by five boys wanting money. I gave them biscuits. There were two hotels on the way, but they wanted 300 and 225 Rs for their rooms. The next 'night halt' I came across was closed, but with the help of an old man, who didn't speak English, I found there was a government one next door. He had disappeared before I could reward him for his help!

Haldwani Tourist hotel was in the worst possible situation, just opposite the station. Many Indian hotels are to be found near railway and bus stations, built there because it is logical to stay where transport is available. The five-star hotels do not follow this logic, of course, they choose sites that are capable of being surrounded by gardens in the quiet parts of town.

My room's veranda overlooked the main street of Haldwani and the back window was directly above a bus station, so I was expecting plenty of noise from the hooting of horns and the revving of engines. I always wear wax earplugs at night to dull the usual night sounds, but at Haldwani I found out that there was the added bonus of a mosque next to the bus station. This meant Tannoy-ed prayer calls from the muezzin at midnight and pre-dawn. I didn't need to worry about not hearing my alarm!

After a tray-tea, I set about my routine of washing, first me and then my clothes. There was always a plastic bucket, and jug, in the bathroom for these operations. Indians abhor our custom of washing in a basin or bath of water because they think we are using dirty water over and over again, even sitting in it! I can remember being amused, when we were students at Leeds University forty years ago, at Ramesh saying the English people used stagnant water to wash in! There are rarely any plugs in the hotel washbasins; they are usually used only for handwashing and teeth cleaning. I used them for teeth cleaning and making my filter water, after checking that the waste pipe would not be emptying on to the floor around my feet.

If the basin was supplied with hot water, a rarity, I would use my 'universal' rubber plug which fits most sinks and use the basin rather than bend over a bucket. Many Indian bathroom washbasins empty through a tube attached to the plughole, directly onto the bathroom floor, or into a channel, leading into a drain or to a hole in an outside wall. There were many occasions when the system didn't work properly, and I would have water swirling round my feet while brushing my hair or packing up my toilet things. The bathrooms I encountered were invariable poorly lit with only a small opening fan light up near the ceiling, or a paint and dirt covered opaque window stuck in the closed position. When there was a mirror, it was usually dirty, so my image was always blurred, ideal for not being confronted with one's imperfections, but just enough to tie up one's hair.

Hanging the washing over the back of a cane chair, and on the veranda railing, I went in search of a telephone. There was a post office next door but no telephone. I discovered I needed Telegraph Office for phones and sending faxes. I wandered down the main street past the usual array of grocery, hardware, chemists and eating places. There were hand carts piled with fruits, and vegetables, and freshly cooked sugary sweets. At ground level, merchants spread their goods on woven mats or sold them directly from circular baskets at the roadside. At Haldwani I saw live hens, in wire cages. for the first time, looking small by our standards, even in their white feathers. It is quite common to see a cyclist with a live bird, its feet tied together, hanging from the handlebars of the bike.

November 9, 1994

Haldwani to Pilibith 103 km/ 64 miles

My tea came at 6.40 am and I was on my way by 7.10 am. I took a boy from the hostel with me because he had no change for my 50 Rs note. The market was only just beginning to open some of its stalls. I bought a bar of Lux soap so that I could get some change to pay him for my morning tea.

After 37 km. I stopped at a petrol station and was told to take the main road to Bareilly via Kichha. It was not really the road I wanted, but at Kichha I could take a road toward Sitaganj. The man at the petrol station offered me tea and wrote the names of the towns in Hindi script for me so that I could follow the signposts. After diverting to Sitaganj I stopped at the crossroads and attracted the usual crowd.

There seemed to be more turbaned Sikhs, than in previous villages. They were part of the itinerant band of harvester workers I had seen on the way, combining large fields of wheat. I had been so surprised by this mechanisation that I stopped to take a photo. The man on the tractor which was receiving the grain jumped down and rushed over to me to ask if I would take another photo of him. I was taken by surprise and as I didn't want to be besieged by all the workers, I said no. I then noticed his silver bracelet and beautiful dagger in his waistband, but I was so hidebound by years of discipline, that I dare not change my mind. I did, however, take a picture of weaver bird nests, looking like loofahs dangling from the branches of a tree.

Whenever I stopped for tea, I attracted a crowd. After bike admiration, the counting of gears, working out the derailleurs, and saying how fat the tyres were, I would start telling those near me what I was doing in India. An old man heard me say I was collecting money from my friends in England. He suddenly came out with the remark that 'leprosy people are bad people'. I turned to him and said quite firmly, in the best Hindi I could muster, that "they are not bad but sick". With the help of an English-speaking Sikh, I told the crowd in general, and the old man in particular, that people with leprosy could be made better in a year and that their illness was caused by a germ. Despite this outburst, I was treated to free tea and invited to stay in their town and not go on to Pilibith. I couldn't see any sign of a hotel and decided that I must press on because I had rather large distances between towns from today until Lucknow

At another break, I asked for an omelette, but the man didn't have any eggs, so I went to a shop, like a wooden wardrobe on legs, and bought three eggs for 4 rupees from the man squatting inside. I took them to the first man, and he made an omelette for me and served it in bread as sandwiches. It was a nice change from tomatoes and bananas. I had squeezed a small lemon into my drinking water, the night before, as I don't like plain water or sweet additives like orange juice, but I didn't like the taste and resolved to try and find some fruit juice to add instead.

Some of the roads were very bumpy – the old patchwork problem, using stones set in the tarmac for a few kilometres and the next section a mass of potholes and broken surface and occasionally smooth tarmac, albeit over bricks. I found out later that the road repairing was done by allotting contracts for a certain distance to different road mending businesses. Some firms would make a good job of the repair, while others would cut corners and use less tar or inferior ingredients or take less trouble to mend the road. Poor workmanship combined with monsoon rains resulted in these rough and bumpy sections of the road. I was grateful to my friends Stanley and Carol for giving me the handlebar and seat suspension, as it absorbed a lot of the vibration through the front forks and rear wheel.

Nevertheless, after several hours on such roads, my neck was very painful, and I had to resort to my surgical collar. I sometimes wore my surgical collar at night and took painkillers and anti-inflammatory tablets. In trying to find the least bumpy surface I took to copying the locals and riding, not on the edge of the road but in the middle, where the surface was usually least worn, because it is straddled by the heavier bus and truck motor traffic.

This was only possible on back roads which had much lighter motor traffic. I knew that if anything came along, I would hear its horn in plenty of time to regain the edge of the road. All Indian trucks, buses and even cars 'drive on their horns'. Hooting means 'I want to overtake' even if it is a bicycle, and even if there is enough room for two lorries to pass. I suppose that as nobody seems to apply the highway code it is only common sense to warn all and sundry. Certainly, in my experience, Indian cyclists, auto-rickshaws, and other vehicles. will stop, turn left or right, and use either side for overtaking, without making any signals.

I developed a 'town riding technique', namely, having one hand on the brake, one on the bell, and one foot out of the toe-straps ready for a quick stop. I am too scared, and old, to throw my leg over the saddle and rear of the bike, to mount and dismount. I have to stop by leaning the bike far enough over to lift my right leg forward over the crossbar, and vice versa for getting on. The other foot supports my list to port!

From Sitaganj to Pilibith was 41 km. Sitaganj and the next village seemed to have a lot of Sikhs and people were speaking Punjabi. At one of my tea stops I was asked by one of the young men in the crowd if I spoke Hindi or Punjabi. I suppose that being light-skinned, though probably sunburned, they couldn't make out where I was from. Punjabi people are often tall and have a light brown skin colour.

People I met on the road, or at tea stops, were predominantly men. Traditionally women would not be out alone. Hindu girls or women would only go out to the market with a male relative, such as a brother or husband. Many of the young men were part of the combine-harvester service that travels down the Ganges valley from the Punjab, and are hired by local farmers to cut the wheat or other cereals and take it to the mills for storing in warehouses called 'go-downs'. These go-downs are government facilities where rice and cereals are stored until the price is favourable for selling, or when there is the need to distribute it in times of shortage. As the monsoon travelled down the Ganges valley from west to east, so too was the date of sowing, and hence harvesting, was later in the eastern states than in western parts of the Ganges valley.

I had already ridden 62 miles. It was 3.30 pm and I started to panic in case it got dark before I reached Pilibith. I didn't fancy trying to look for accommodation in the dark, as it would be difficult to find my way around nameless streets. Indian towns, at least in the parts I'd been in so far, rarely used road names. It is easy to make out the main roads because they are named after the next large town on the route, but apart from this, I was completely at a loss. The central streets are often named after well-known people, and as India has a rather small repertoire of 'surnames' they must be distinguished by the honoured ones' initials, so that it all becomes rather a mouthful when used in full, and a mystery when abbreviated. For example, S.P. Marg stands for Sardar Patel Street. He was Sardar Vallabhbhai Patel, an Indian independence nationalist, known in India as 'Freedom Fighters', a barrister and former Deputy Prime Minister of India. All of Bombay's, now Mumbai, Raj-era roads have been renamed, but people are not consistent in using them, preferring the former English names like Marine Drive rather than Netaji Subash Marg.

From the Pilibith end of the by-pass, I was directed into town just as the sun was casting an orange glow in the sky. I asked a policeman, on traffic duty at a roundabout, if he could recommend a hotel. He said I should try the Anand, which translates as 'joy'. I wondered what joys were in store for me at this my first Indian hotel that was definitely off the Western Tourist track. I found it near the crossroads leading to the main Bazaar and booked into a room costing 175 rupees. The geyser didn't work and, when I asked for clean sheets, the little man selected some from a pile in the corridor. They hadn't any iron marks on them, and I think they were just recycled without washing. He picked up towels from a pile on the floor, holding each one up for inspection and finding the least dirty! I didn't need to rely on their sheets and towels, but it saved mine if I could get clean ones - after all, I didn't have time to dry towels overnight.

My bicycle was brought up the narrow stairs to my second-floor room, which had only an interior window, in other words, the window would open onto a corridor, if it opened! It had an air-conditioning unit, which I put on slow-speed, and a man appeared with a bundle of joss sticks and stuck them into the window frame. Whether. they were designed to keep mosquitoes at bay, act as air fresheners or be for my religious needs, I didn't know

After a wash in tepid water, a glass of tea, and filtering my water, I went in search of a chemist shop to buy some Canesten, a treatment for fungal infections of the vagina. The pharmacist told me that 'Indian ladies don't get that infection' when I told him what was wrong with me. If that is the case, why is Canesten sold at practically every pharmacy? He either thought that fungal infections had to be sexually transmitted, or he was just against me as a foreigner. I asked him where I could find another pharmacy and he directed me to the market area.

The next shop was out of stock, but the owner very kindly co-opted a man he knew in the street and asked him to take me to a large 'medicine hall' in the chowk area of Pilibith. I was just going to follow this man when a couple of ladies in a rickshaw, loomed out of the power-cut and stopped me.

The younger of the two wanted to know where I was going with the man, and when I told her she said that I was doing a very dangerous thing. She said that the man would only want money from me. I tried to protest, saying that it was the pharmacist who had chosen my guide, but she was adamant and so embarrassingly noisy, that I capitulated and accepted a ride in her rickshaw to the next chemist's shop. This time I was in luck, and I was able to buy six pessaries for 25 Rs, a tenth if the UK price. I had to ask for an inserter!

My 'guardian' asked me to go to her house for tea and, as she had been well-intentioned, I thought that it was the least I could do. She was married to a doctor in Punjab and was visiting her mother and father in Pilibith. I met her daughter who was celebrating her first birthday. We were joined by her mother and younger sister for tea and had a birthday cake, 'cooked without eggs', 'because they didn't eat eggs for religious reasons on Tuesdays" This was news to me, and I made a note to ask Ramesh about it. I took their photos and promised to send a copy. Sweety asked me how to get a visa for the UK – not the first time I have been asked! I was invited to stay for dinner but declined because I found Sweety a bit overpowering!

I went back to the Anand hotel and had a look at the menu. I decided to risk having chicken, it was probably well stewed and so small that the heat didn't have to penetrate far anyway. I was surprised to be offered chicken in this north Indian area where Hinduism predominated. I remembered seeing white chickens in Kathgodam, on my first foray to a 'night-market'. They were the size of pullets in the UK.

I saw ducks on a village pond today! My short wander around the night-market had been in the dark because there was a power cut, not at all unusual in this area. I was amused to see a gaudily painted sign over one shop, "Hare Drasher", no relation of Hari Krishna, but a hairdresser! The road was flooded at the crossroads near my hotel, and I gathered from Sweety that this was a long-standing event. I learned the next day from the Times of India, that there had been an escape from Pilibith Jail under cover of a power cut and five persons had escaped.

Pilibith was still sugarcane country and the chaff, from the canes which have had their sugar boiled out of them, is spread over the fields to dry. It is turned over by being walked through and making lifting and swirling movements with the feet. Bullock carts with wooden wheels, and their sides extended vertically, with an arrangement of bamboo and sacking, take the chaff to factories where it is made into strawboard for use in the building industry. Sweety said that I should ask sugar factories for accommodation as they all have 'guest houses' and that they should help a foreigner! I wouldn't have the nerve, but I suppose in an emergency I might.

For those without the luxury of hiring a combine harvester, the threshing of the grain from the stalks, is done by hand. Using both arms to grasp a bundle of stalks and starting from behind the neck, the bunches of stalks were brought over the head to be whacked six or ten times on a stone, a wooden bed, or a bench. These are occasions when a group of women will work together and sing as they beat the stalks to release the grain The piles of grain fall out onto the ground and are then collected up in shallow trays to be winnowed, often using hand turned fan to create wind to remove the dust and bits of stalk from the grain, as it is jiggled in its tray. I had had a go at this process in my Bihari friend's village!

I had to reach Shahjahanpur the next day, so I washed the bike, before taking Nurofen for my painful neck. The fan part of the air conditioning unit was very noisy. I turned it off when I was ready to sleep. I ordered tea for 6.15 am and breakfast for 6.45, omelette and toast.

I had noticed that there was 'Nes' coffee on the menu, as well as 'espresso'. I ordered some. After dinner I was told, "Sorry madam, this is my experience of machine, plain!". The contents looked like bad milk in tea – then I remembered I'd ordered Espresso coffee!

November 10, 1994

Pilibith to Shahjahanpur 85 km/ 53 miles

Leaving early, I made my way to the Shahjahanpur road, in an autumnal mist that was slowly clearing. Ghostly figures, wrapped in their winter shawls and wearing balaclavas, were warming themselves over little fires in the streets. These fires are often fed with old rubber tyres, and the smell is awful. The early-bird tea shops had got their stoves going, fuelled by cow dung road sweepings, and little balls of coal dust, giving off clouds of acrid, tear-producing smoke. Men were trying to warm themselves, hands cupping little glasses of tea, accompanied by much coughing and hawking. With the absence of wind and the heavy layer of mist the fumes swirled around at bike level. I was glad to reach the area of motor and agricultural repairs which signalled the outskirts and end of Pilibith.

Most Indian towns have motor vehicle repair areas on their outskirts. Rainbow-coloured puddles of petrol and oil surrounded by mud. Vehicles in various states of disassembly litter the area and indicate that a town is imminent. Transport offices often congregate in the same area with huge lorries that ply the length of India. Lorries have a driver and a mate, who is the indicator, leaning out of the door to signal to turn. Lorries in India, in 1994, did not have much in the way of working lights and instead of signalling they used their horns, loud vacuum-assisted claxons! On the back of a lorry, it would say

"Horn Please", the Indian way of giving instructions that you wanted to overtake.

Policemen at traffic junctions were quite good at giving me directions, though they would say 'straight on', even if there were several roads available at differing angles. Cycles and rickshaws, as well as cars and lorries, often drove without lights at night. What seemed like a motorbike headlight could well be a car with only one light working! A lorry without lights would give itself away by the noise of its engine. If there is a highway code no one knows it or uses it.! On encountering a bad stretch of road, or a pothole, the accepted rule is 'go around it'. Bridges often had bits of their balustrade missing – had a vehicle gone over into the river?

There was no shade on the road today and it reached 40 degrees. I managed to buy two bottles of Bisleri water. It was only available in larger towns, or on railway stations, frequented by businessmen and tourists. After two and a half hours I reached Bisalpur, and stopped for my morning cuppa. I chose a small tea shop at the end of the village and sat, as usual, on the bench on the street side of the counter. For some reason, there were a lot of flies on the ground and in the air. Unusually, no one spoke to me, and I didn't attract a crowd. Either they were very shy, perhaps embarrassed, or just stunned, at a white woman invading their village tea stall. I left as soon as possible. There were lots of fires outside shops and houses this morning, a sign that winter is coming. Any old rubbish gets burned, including discarded rubber flip flops which burn with an acrid smell.

Soon after leaving Bisalpur, I met a doctor going to his dispensary, in a distant village, and we rode together for eight kilometres, as far as the Katwa Bridge Octroi Point, where he had to turn off the main road. An octroi was a government post that levied a tax on certain goods as they entered a municipal area or a state. The barrier across the road functioned like a toll gate. The red and white bamboo pole was weighted with a huge rock and raised and lowered for traffic to pass. They were made obsolete in 2017 by a new online tax system. The doctor asked me to stop, and the men manning the taxation point made tea and invited us to sit on the bench outside their hut. Anyone who wasn't in a hurry stopped as well. I was given a packet of peanuts in their shells, but I didn't eat many of them because I didn't feel comfortable throwing the shells on the ground. Everyone wanted to know where I was from, and they were amazed that I was going all the way to Calcutta. The doctor told me that the main diseases he has to deal with are dysentery, cholera, and typhoid, all waterborne infections. He estimated that leprosy affected five percent of his rural population. Everyone was pleased to pose for a photo, and I continued on my way to Shahjahanpur.

It was still a sugar cane, wheat, and rice growing area with villages of mud-plastered cane and straw huts in little walled compounds. Some had relief decorations of doll-like figures, one had a pattern of a mirror on a stand, like the one Kailash had tried to give me, I found out, when I visited a museum in Ingraz-Bazaar, that this symbol is associated with Parvati, Shiva's wife.

The open countryside was replaced by thick woodland. The road had been newly tarmacked, jagged two-inch stones embedded in its surface. I bumped along until I came to a T-junction where there were no signs. A jeep was parked nearby so I went over to ask whether I was on the correct road. After confirming my direction, they asked me if I was alone, and for the first time, I felt uneasy. I said that I was meeting Indian friends in the next town, and hurried on my way. The enclosing effect of the tall trees and the fact that there wasn't much traffic may have added to my sense of loneliness, which until then I hadn't experienced.

After a while, I crossed a river bridge and the road became more open, and I could see the distant horizon where the tree cover was thinner. While I was having my lunch of tomatoes and bananas, at Lal Kuan Junction, an oxcart trundled slowly towards me. It was an ancient-looking wood and string contraption. I jumped up to get my camera and asked the driver if I could take a photo of his solid wooden wheeled cart, no rubber rims or pneumatic tyres on this one! While I was getting my camera a man in a bright yellow tee shirt joined us. His bicycle had a large flat cylinder on top of the rear wheel, so I asked him if I could take a photo of his bike too. He said "No!" and I was disappointed. Perhaps he thought I would put a jinx on it. I knew that some people think the camera takes the spirit away, so I respected his choice. Typically, another man arrived to join us, strangely I hadn't passed anyone in the last hour and now we were four! He was balancing a large cloth-covered dish on his head and the carter told me that it held goat meat.

Meanwhile, the bicycle man had propped up his bike on its stand and set up his machine so that I could see how it worked. He had wanted my photo of him to include his machine, that was why he had said "no". He had fixed a belt from the drum to the pedals – it was a candy-floss machine! He was now posing proudly beside his bike, and he let me reposition him to get a view of him and the wonderful machine. There were smiles all around when I took another photo of the three of them, this time with the polaroid camera. Once again it was a pleasure to see the amazement on their faces as the picture developed before their eyes. Of course, I had to decide who to give the photo to, but as they probably came from the same or at least neighbouring villages, I chose 'Yellow Tee-shirt' as custodian, for all the trouble he had gone to in assembling his machine.

Further along this road, I was greeted by a young man on a scooter, he was going the opposite way to me, but he stopped to say hello. On enquiring what he did I was amazed to hear that he was a Glaxo representative. My immediate response was "my husband worked for Glaxo". He must have thought I said 'works' because he turned his scooter around and invited me to take tea at the next village. Sunil Datt rode slowly alongside me. It was a relief to have someone who spoke good English to chat with. When we reached the village he took me to an indoor tea shop, the first I'd seen, but the bike had to be left outside on the road. I kept looking anxiously to see if the crowd of men and boys were touching the gears, I dreaded them being put 'out'. Sunil suggested that we try to find somewhere quieter. It was too much of a strain for me to ride fast enough to keep up with the motor scooter, so I suggested that he go ahead and that we meet at the next dhaba, which he told me was by the railway line.

When I got there, it looked quite normal, but there was no sign of Sunil. Well, I thought, he has probably changed his mind and gone off to do his rounds. However, he was just up the road waiting for me, because he didn't think it was a suitable place. I think he is a city man at heart and thought the shack was too lowly. They are village talking shops and perhaps it wouldn't be good for his career to be seen with me at one. (I forgot to ask him). It must have been difficult for him to ride the scooter at my cycling speed. I suggested that he had better carry on with his visits as I would take at least two more hours to reach the town. I asked if he could recommend a hotel in Shahjahanpur and he recommended that I check into the Durga. We agreed to meet at 6 pm.

Many of the ponds, at this time of the year, are covered with a floating plant like a water soldier. I think they might be some kind of water chestnut. Their Hindi name is 'Singara'. I saw a man in a little boat made of flattened corrugated iron. By the time I had stopped, parked the bike, and fished out the camera, he was no longer in the boat, but coming up the bank towards the road to join his friends. When they realised what I wanted, his friends insisted that the poor man get back into the boat, even though he had to bail it out, before he could paddle it out into the pond again. He used his hands for paddles, sitting in the stern and steering it to face the camera! The singara have fleshy leaves and the fruits are covered with thick dark green or reddish-black skin. This peels back to reveal a waxy, heart-shaped fruit that is crisp and slightly bitter to the taste. I'm not keen on them, but the polluted state of the pond is probably putting me off them. My Bombay friends relish singara as a delicacy.

It was very hot, my thermometer registered 40 degrees C in the shade, not exactly the winter temperatures I'd been expecting. The full force of the sun is felt when you stop. Just a few minutes rest for a water stop and the heat became noticeable, and I was glad to be on my way again. In fact, this cooling effect of riding, and the desire to always find accommodation before dark, was the reason why I didn't take long breaks, even in the hottest part of the day, which I had thought would be necessary when planning my trip. I became part of the "mad dogs and Englishmen" brigade. My watch was set to give an alarm signal every hour to remind me to drink water. I don't like water in England, and it required real effort to drink my filtered water here in the hot middle of the Gangetic Plain.

There are recommendations about drinking a pint for every pound of weight lost, but I wasn't going to be able to access scales for several weeks. Try as I might, I couldn't manage a pint of water – for some reason, I don't have this trouble with lager when I go to the pub! Unfortunately, alcohol aids dehydration so that was out, even if it had been available! I probably drank about half a pint at each stop. I knew that if I didn't then I would suffer from dehydration. The signs and symptoms range from headaches, nausea, and (more than normal for me) wandering of the mind, blindness, possible collapse, and death.

I remember seeing Greta Kristianson staggering into the stadium after one of her marathons, weaving all over the place like a drunk – that was dehydration. Whenever I had exhausted my overnight filtered stock of water, I would look out for irrigation pumps in the fields, which gushed water with the aid of electricity, to crops like sugarcane and newly planted rice. There was usually a hand-pumped supply at the larger dhabas. In villages I would ask before taking water, in case I infringed any caste laws and thereby, defiled the water supply. In one village there were separate supplies, a hand pump for drinking water and a well with a bucket for washing cups at the dhaba. I wondered which source was for washing people.

My road was brick-based, with tarmac over the top, but applied by hand rather than by a machine, hence the road was a series of coalesced bumps. Road improvements usually take the form of widening the road by three feet on one, or both sides. Broken bricks or stones of decreasing size are hammered into the excavated soil and then embedded with the sandy waste before being coated with tar. A blackened boiler on wheels, like a rusty steam engine, would be fired up with branches chopped and broken from wayside trees. To this fire, old rubber tyres are added, producing carcinogenic, black, stinking, smoke. Rusty drums of tar are melted on this contraption. Often barefoot, half-naked, skinny men, carrying pierced former ghee or cooking oil tins, take the molten tar to the required destination, where it is dribbled over the stones to embed them.

Sometimes ready-tarred stones are carried on small stretchers to a pothole, which had been dusted out by the foreman-hole-spotter and dumped into the hole to wait for a passing vehicle to do the road rolling. I only saw a few road-in use, mainly near Gaya where the already reasonable road was being widened. The area has many Japanese tourists to its Buddhist shrines, and the state, or national government, wants to make a good impression on them and other foreign tourists, who come to this popular religious pilgrimage area. Most of the road-rollers I passed were broken down, vandalised, and judging by their condition, had been abandoned for a few years. This tied in with what my Bihari friends told me about roads not being repaired since 1992.

I must confess that most of my journey was through the poorest states of India, Bihar, and Uttar Pradesh, perhaps it is better elsewhere? Many road repairs use three-inch sharp stones, of limestone or granite, which when embedded in tar are very uncomfortable to ride on and a puncture hazard. Calcutta had this kind of road treatment. I began to dread seeing piles of stones beside the road, as harbingers of neck pain and general bone shaking. I would put my foam neck collar on, to help me keep the best possible posture to withstand the bumpy road and lessen the potential pain.

I was surrounded by a crowd of curious children when I stopped at an irrigation pump to filter water, admiring the bike of course! I got to Shahjahanpur by 2.30 pm, having had a 7.10 am start. I felt stronger but the road was very bumpy, being brick-based and hand-tarmac-ed over the top. Piles of stone chippings at the side of the road, with a line of white paint, drizzled over them in a cross, indicated forthcoming road widening and improvement. The cross was to indicate if any of the stone had been stolen from the pile, as the remaining stone would move and disturb the white paint lines. Wherever possible I rode on the sandy strip at the side of the road. When I felt the bumpiness in my neck, I put my collar on and it was better.

The Durga Hotel was easy to find, after all, true to tradition, it was near the railway station. The janitor showed me rooms at 100 Rs, with no window, a single deluxe for 125 Rs, and a double, festooned with plush red velvet, which he informed me was for foreigners, at 250 Rs. I settled for the de-luxe with a real window. The sun shone into the room, which was faced with marble, floor, wall, and ceiling, in swirling patterns of black and white. As it was on the third floor, I didn't have my bike with me, but the receptionist assured me that it would be safe. All I could do was hope it wasn't being ridden around behind the scenes. I wasn't worried about the riding, just fiddling with the gears and throwing them out of alignment. Adjusting them was my Achilles heel. The front changer would not move over the chain on the largest chainring. I made do with the middle and lower range of gears, which with my luggage made me about the same speed as the sturdy Indian bikes. I could overtake them or fall behind, according to my mood and energy levels.

After a bucket shower, I did my washing and was brought a tray-tea by a very pleasant Nepali man, who spoke quite a lot of English. The tea was the best yet, not too strong, and a good three or four cups.

As I was on the third floor my room was much cooler than those on the lower floors and more mosquito free. Luckily, the bathroom window opened, and I put my leggings on the railing and my Lepra tee shirt on a clothes hanger at the open window. I would have to remember to close it at dusk or close the bathroom door. The downside was that the hotel was near the bus station and the railway station but I would use earplugs as usual.

I saw myself in a good light for the first time in weeks and I was horror-struck! Sprouting whiskers! Very grey hair! My bones stuck out of my skin and the tops of my arms had atrophied. What amazed me most was that my face had become very thin! I must have lost a lot of weight, but I had just covered 84 km. in good time, despite riding on the sandy tracks alongside the road, where it was slower going, but where there was less vibration.

I had half an hour's rest until 5.30 pm and went down to reception, where I read the Times of India among many mosquitoes. Sunil came at 5.45 and took me to the market area. I needed something that could be worn with the collar up to protect my neck from the sun and bought a green Swiss cotton shirt for 180 Rs. There wasn't much choice as it was now the winter season in India.

Sunil invited me to his lodgings. I told him that I wasn't in the habit of going to men's rooms. He told me that "there are two kinds of men, those who respect women and those who don't". He said he belonged to the former set and came from "a good family" in Delhi. I relented and we went along narrow brick paved alleyways to his room which he rents for 800 Rs a month, all in. On the way he told me about his family, and how he would like to work in Delhi, not in this rural backwater, where he had been for three years. His room was just about as untidy as my 20-odd year-old son's room.

His bed was not exactly made, clothes lying around on chairs, a half-open packet of bread on the table, which doubled as a desk, and a portable radio which looked like something before design became a feature. He made very good coffee, despite the pre-sweetened dried milk powder, and we talked about English, education, and medicine. Sunil told me that he had been working for Glaxo for three years and that he earned 3500 Rs a month and lives on banana sandwiches for his dinner - kindred spirits regarding Glaxo and bananas! He showed me a Glaxo report about the plague which was nearly over when I arrived in India. Four distinct varieties were mentioned whereas we had been told only of bubonic and pneumonic variations. The plague, Sunil said, was an example of the new openness of the Indian government about problems, at least medical ones. A friend, also called Sunil, joined us. He too was a medical rep for another company, Hoechst.

Sunil said that it was difficult for middle-class and educated working-class people to get jobs. The government operates a quota system, which gives people from the lower castes, and tribal people, priority in employment and education. The basic idea behind the system is to enable poorer people to get jobs and college places and thereby, increase their standard of living. The problem is that the quota is set high, for example, 70% of places in the Civil Service are for these 'reserved and scheduled castes.'

The two young men walked me back to my hotel and I watched TV in my room. This was the first time I had one – obviously part of the 'de-luxe' room. I tried to understand the news and weather in Hindi. There was a state-by-state news round-up, and some USA, Sri Lankan, and Kuwaiti items. The presentation was very boring, with just a newsreader and a map of the state in the background. I saw adverts for Pear's soap, a back-pain cream, and one about saving water while shaving, by not leaving the tap running.

There wasn't a dining room in the hotel, something I came across many times in Indian hotels, as opposed to international hotels, consequently, I chose from the menu card in my room and it would be brought to me. I ordered a Moghul vegetarian dish for my supper, a Navratan, which should be mildly spiced and cooked in yoghurt. For a treat, I ordered a bottle of Limca which I was going to drink in bed – real decadence. I may have to drink it in the dark because, according to Sunil, there is only electricity for ten or eleven hours a day. He has a portable, rechargeable neon light because he has to be able to write his reports at night.

When he came to collect my plate, I asked my Nepali man for tray-tea at 6.15 am the next morning. He told me that he wouldn't be on duty then, so I gave him 10 Rs. He didn't ask for it so I was pleased to give him a good tip.

November 11, 1994

Shahjahanpur to Sitapur 80 km/ 50 miles

I saw bullock carts with string sides, others with pneumatic tyres, and quite a few pony traps today. The first half hour of cycling was terrible on a brick road. I was beginning to think I'd never make it to Sitapur because of the vibration through every bone of my body, when the road joined a National Highway and by-passed Shahjahanpur, it was then a mostly good surface and I did 24 kilometres in the first two and a half hours, including the brick road section, a drink stop, and a bread and banana shopping stop. I was sitting on a little track, leading to fields, when a woman complained that I was sitting there, but on saying "Namaskar, I'm going to Sitapur" another spoke in my defence. Men were measuring a field with a stick yesterday - it is still sugar-cane country today. A swineherd just passed me. Lorries are stacked high with cane and are sounding their horns to say 'hello' but it is very wearing, as the sound goes on and on!

I was having a picnic lunch in a quiet spot under a tree, when I was surrounded by about 50 youths, and some older people. I was facing the fields, and they came up behind me, from the road. They kept their distance until I started to move off. and then they surrounded me and followed me on their bikes. After 5 km they were still there – I didn't speak and a 16- to 17-year-old youth, who was the ringleader, tried to make me fall off my bike. I stopped and followed a family who got off a bus, down a track towards a village, but the youth followed me. I was near to tears. The family moved off. I told the youth to go away and started to write in my book. He came up behind me, so I got up and told him again to go away. He touched me on my breast, so I hit him in the face, and he returned it! Then I tried to kick him but wasn't near enough and I wasn't going to let go of my bike. An older man came from the village, the youth spoke to him, and they both smiled. I went back to the road, determined to flag down a lorry when I heard another youth say, "let her go to Sitapur ". My arm and chest were quite painful after this experience, and I wondered if it was muscle strain or my heart causing the pain.

Hotel Mayur was signposted on a hoarding. It was the only one and quite dirty, but I took a room. My room was very dusty with no glass in the window, only metal mosquito netting. When I swatted a huge orange wasp, its body and trailing legs measured about two inches, and hit the mosquito netting a cloud of dust filled the room! The sheet looks ironed and clean, but the blanket was dubious – I'd use my sleeping bag tonight – I'd been bitten quite a lot last night. I asked for a mosquito machine, thinking I might be given an electric mosquito repellent, but a man brought Flit – a pump action gun that sprayed liquid under my bed and stank of paraffin.

Outside the staff were watering the ground to lay the dust. There was a restaurant, but I didn't know whether to bother. There was an ice cream shop too! My bike was inside the hotel where I was assured it wouldn't be touched.

Earlier today, when I was photographing a doorway with a lion or cougar picture, in relief, on the front of a house, two or three boys asked me if I drank tea. I said "abhi?", 'now?', and they took me to their dhaba next door. Their mother and they admired the bike, and we had a conversation. She had a nice face with dimples, and was about 40 years old. The boys wouldn't accept any money for my tea. The only English they knew was 'ta-ta' and 'bye-bye'. We probably got 'ta-ta' as children's talk, from India, and 'nana' which means grandfather!

The road was quite shaded today and mostly good. It seemed to be going slightly uphill, but I think it was an optical illusion. At one stage I was on the biggest front chain wheel, but I'm mostly use the second one. A Sikh man in a maroon turban and khaki jacket and trousers, has just gone along the road on a maroon motorbike. He looked like a praying mantis – I think because the bike frame was so huge, and his legs so long and skinny. There isn't a garden or anywhere to sit inside the hotel, so I'm sitting in front of the hotel, about 20 feet from the main road. There is a police training post opposite the hotel, and they are square bashing. They are almost lost in the clouds of dust raised by their stamping feet!

A man staying in the hotel told me he lived in Southall for 6 years, and offered me some tea. I tried to decline, saying I was going to the STD box, but he immediately poured half his cup into his saucer, drank it, and gave me his cup!

Ramesh will try to arrive in Lucknow on Monday at 12.15 pm. His friend, Mr. Dass, is expecting me to stay with him and his wife.

November 12, 1994

Sitapur to Lucknow 88 km/ 55 miles

I'd left Sitapur at 6.55 am after having only tea, so I stopped at the first dhaba where I could see eggs on the counter, and ordered an omelette, it was 7.20 am. Carts and bikes were taking long green cucumber type vegetables to the market. Lines of parked trucks were disgorging sleepy drivers and mates. It was their 'wake up and wash time', balaclavas, shawls, hand-knitted pullovers teamed with bare legs and sandals, looked very funny to me, but at least the speed fraternity were off the road for a while. After sandwiching my omelette between two slices of bread I carried on. At 9 am. I had a water and banana-sandwich stop.

I had done 26 km in two hours, including my breakfast stop. At 11 am I had a tomato-sandwich, filter water and chai (tea) stop, much to the amusement of the locals. There was less sugar cane growing now, and more rice growing and a market-gardening. Orange groves and guava orchards began to appear as I got nearer to Lucknow. Bananas only seemed to be sold in small towns. At 1 pm I had three bananas, and a water stop. I had only 14 km to go.

I found my way easily to the town centre, crossing the Gumti river, where a red sandstone building with pretty towers stood beside the river. The streets were filled with rickshaws, cars and cycles like all Indian towns, but here in Lucknow there were lots of wide streets and beautiful classical buildings, surrounded by trees and parkland. Some of the former palaces of the Muslim princes were now offices, and as such, they were set upon immaculate lawns and were freshly painted, in pastel yellows and pinks. I passed a church which might have been transplanted from an English village, stone tracery, stained glass windows and spire! There was a church built like a Noah's Ark, as well as a sedate, lime washed cathedral, surrounded by shrubs. Protestant, Catholic and newer American sects were well represented in this state capital of Uttar Pradesh.

Outside the cathedral I asked a group of rickshaw wallahs the way to Vikram Aditya Marg, and they directed me to the district known locally as 'Diplomatic Marg', for its abundance of embassies and ministerial residences. It was literally 'straight on' across each roundabout and road junction in this newer, geometrically laid out part of Lucknow. I was being given conflicting instructions by two policemen when, by chance, a teenage boy came by, who knew the Dass family. It transpired that his mother worked for them, so I was escorted by this young man in the red shirt, to their house, just off the main road opposite the Russian consulate, with its huge statue of Marx.

Mr Dass was in London at the Indian High Commission from 1956 to 1957. Mr. and Mrs. Dass travelled widely in the UK, Scotland, and

Europe. Mrs Dass was now acting principal of a Montessori school for fee paying 6- to 11-year-olds. She trained in London. Her mother lives with them, and is a very spritely 84-year-old, whose husband died recently at the age of 90. Nirmal and her mother have the same beautiful faces, high cheekbones and long noses. They certainly don't look their ages.

I was shown onto the veranda, overlooking the back garden, and brought tea by Mr Dass, to be joined by his wife when she returned from school. I had been given their son's room, as he was going to Delhi. It was suggested that I rest for an hour. Needless to say, I didn't feel able to rest, so I did some pre-washing, in case the dhobi got a shock at the colour of my traffic-grimed leggings, shirts and socks. There was an electric boiler in which to heat water for my bucket shower, so I was able to heat water for clothes washing. The windows had mosquito netting, and the double bed had a pretty patterned sheet and quilt set. My panniers occupied one corner of the room, which connected to the kitchen by a small corridor, where cooking utensils were arranged on newspaper-covered stone shelves, and led to the front porch-cum-veranda by a pair of double doors. The bathroom opens off my room and also leads directly to the outside, so that the bathroom cleaner can enter from the garden and not through the house, thus avoiding any caste infringements, and making the sluicing of the bathroom easier too.

Mr Dass said he would take me sight-seeing the next day and I made a mental note to ask him about church and collecting my case from the station. Ramesh would arrive on Monday. I will have to clean and maintain my bike on Monday morning. A little servant girl peeped in through the mosquito netted window. She had been watering the garden. I could hear a baby crying somewhere nearby.

I had a bit of a cold – it started as a sore throat and earache, though it could be from lorry fumes. I had been retired for an hour, so I had a shower and washed my hair. I ran out of shampoo and made a mental note to ask Nirmal where I can get some.

Yasbir Dass, his wife Nirmal and Mrs Dass's mother were very kind. They introduced me to many kinds of Indian dishes and even gave me a beer from the Diplomatic coffers on my first night! Mr Dass's son was leaving to return to Delhi, and we went to town to choose his Diwali present for his mother – a new sari. Nirmal chose a dark coloured one, which she said was most practical for teaching.

Sunday November 13, 1994

Exploring Lucknow.

Mr Dass's son had told me where the church was, but it turned out to be one of the hot gospel sects of America. I had walked there and went further towards the town to locate a Roman Catholic church. It was getting late when I found the cathedral. I went in. It was very much like the Roman Catholic service, except that the priest wasn't facing the people, and it turned out to be the Church of North India. I stayed until the end of the service, on the principle that something was better than nothing. The service was what my daughter would describe as "high" or Anglo-Catholic.

The Dass's took me sightseeing after my return from church. I was taken to see some of the elegant mausoleums dedicated to the early Princes, (Nabobs or Newabs) of Avadh (also spelt Oudh by the British) dating from 1850, set in parkland and popular as a picnic spot, judging by the litter lying around the site. Round-abouts were decorated with tinsel and preparations were being made in a nearby park for National Children's Day to be celebrated the next day, with outings and picnics for children on the anniversary of Nehru's birthday. Nirmal's schoolchildren are going to a village school and taking bananas for the seventy children on the register. She told me later that one-hundred-and -forty children turned up for free bananas!

91

The highlight of my tour was my visit to the ruins of the British Residency. The whole complex had been left as it was at the end of the eighty-three-day siege by Indian mutineers from the army, supported by local militia and residents of the city. The former British Residency was home to 2000 men, women and children during those hot, gruesome days in 1857. The women sheltered in the underground rooms in the building which today houses a dusty model of the besieged site and some ill-displayed etchings of old Lucknow. Only 976 survived the entrapment, including the force which was sent to relieve the British contingent and was itself trapped and obliged to remain in the besieged outpost. The walls bear the marks of the shot and cannon balls; the tower and walls of the main buildings are shot away. It was a widespread but unsuccessful rebellion against British rule in India from 1857 to 1859., Known in Britain as the 'Indian Mutiny' and in India referred to as ''The First War of Independence''. There was a memorial saying,

"Erected in Memory of

The Devoted Gallantry and Fidelity

of The Native Officers and Sepoys

of The Hon. Comp. 13th Bengal Native Infantry

(Garuda Pultun)

Who Fell in the Defence of Lucknow".

'This monument is Erected by the Surviving European Officers of the Regiment

in the Bailee Guard Post

which was held by the Regiment

throughout the Defence'

It mentions fifty-one personnel of various ranks including five 'drummers'

It was not until a few years later that I read an account of the siege of Lucknow and its relief, in great detail, in a diary of daily events by Lady Julia Selina Inglis – whose father and husband commanded the British troops. She had three children under five with her at the time.

Mr. and Mrs Dass not only introduced me to Lucknowi cuisine, but also to the famous Lucknowi crafts and etiquette. On Sunday evening I was taken to meet an old lady who lived in a mansion, surrounded by antiques, with her unmarried son. She was a lady of an 'established family', now possibly in reduced circumstances judging by the on-going redevelopment of their garden. Her son wore a kurta of the finest cotton I had ever seen, almost transparent, hand embroidered and tucked, and secured with diamond buttons. Lucknow specialises in this kind of embroidery called 'chickan'. They spoke a very pure form of Hindi with the formal etiquette for which Lucknow is famed. 'Apne aap' after you, and 'Pehle aap', ' You first', and 'after you' are said at every opportunity.

Mr. Dass does the vegetable shopping for his wife, either from vendors who came to the house, or from a small suburban market. He took me to the market each day and would identify strange fruits and vegetables for me. He showed me gourds, thin green cucumbers, marrow-like lowki and kerela (very bitter but good for diabetes) In a village outside Lucknow I had seen a garlic seller and. 'turai' a yellow flowered gourd growing on roofs and on stacks of cow pats.

In different parts of India women make cow-dung pats into specific traditional shapes. The cowpats are semi-circular in the Lucknow region – like Cornish pasties! In the Allahabad area they were flat circular discs, in the eastern part of Bengal they were wrapped around jute sticks like elongated lollipops or kebabs. The storage of cow dung also varied across the continent. In many places they are slapped on walls and stick like discs, with the owner's handprint for identification. In another parts of India, they are stored in beautifully decorated rectangular or circular mud huts.

Although Mrs. Dass Senior knew about as much English as I knew of Hindi, we got on very well, holding long conversations about her childhood, and my life in England, Although Mrs. Dass senior knew about as much English as I knew of Hindi, we got on very well, holding long conversations about her childhood, my life in England, including details of the cost of living in our respective countries. We were often alone together when Mr Dass was working, he too was amazed by our conversational prowess. She was so charming that we managed to understand one another. Mind you, if I had known that Mr. Dass was able to hear my efforts through the open window of his office, I would have been more reticent!

On Monday morning Mr Dass and I tackled the suitcase problem. When it left Ramnagar the station master had said it would take either two days or two weeks to reach Lucknow. I thought he was just trying to pull rank on the police officer, who asked how long the journey would take. Luckily the case had not been put on the wrong train at the mainline junction, neither was it languishing in some siding – possibilities which Mr Dass thought highly likely, no doubt borne of long experience as a government official

The suitcase was indeed in Lucknow but it had incurred extra charges, for remaining there uncollected, even on days when the luggage department was not open for business. Mr Dass had words with the various managers, the commercial manager and the station manager, whom he knew personally and the case was eventually declared located. I had to write a letter, dictated to me by an official, the Railway Superintendent, for charges to be waived.

Personally, I would have gladly paid extra charges just to get my case, but I followed Mr Dass's instructions and we were eventually taken by yet another man to collect the case from a point outside the station. I wondered if the waiving was for an ex-government official, or for a foreigner!

I was having Indian food morning, noon and night and eventually, on Sunday night I succumbed to a tummy bug, or more likely a reaction to the surfeit of spices, for my constitution. My headache had become more persistent too. Ramesh was due to arrive at Clark's Hotel at 6 pm. I made an appointment for a manicure, pedicure and leg wax at his 5-star hotel. The leg wax used lemon and sugar and was given with me sitting with my leg on a stool, spreading the mixture on long lengths of cotton sheeting about 5 inches wide – three applications for each leg! Another new experience!

Ramesh arrived before I had finished my treatment, but we were able to have tea, before leaving for dinner at the Dass's house. He was shocked to see me looking so thin, but I did not dare tell him I felt ill. He had brought a new Pentax camera for me to use while I was in India, because mine had packed-up on the plane, or through the x-ray machine in Delhi, and it wasn't possible to repair it in Bombay. I had been using Prem's camera since Gangotri, but it too had a fault with the zoom lens, and I was anxious to get some good photos.

Ramesh came to collect me the next morning to go sightseeing. We saw La Martiniere college, a palatial building, a mixture of architectural styles, that was built as the country residence of Major Claude Martin 'the richest French man in India'. He made his fortune in the service of the East India Company and for the Nawab of Audh. He left his fortune to the creation of the school. There are now ten schools named after him in India and France. We also went to see the 18th century Imambara shrine, with its huge arched hall and a maze of tunnels, with city views from its upper balcony.

I felt worse, having been up with diarrhoea in the night, and had a temperature. Ramesh called a doctor. He also arranged for me to have an x-ray on my ribs, which had been hurting for some time now, and I also showed the therapist my neck problem. The tablets I was given made me sick but my head got better in the night. Ramesh stayed an extra day in Lucknow. He took more of my luggage, sleeping bag, mattress and fleece to Bombay, and persuaded me to go to Allahabad by train. When I felt better Mr Dass booked tickets for me and the bike to go to Allahabad.

November 17, 1994

Lucknow to Allahabad by train

The train only stopped at Lucknow for a short time, so I hurried along the platform with my bags looking for my second class, air-conditioned carriage, while Mr Dass made sure they loaded the bike in the luggage van, at the rear of the train. Mr Dass was a Chief Government Secretary and had a lot of influence –he knew the systems, and arranged my x-ray, and circumvented the station shenanigans when we collected the case. I had noticed that other people were polite to me when I was with Mr Dass but hardly gave me a glance when I was with Ramesh. I just had to hope that the bike was not squashed by boxes and crates when it stopped at later stations, and more luggage was loaded. I had tried to pad the gears but there was no foam available this time. Later on, I saw scooters protected with wads of straw.

I took my allotted seat in the correct carriage, and managed to have a two-hour dose on the train, then breakfast –a flask of tea, vegetable cutlet, bread and butter. I had ordered an omelette and toast but this is India! There was a western style toilet on the train and it was actually clean, and there were hardly any passengers on this 2nd class sleeper train. There were no other tourists around either– though I had seen American and German business people in the hotel, including a woman clutching a UNICEF envelope. It is only 160 km from Lucknow to Allahabad, but it takes six hours by train. I was in a window seat and the air conditioning was very cold, so I changed my seat to sit under a permanently lowered top bunk where there was a free seat and I was sheltered from the blast of cold air!

I saw a man broadcast sowing a field. The crops were 90% rice alongside the railway track, but I also saw rows of potatoes and huge cabbages. The field sizes are about 40 x 20 feet and multiples of this. Trees were protected by circular walls of brick and village houses had walls of cream coloured mud. The soil was whitish. At Khudaharanaganj station I saw a one horse, two-wheeled cart, with a covered seat on top. It is called an 'Ekka', meaning one! Ponds have white lotus flowers in them and I saw three boys on a bike, one sitting, one standing, one on the carrier holding the seat man's shoulders. There were mango groves protected by mud walls about two feet high, and I saw my first camel being ridden through fields near Phaphanali Junction. On the whole it was a painfully slow journey.

On arriving at Allahabad Junction station, a hotel tout attached himself to me and proved most useful in re-claiming my bike. The process took an hour instead of the usual three, as requested by the parcel office. I paid a coolie 15 rupees to take me and my bags to the parcel office where I handed over my chit. I then had to go to the platform again to find the bike. It was in a wire cage under some stairs. The tout carried my bags and I gave him 50 Rs with the sheer relief of getting my bike.

His 'hotel' was full and the Government Tourist hotel in Allahabad took an hour to find, as it is known locally as Hotel Ilawat, with no mention of 'tourist'. They only had one night available so I was recommended to try the Samrat hotel which wanted 500 Rs. Another said no, so I ended up at a 132 Rs, Raj period hotel, which had decayed a lot. It looked like an army barracks inside, with 40 feet ceilings. The manager said it "was Barnard's"! I was given a mosquito coil, towel and blanket. I turned on the bathroom light and found there was a geyser for hot water but I dared not turn the light off, or touch anything electric again, as the fittings were broken off the wall, and were dangling dangerously on the ends of their electric wires.

I went out to buy some apples, 'musumbie' oranges and tomatoes. I couldn't find any tomatoes! There were lots of restaurants, some places with espresso coffee machines and a nice-looking sweet shop. I would have to go out again with more money. My foot was already bitten so I might as well risk a few more bites!

I decided I would visit Anand Bhavan, the Nehru family home, the Fort and religious Sangam the next day. An old man insisted on giving me 30 Rs in coins- tomorrow is a special festival.

There were no meals in my hotel, even the tea had to be brought in from outside, at 6 rupees a glass. The bed felt like hair- probably Raj era, and the pillows were lumpy. At 6 pm I saw a huge rat run round the room and hide in the rolled-up carpet. I had visions of more rats coming up from the sewers, into the squat toilet bowl. I went to the reception to say I was leaving, saying 'British Memsahibs did not sleep with rats!' He would only return one of the two nights charged.

I went to Hotel Tippo, on the opposite side of the street, for a recce. The room looked OK and was supposed to have hot water. It turned out to be only cold. I was later given a bucket to get hot water from the kitchen. I paid 225 Rps, and had lost 132 Rps .at the other place. I spent half an hour trying to kill mosquitoes until I was brought coils, that burn smokely and slowly to discourage the mosquitoes. The janitor started asking me questions, "where was I from?" and so on. He then surprised me by asking if I had a husband. I said my husband had died 6 years ago. He immediately said, "No sex for 6 years! I will be your special friend" This was the first time I had heard any Indian mention sex to me and I was very surprised. He seemed such a mild man, so I said I was very old, but he was probably very confused, because I used the wrong word for 'old'. I used 'purana' which means old as in antique, instead of 'burhiya' meaning old age. The door to my room had a bolt which fitted into the thickness of the wall and was not at all secure. Not sure how far his offer of 'special' might extend to, and worried that he might try to come into my room at night, I wedged my bike against the door when I closed it for the night.

I set up my own mosquito net for the first time. With nothing obvious to anchor it to, I used the bike handle-bar-ends to hold the top of my net and slept with my head at the foot of the bed to be near the bike. I slept well for the first time in days, despite rows and noises about someone in the adjacent kitchen, who was sick from drinking. The noise went on until midnight!

November 18, 1994

Allahabad

The main reason for spending two days in Allahabad (pronounced, illa'ha'bad) was so that I could visit the holy Sangam, the confluence of the Ganges, the Yamuna with the mythical river Saraswati. All the places where other rivers enter the Ganges are of special religious significance and are known as Sangam or Prayag. The old name for Allahabad was Prayag.

I walked up my street, the main road of the modern part of town, called MG Marg – Mahatma Gandhi Street. Indians are very fond of using initials for streets and buildings. I think every town in India has a MG Marg! I was wearing a beige tee shirt that I had bought in Lucknow – it was cooler with my crinkle skirt and my black woollen jumper.

The newer part of Allahabad, and other towns too, where once troops were garrisoned in 'cantonments', are called 'Civil Lines'. The Allahabad Civil lines were as dusty as Lucknow's, but there were quite a lot of raised sidewalks, and there were brick-paved areas in front of modern shopping parades at each intersection. To ride along such main roads, where at the intersections, a policeman controlled the traffic to some extent, I would have one hand on the brake, and one foot out of the toe straps ready for a quick emergency stop!

The old part of the town, referred to as the 'chowk' was on the other side of the railway line and was the usual jumble of dhabas, shops, cheap hotels, open drains and dirty roads, chock-a-block with cycles, cycle-rickshaws, pony traps, and cattle, not to mention people.

I passed the Tourist Hotel where I had been refused accommodation, because it was fully booked for a wedding, and asked at the bus station next door, about a bus to the Sangam. Apparently, it was only for long distance buses, not local ones. I was told that I should take a cycle-rickshaw, or an auto-rickshaw to the Sangam and the adjacent Fort. Of course, being foreign, I attracted several offers of transport at exorbitant rates, like 50 Rs., so I kept on walking, looking for someone to ask directions from.

I met a man who told a hovering rickshaw wallah, and onlookers, who seemed to have appeared from nowhere, that "we must be good to foreign visitors". He told me, and wrote down in Hindi script, how I could get to the Sangam by auto-taxi. This was to be another 'first'.

They are larger versions of rickshaws with open sides holding six or more passengers on bench seats, facing one another across the width of the vehicle. The driver often has a mate, who collects the money as the fares get off. I was told I should pay between two and four rupees per leg of my journey. There are set routes, but not designated stops. I had to change about three times and still had a long walk to the place where the boats left for the actual confluence.

Preparations were being made for the 'Kumbh mela', a religious gathering of priests, holy men, representatives of various sects, millions of pilgrims and other hangers-on. It was to take place on February 14th. The event rotates with four other cities over a period of twelve years. (Hardwar, Nasik, Ujjain and Allahabad). The huge flat area of sand and silt, which is the dried up river bed part of the Ganga and the Yamuna were being divided into compounds by corrugated iron, bamboo and other temporary material fences, for thousands of holy men, gurus and other religious leaders. Pilgrims come for ritual bathing in the river, to gain release from the cycle of reincarnation.

Tens of millions come to a special Kumbh' mela festival every twelve years at Allahabad. The smaller mela is ever three years. Pilgrims live in tents and hear talks, sing hymns and pray and bathe. Water pipes were being laid, and latrines constructed, electricity and loud-speaker systems were being laid on, and roadways of steel sheets, led to pontoon bridges, that connected the mela area with Allahabad's main road network. Shrines were being built in the compounds, tents for people, and even housing for elephants. The army and the police are involved in the construction and supervision of the millions of visitors who come to this fifteen-day festival.

The Red Fort of Akbar wasn't as high as I'd thought it would be, having seen Delhi's Red Fort, but I only saw the confluence side. Trees and greenery were spilling over its red sandstone walls, as I imagined the Hanging Gardens of Babylon might have looked. The boats, going to the spot in the river where the three waters merged, left from the far end of the road which skirted the Fort. There were about a hundred boats of various sizes and physical states, arriving and departing, with decks only a few inches above the water line. Generally, the boats were about 20 feet long and 6 feet in the beam. Some had arches of bamboo over them. The poshest looking boats had the fewest passengers.

I was offered passage for 100 rupees to begin with, then 50 rupees and finally 20 rupees. I was trying to tell the boat master that I wanted to go on a boat with twelve to twenty passengers on it, not on the already almost sinking craft, with fifty to a hundred pilgrims on board. Not getting very far with language I drew two boats on the cover of my journal and filled one with twenty stick men and the other with about ten figures. The boat master interpreted the people as money, and offered me a seat for 20 Rs. I had often read in the Indian press of boats foundering with hundreds of passengers on board – grossly overloaded for the sake of a few rupees! I was directed to a boat with ten people on it. It was just leaving so I had to run, and jump to get on board, as it left the shallows.

My zinc covered boat had a wooden deck at gunwale height and was propelled by two young oarsmen, in the prow. Their oars were crudely made from bamboo poles with pieces of hardboard nailed to them, to form the blades. I took my place on the deck facing the oarsmen, who sat in a well, below deck level, and was able to sit on the deck and let my legs dangle into this well – much more comfortable than sitting cross-legged on the deck like the other passengers.

The pilgrims were all members of one family, from Madhya Pradesh. An ayurvedic doctor, Mr. H. Pal, with an uncle, his three sons, mother and sisters. They were accompanied by a pujari (priest) who led them in the performance of the Ganga Puja all the way to the Sangam. He had brought a little flower-pot with a holy basil, 'tulsi' plant in it. It was a marvellous opportunity for me to observe the details of the ceremony and to take some photos.

Large plates, made of dried and pressed leaves, were placed in front of each man, as they sat cross-legged on the deck. Two containers of Ganges water were used to sprinkle the rice flour which was ladled onto the plates. Each man proceeded to make dumpling sized balls which were then divided into nut sized pieces. Coloured powders, rice and wheat grains, mica chips and seeds, were added to the plates. Water was sprinkled on each of the four men (the women sat at the back of the boat), carefully wetting the little tufts of hair on their otherwise shaven heads - a sign that they belonged to the Brahmin caste. After this, with thumb and ring-finger together, they put the water on their eyes. Cupping their hands they cradled marigolds in their water-filled hands. The pujari intoned the prayers. I could pick out the names Ganga, Haridwar and Saraswati, the men repeated 'Om' after each phrase. Little newspaper parcels were produced and unpacked to reveal small chips of silver, coloured powders, seeds and spices. Coconuts were introduced into the proceedings and dipped in the river.

At the confluence everything was thrown into the Ganges-Yamuna-Saraswati with a prayer. The confluence itself was not as vivid as that at Devprayag, mostly because viewed from the boat deck, the different colours of the rivers were not obvious. There was just a band of ripples where the calmer, slightly greyer Yamuna reflected the late morning sunshine like a shimmering ribbon.

My journal fell overboard at one stage and was noticed by someone in the next boat, and rescued by the pujari. It soon dried out in the sun.

When the boat arrived at the recognised auspicious part of the confluence, (a shallow sandbank, where a pontoon and poles allowed the hundred or so boats to moor) pilgrims, men, women and children left their boats and washed themselves in the river. Men wore underpants or shorts, children were naked and women wore their saris, blouses and underskirts. I noticed that the men generally frolicked around in the water, while women stood and prayed with clasped hands and serene looks on their faces.

There was a very old, extremely frail lady in the boat next to ours. She was having difficulty negotiating the well part of the boat, yet the oarsmen made no attempt to help her. I leant across and tried to give her some support – she was so small that she could have been carried by a man, and I wondered why she wasn't helped in any way. Was it men's attitude to women in Indian society or just ignorance? I dreaded to think of the trouble she'd still have to face stepping the two feet down onto the sandbank.

Ladies dressed themselves in dry saris with the utmost decorum – either on the landing stage or back in their boats, and the men changed into dry dhotis – a much easier task. I noticed that the bamboo hoops over some boats were used as washing lines for wet clothes, at the same time providing shade for the return journey to the Fort, at the end of the mela ground. On the return journey I tried to talk, in my poor Hindi, to the Doctor telling him about my journey and asking him if he had ever been to Gangotri. He told me that he had been to Allahabad once before – they only come here and have no intention of visiting Benares, another holy city (equally near for them from Madhya Pradesh in their van). I promised to send them photos in February and Dr Pal gave me his card, all in script, which I had to get translated. (He wrote to me a few months later, in English, and invited me to visit if I was ever in his neighbourhood).

When I disembarked, I paid my 20 rupees as agreed but was told that I should only pay 10 Rs. – a bit of a contrast to the 100 Rs that I was asked for at first!

I made my way back towards the city, along the long line of beggars. Vendors with portable cane stands, on which trays were placed, displayed their wares. Little tin oil lamps made from empty food tins, fitted with a spout like a kettle, were attached to the stands, so that they could continue selling at night When moving around the trays were carried on their heads. The hour glass shaped cane stands were tucked under an arm. Living as I do in the "west" in such a consumer-led, throw-away society, where obsolescence is built into the manufacturing process, I am always pleased to see how ingenious these poor people are, making use of seemingly useless bits and pieces. There were more stalls for the 'pandas', pujaris who kept the pilgrims' records and took care of the donations. I tried to find out why one of them had a bicycle on his saffron flag, flying at the top of a long bamboo pole. I knew that political parties adopt a utilitarian sign on their flags and voting papers, to represent their party among a largely illiterate population, but this was the first time I'd seen a bike on a religious banner.!

Old and deformed leprosy sufferers were sitting on their wooden carts begging from pilgrims.

Taking an auto-taxi again, this time sitting next to the driver and his mate, my head banging on the tin roof and glassless window-frame. I was quoted 40 Rs. for the journey to the Nehru House Museum, known as Anand Bhavan 'House of Joy'. I decided that at 5 foot 9 inches I was too tall for Indian public transport vehicles! Forty rupees was very much over the odds but I was hot and tired, and they were going to take me all the way, so that I wouldn't have to keep changing vehicles.

I learned later that I was a 'reserve' passenger. At Anand Bhavan there was a crowd around the gate, watching a man literally hacking limbs off a tree with an axe. I thought the crowd was waiting for the place to open after the lunch break, and was disappointed to find out that it was Guru Nanak Day, the sixth Sikh Guru, and was a religious, national and bank holiday.

After buying some fruit and a glass of tea, I managed to find a cycle rickshaw who took me all the way back to Hotel Tippo for 10 Rs. I was so pleased at not being ripped -off that I gave him a 10 Rs tip. The problem with tipping is that if one westerner is willing to give 20 rupees he might as well ask 20 rupees from the next fare, and so the charge winds up the rupee spiral ladder.

I ordered a pot of tea, 16 Rs and lit some more mosquito coils in the ashtray in my room. The advertising on the packet said that the mosquitoes "will rush out of doors"! They weren't very effective as far as I could tell. I'd have two or three smouldering away and they would often go out when I wasn't there to relight them.

To get away from the smelly coils, I retreated to the Jade Garden Restaurant, garden where I wrote up my journal. I was sitting on the grass when the little janitor who looked after me rushed over with a chair. He had also been looking after my washing, which I had left drying on a hedge outside my room, turning my woollen jumper to dry it thoroughly and keeping it in the sunshine. He then brought me a still blind puppy - I told him to take it back to its 'mother'- unfortunately its 'mother' was lying in the sunshine and had great trouble carrying the little thing back to its bed in the shade of the trees. She kept on dropping it.!

In the morning, I was going to Mirzapur 91 kms (58 miles). I didn't know if I could do it in one day. I met an American Indian in the market, who had just arrived in Allahabad, and he helped me to get directions for Mirzapur. I knew I had to cross the Yamuna River. Just to be certain I asked the waiters in the restaurant and the decision was unanimous that it was "over the Yamuna" and turn left!

I was not sure where to eat but decided to try the Jade Garden Restaurant, which probably belonged to Hotel Tippo. There was a very nice large, but not dark room with clean table cloths. A table was cleared for me. A spot light was turned on me. The staff had probably seen me writing in the garden and thought I might do so again. I ordered a nimbu-soda to drink, chicken spring roll, mutton korma, Navratan, rice and Kashmiri Naan for afterwards. I imagined the later would be like the sweet Peshwari naan at home.

At the next table were a mother, father and son. I thought he was 'trendy' because he was wearing a check lumberjack flannel shirt and probably jeans, and a black scarf (nearly all Indian men sport this item in winter weather). The father's hair was orange in places, probably through having grey hair that had been treated with Henna paste.

My meal was beautifully served and presented, well cooked and only 157 Rs. I had to leave two-thirds of the naan, half the rice and half the coffee. I remember that the fruit filed naan was decorated with bits of silver leaf.

My bed tea was late in the morning but I got a separate jug of hot water. The geyser was also giving warm to hot water in the bathroom – better late than never

Chapter 5

Carpets and Rock Paintings

November 19, 1994

Allahabad to Bisunderpur 91 km/ 58 miles

I was out of Allahabad and over the Yamuna bridge by 7.30. Whenever I stopped, to fill my water bottle or filter water, I was surrounded by people, and didn't get many chances to eat. It turned out to be a 'three tomato and three oranges' day. Often cyclists would try to keep pace with me and after a 'hello' or 'namaste' would feel free to chat to me. I cycled some distance with an 'only-Hindi-speaking' road worker. We met the Ganges again, it was very peaceful and calm, and he took me to a short cut over the old bridge, instead of the new one, on the way to a place called Major Road. He let me stop to buy tea for one rupee and a packet of biscuits for four rupees 75 paisa. He wouldn't have a biscuit or tea himself. At his destination he asked for one biscuit. The small packet fell apart and two biscuits fell on the road. These he gave to bystanders - road workers. I gave him four or five and again he distributed them around. At last, I said, 'for you' and gave him two. I think he wanted the whole packet

A further ten kilometres out of Allahabad, I cycled alongside a chartered accountant who used to work at the Rajmahal Hotel in Varanasi, and now worked at a plastics factory. I had to keep cycling and there were not many re-fuelling chances, because a crowd always gathered, and being the SH 44, there weren't that many dhabas, they seemed to be only in villages. A student of the Indian Civil Service told me that the road we were on was 'a bad road' because 'scheduled caste people' lived along it! What an attitude for a future Civil servant to have!

I met the Ganges again. It was peaceful and calm, and it ran to Bisunderpur where my next stay, at the Obeetee Carpet offices and residence, were situated. I had been invited to stay in their guest bungalow. I found 'Obeetee's carpets' with the help of an old man in the STD phone shop. He wrote their address in Devanagari script for me and said, 'straight on past the Civil Courthouse'. I didn't ever see the court but asked all and sundry about the road and eventually at about 4.30 pm arrived at the compound gate.

A security officer said Mr Oakley was at the factory in Gopalganj, with guests who had arrived that day from Varanasi (Benares). However, he phoned the office, and handed me to a Mr. Das, who took me to my room in the Obeetee Guest Bungalow.

It was a palatial Raj style bungalow with 20-foot-high ceilings, white-washed inside and out, its windows and doorways draped with white cotton curtains. My room was a suite! Twin beds in the centre of the room under a fan, a dressing room and a shining clean bathroom, with a real bath and shower. The whitest, fluffiest towels hung on stands and rails, and a white face cloth was perched on the hot tap of the hand basin. There was Bisleri water on the shelf. A bucket stood next to the bath, into which I put my dirty clothes, hoping that this was what it was intended for.

The bedroom ceiling was 16 to 20 feet high and the doors eight feet high and of panelled oak. Before my bedroom was a lounge with magazines, before that, a dining room with a table that could seat twenty, with a kitchen off to one side, which overlooked the gardens and the porticoed porch. The lounge had books and games, including my favourites, Scrabble, Othello and Trivial Pursuits! My cycle had been brought here, and my water bottle was put in a fridge. I was offered tea by one of the Muslim servants with the query, "inside or on the veranda?" I chose the veranda "in 20 minutes " to give myself time to bathe and wash my hair. Despite the hot water and liberal scraping, I found that I'd still got dirt behind my ears – which went onto the white towel. I felt ashamed! After my bath I wandered into a room which was like a lecture room, having four desks in rows and adorned with hunting trophies - leopard heads shot between 1951 and 1953.

Tea was served on the veranda, which ran all-round the bungalow. A servant put the lights on, and started the fan above me. The garden lawns were immaculate and edged with rose beds. I had admired a posy arrangement of roses in the lounge, in pinks and reds, which smelled lovely. I was told later that the roses had been brought to India from England by Mr Oakley's mother. One lawn had a selection of citrus fruit trees in various stages of flowering and fruit ripening. There were grapefruit, oranges, limes, lemons, satsumas and my old friend the musumbie. Chrysanthemums, in flowerpots, stood sentry on the steps of the veranda, where there are at least three seating arrangements of tables and chairs. The cane upholstered arrangement where my tea was served, was symmetrically arranged, including side tables with large, matching, pewter ashtrays. Even the tea strainer was silver! The tea tasted the best I had had since arriving in India. The biscuits were Nice but not crisp – this was a surprise!

Ramesh phoned to see if I had arrived and told me that Edward was having lunch with him the next day in Bombay. They knew one another in the early 70's and hadn't met for 20 years

A servant has been round with Flit, yes! there are mosquitoes! I'd love to stay two nights but will need a good excuse.

Mr Oakley arrived with Emma Duncan, and his godson, Daniel Randall. Emma was researching the carpet industry in Uttar Pradesh, for an article she is writing for the Economist. Daniel is in India to see if he would like to live here permanently, and eventually take over the business. It is a coincidence that Emma is a god-daughter of Mr Pemberton of Mill House, who lives in my village, Grantchester. I was able to report that he had made a donation to Lepra when I approached him for sponsorship for this bike ride.

Edward Oakley was in his fifties and a bachelor. He was obese, and a heavy drinker and smoker. He boasted that he exists on about 5 hours sleep a night and a siesta on Sundays and on other days if possible. He has two lovely Labradors "aren't they sweet?" We all went to his bungalow for drinks. He was very frank about his sexual life.

We watched a video about the company, in his new house, which seems to be underneath the office building. The conversation turned from business to more personal things. Edward talked of a former girlfriend whose marriage was on the rocks and whom he would like to contact again. The problem of bringing an English lady to live in India was part of the discussion. Edward and the young people were very frank, and, with their tongues loosened by generous amounts of whisky, their language embarrassed me. Daniel was obviously going to face similar problems if he settled in India and I could sympathise with their aloneness. Love of work must compensate for, and replace, the love of a partner. Social life revolves around alcohol, no doubt dulling both the physical and mental pain. Edward's children were his dogs, and his company his bride.

At a quarter to midnight, *I had* to mention hunger, - the servants had laid the table and prepared the food hours before, I had only had fruit all day! Dinner was fish, guinea fowl, orange syllabub and coffee.

November 20, 1994

Morning Mist over the Ganges

I thought I'd get up early to view the Ganges, so I told Daniel, and he gave instructions to the servants to bring me bed-tea at 6.15 am. I was served freshly squeezed orange juice and luxuriated in the presence of the silverware and china on my tray, enjoying several cups, before I set out, via the secret gate in the high wall that surrounded the compound.

By 7 o'clock I reached the village of Bisunderpur and asked the way to 'Gangaji'. – the respectful name for the Ganges. I was shown the way to the river, along brick paths laid in herringbone pattern, past houses and through side lanes, downhill to a shrine, perched some 20 feet above the level of the river. Huge cliffs of sandy soil had been eroded and sculpted by the great river in its spate, but that morning the scene was a tranquil one.

There wasn't a path down to the riverbank, it was a steep descent over soft sand, which I zig-zagged down to avoid falling. In the river a woman stood waist-deep washing herself. Further along, facing away from the bank, a little girl, about 9 years old, stood waiting, arms clasped to her shoulders, a shawl around her head and shoulders, over a knee length yellow cotton dress. Women were washing in a separate area from the men's washing place. Dhobis were washing clothes and men were bathing or squatting to perform their toilet. There was still, at this hour of the morning, a mist over the river and I remembered that there had been a heavy dew on the lawns around the bungalow.

On my way back to the village, I met a fisherman with a very meagre catch of about twenty-five, tinned-sardine sized fish, in a woven cane basket. He was wearing a brown canvas jacket and had a pink and white scarf, wrapped turban-like around his head. His neatly trimmed beard and moustache were white, his face thin, with deep set eyes. His boat was anchored below, a 15-foot canoe-like structure, with a tent of canvas over part of it. There wasn't a sail, he used his single oar to propel the boat through the water. In his spare hand he carried a piece of driftwood – fuel is very scarce here in the plains, hence the use of cow-dung and leaves to cook with. I took some photos and returned to the village.

The villagers followed me and posed smilingly for photos; adults, teenagers and children carrying their younger brothers and sisters. Some were well wrapped up in shawls or wore jackets and pullovers, others just had one thin layer of clothing. At one house a young boy wanted me to take his photo with a little kid. The whole family joined him on the front veranda of his little single storey house, mother pushing forward a plainly frightened toddler. She covered her head with her yellow sari for the photograph, but I could see her arms, and they were decorated with a dozen red, black and white bangles. Other women covered their heads, but I could still see their smiling laughing faces. Most of the villagers were barefoot.

I was back at the guest bungalow by 8.30 to join Emma and Daniel, for a breakfast of scrambled eggs, toast, jam and coffee. Emma was being taken to see a carpet producing village and I was pleased to be given the opportunity to accompany her.

We were taken by one of Edward's managers, Daniel accompanied us. Emma was on a fact-finding mission, and she was allowed to ask any questions of whomever she pleased, with the manager as interpreter.

Madhapur village was an 'open plan' village- there was no physical feature like a river to enclose it, and there were no brick pathways. The houses were scattered here and there as if some giant hand had tossed dice on the ground. Madhapur village had three or four looms, set up in brick buildings with electric light. The minimum wage has been nationally agreed, based on the work study at a mechanised carpet factory, at 50 rupees per 8000 knots tied. The looms are owned by a loom master, he is often a weaver himself, and he gets 20% extra pay. Men do the weaving, and it is regarded as a semi-skilled job. Some men only want to work for a few hours if there is something else to do. Others work slowly at knot tying.

The pattern of the rug is supplied by the design team at Obeetee, and the colours used in the design are suspended above the loom from bamboo poles. The warps are laid out in the open air, before being transferred to the loom. Obeetee doesn't use any child labour in its carpet production. Boys have to be over the age of fourteen.

Emma was investigating the carpet industry because a German TV programme had revealed that child labour was being used in their manufacture. This led to a boycott of hand-loom carpets in Germany and had also been reported on in the USA and the UK. To combat this adverse publicity a labelling system is being devised, 'The Rug Mark' to be used by those whose production is open to inspection and can prove that they do not employ children.

Madhapur village had only two castes, Javan's and Binds – there were no harijans. The weavers are paid an average of 25 rupees per 4000 knots tied in the carpet. The weavers work an eight-hour day with a one-and-a-half-hour lunch break. It can take six months to 12 months to finish a 12 x 9-foot, close knotted (high quality) carpet.

The wool for weaving is a crossbred merino wool from New Zealand which is mixed with the best Indian wool. The hanks are wound by both men and women, and hung above the loom according to their place in the pattern, The pattern 'nauksha' is drawn in colour on graph paper and is supplied to the loom master, together with the wool from Obeetee's depots. There are forty of them in the 1000 sq. mile carpet producing area. Some are as far away as the Nepal-India border.

We went to another village where the carpets are washed. The unit was developed by "a very enterprising man" who is now headman or 'Pradhan' of his village. He was immaculately dressed in a long white kurta and dhoti, supervising the workers. There was a concrete floor where the carpet was placed before being rolled into the tank of water along-side it. In the next stage the water was squeezed and beaten out of the carpet by men wearing plastic shoes, using foot square wooden paddles, at the end of long poles – rather like the fire-fighting beaters seen in forestry commission areas in the UK. Two men work together on a 12 by 9 carpet; more were needed for larger ones. Chemicals, sulphuric acid and caustic soda, are flooded onto the carpet. The length of time for this treatment is crucial. The carpets are then rinsed, with clean water from a very deep tube well. The carpets look like felt at this stage.

After being spread out on the grass to dry in the sun, the back of the carpet is singed by a flame, and the front pile is cut with shears to reveal the pattern again. The carpets are meticulously inspected by a man who moves any fibres which have become misaligned, and so the pattern is clearly outlined again. The carpets are then taken to the Obeetee factory in Gopiganj, to finish and pack them. Being Sunday the Gopiganj factory was closed, but we had lunch at their guest house, before returning to Bisunderpur. (I had seen young children tying knots for the fringes on silk carpets in Rajasthan but was told that the children had part time schooling).

Madhapur village had a population of 2000, and 200 children were in school. The first to the fifth grade covers ages 6 to 11. Only 10% of children go on to higher education in neighbouring towns, and most stop school at 10 or 12 years of age, to work in the fields, or in the home. There is an old private school that charges 10 rupees a month and this village is having a new government school built.

When we got back to the bungalow Daniel and I were taken round the rest of the Oakley estate, twelve acres of which, are devoted to horticulture. Edward has a contract to sell the produce, which earns enough to pay for the upkeep of the whole estate. The banana plantation is the most profitable. Every year the trees are cut down after fruiting and they regrow to give a new crop each year. Three kinds of mangoes are grown, langar, Dussehra and Chaurasia, as well as evergreen gooseberries, which have red and white fruit. Turnips, marrows, cauliflowers, cabbages, broad beans, Swiss chard and small sweet oranges are grown for the market. Women work in the garden under the guidance of a head gardener (mali) from 8 am to 5 pm and they are allowed to take produce home.

One more coincidence was that I overheard Daniel talking on the phone to his girl-friend in England. She had the same name as my daughter, Sarah Maris!

Monday November 21,1994

Chunar Fort

I said goodbye to Edward, who was off on his business trip to Bombay, and to Emma. Daniel and I went sightseeing to Chunar Fort, some Mughal tombs, and for a picnic at a reservoir in the hills. We travelled by van as all the cars and jeeps were in use.

The Fort overlooks the Ganges and was built on a spur of the Kaimur hills, at a height of 53 metres above the plain and was obviously a place of strategic importance, changing hands a number of times. Akbar recovered it in 1575, and the Mughals held it until 1750 when it passed to the Nawabs of Oudh. The British stormed it in 1764. Today the fort is used as a barracks for training sepoys, and we were accompanied by several young men as we looked around.

Down by the Ganges we could see a cremation taking place beside the river, next to the pontoon bridge Like the one at Ramnagar, this was constructed of lashed together bullet shaped tanks, topped with metal plates to form the road surface. In the monsoon season the bridge could be withdrawn from the river.

On the inland side of the fort, we could see an old British cemetery with monolithic headstones and grave architecture surrounded by a stone wall. Daniel and I had to suffer the embarrassment of borrowing money from our driver to give a tip to our guide – we had both forgotten to bring money with us.

Daniel had heard about a pottery bazaar which was open 24 hours a day. This turned out to be identical stalls of garish glazed plates, vases and statues which were displayed at the roadside day in, day out, being too heavy to move away. Apart from a few pieces of Jaipur pottery it wasn't to our liking. We reckoned that their trade must come from coaches travelling up and down to Varanasi from Calcutta.

We made enquiries from several people about Muslim tombs, and eventually managed to make ourselves understood and found them near the Fort. Again, we had nothing to give the custodian, but he let us look around all the same. We drove 10 km. into the hills for our picnic, -plenty to drink but very light on food – only three sandwiches each!

Back at the guest house Daniel and I played Scrabble and were offered drinks before our dinner. After dinner our host for the next day came to visit us. He was Mr. Raj Dutt, the owner of another carpet firm. He was interested in archaeology, and offered to take us to see some rock paintings dating from 8000 BC, at Mukka Falls, a beauty spot in the Vindhya Hills.

November 22, 1994

Mukka Falls

Raj Dutt drove us in his own car, a cross between a jeep and an estate car. A high clearance between body and road was necessary once we left the tarmacadam road, and were driving along soft sandstone tracks, which had been badly eroded into gulleys by the last monsoon rains. We had to stop several times and Daniel, and a local guide, whom we collected en-route, reconnoitred the way so that we didn't get the car straddled across deep ruts, or onto the chunks of rock strewn alongside the deep ruts, and damage the underside. After an hour we parked the car on a rocky plateau and set out to find the Mukka Falls. The sandstone rock of the hills was laid horizontally, and water has percolated down through the rocks, running out as numerous small silvery waterfalls, descending a staircase of black and gold rocks, to join the river in the gorge below. It was a very beautiful scene.

We walked along the horizontal bands of rock above the river at different levels, sometimes under overhanging layers of rock. It was awe inspiring to imagine our ancestors crouching here intent on fishing or hunting. Man's earliest attempts at art would have been hand prints, and tracing outlines in mud. He could paint and draw at least 20.000 years before he could read and write, depicting nature and the world around him. The animals he hunted were very important to him and were frequently the subject of his art. His pictures were intended to help him hunt them down and guarantee success in hunting.

Raj told us that there are many of these stone -age paintings in the Vindhya Hills south of Varanasi and in the Son River valley in Mirzapur district.

The paintings which we found were on the sides of the gorge, fully exposed to the ravages of climate but thankfully, little known to locals or tourists. The figures were painted in black and red. Water, blood and milk would have been used to dilute the ground earth colours and they would have been applied with fingers, twigs and pieces of bone. Buffalo, camels, deer, goats, dogs, pigs and trumpeting elephants could be identified. They were grazing, galloping and sometimes pierced with arrows. Between the animals, portrayed with a side view, were human figures in animated positions – arms raised up, legs 'walking', with bows and what might have been 'offerings.

The paintings were in rows, six feet long and two feet high. After studying the paintings that Mr Dutt knew about, we set off to search for more and I managed to find some on the opposite side of the gorge. Sadly, someone had chipped a layer of rock away to remove some of the figures, completely unprotected from the elements.

Many of the paintings seemed to have a thin white film over them, and we wondered what it could be. In some places the men and animals were interspersed with symbols, especially squares with a checkerboard pattern on them with projections at each corner, looking like charpoys squashed flat!

Roots of trees and other vegetation had grown between the horizontal fractures of the rock and the fine banding of the original sandstone formation, ran through the painted areas

It was a truly exciting and magical experience for me in 1994, just as it probably was for the first rock painters of stone age India.

Mr Dutt had yet another treat in store for us when we had eaten our picnic. at the foot of the Mukka Falls. He took us in the car to an isolated temple devoted to Shiva, and he told us we would be seeing something very rare. Removing our shoes, we climbed to the platform which surrounded the central room in which the deity was kept. We

119

were allowed in as Raj Dutt's guests. Inside it was very dark but we could just make out a statue of two gods, Shiva and his wife Pavati.

There was a red cloth draped across the front of the black stone statues. Mr Dutt asked for lights but they did not have any, so we used candles and torches to see by. The temple priest removed the cloth and there before us was, according to Mr Dutt, only the second known in India, portrayal of an erect Shiva fondling Pavati. Mr Dutt told us that the carved statue was 2700 years old, from 400 BC, and made of the black stone that goldsmiths test gold on.

Outside the temple a holy man, painted with bands of sandalwood paste, on his forehead, chest, arms and legs, sat cross-legged in lotus position, his hands joined in prayer. He anointed our foreheads with tilak marks when we came out of the temple. There was a tea stall near the temple and Mr Dutt arranged for a 'kettle' of tea to be brought to us, the temple priest and all who had gathered around us. We drank the tea in the little red baked-clay handle-less cups called 'coulars'. When one has finished drinking, the cups are thrown to the ground to break them – so that nobody can be defiled by drinking something touched by another person, who might have been of lower caste, or none at all – like me!

On the way home Raj Dutt pointed out the ruins of a fort and moat, where he says he has found 5th century antiques by turning over stones lying about the site, half hidden by vegetation. He told us that if such sculptures are placed around a tree, he doesn't touch them – they are adornments to a tree and devoted to a god, like a temple.

We called in to a village, to see a doctor friend of Raj's. He invited us to take tea and Raj brought some biscuits to hand around, while we drank our tea from coulars again. Raj told us that this doctor of ayurvedic medicine wanted to start a project to distribute calcium and vitamins A and D, to the poor in his area. I asked about leprosy, and he showed me some herbal balms which he prescribes to treat the disease. I noticed that he did have a stethoscope, and he showed me books of ancient recipes for making medicines. They were written in script and Raj had to tell me that I was holding the newspaper-covered book upside down! Raj said that people are so poor in this area that they only possess one sari, so Raj collects clothes to distribute the poorest tribal people.

It was a long journey back to Bisunderpur and quite dark when we got back. My neck and back were a bit fragile from the vibration of the car. I was grateful to Raj Dutt for taking me to see such wonderful works of art.

Raj Dutt was in his sixties, and he told me that every year, on his birthday, he goes trekking in the Himalayas for a week. He invited me to accompany him and his friends next September. He told us so many jokes and stories on our drive that I'm sure his treks must be good fun, and interesting too. I did join him in 1999!

Chapter 6

Chai Pilo!

Bisunderpur to Varanasi 51 km/ 32 miles

I said goodbye to Daniel and the luxury holiday I'd had as Edward
Oakley's guest at Bisunderpur. One of the servants came with me until
we reached his house, "because his wife and family wanted to see
me". I said a brief hello to his wife who was feeding her baby, and he
showed me around his little house, taking me up onto the roof to view
the Ganges. After showing them the photos of my family, I made my
way to the bridge which crossed the river, to the north of Mirzapur.

A relatively quiet 12 kms. later, I reached the junction with the
Grand Trunk Road and was back among the heavy lorry traffic again.
I stopped to take a photo of a road sign, the first one I'd seen to
mention Calcutta! It was 124 kms ahead of me if I kept on the GT
road. After Varanasi I would be leaving National Highway 2, to visit
the leprosy centre at Bhabua then heading north to Patna and
following the Ganges again.

Just as I was getting on my bike, a tea stall owner on the other side
of the road shouted out, "chai pilo!", 'drink tea!'. I liked this
spontaneous command, and he poured me tea in a coular and
proceeded to offer me biscuits from several packets which he tore

open. He wouldn't accept any payment, and he and his customers gave me a cheer as I set off.

It was busy on the road, with bicycles and children going to school. I had to make an emergency stop outside one and promptly overbalanced as I tried to get onto the sandy shoulder. I fell, trapped by the bike and the luggage – most embarrassing, and with an audience!

Some twenty-five kilometres down the road I stopped to photograph some pink lotus flowers – like water lilies on stalks. A man came up to me and told me that there was a better display of them further along the road, and he was right!

I battled my way along the GT road into Varanasi, looking for the Junction Railway Station. I crossed several bridges but missed my turning. However, using the sketch map in the Lonely Planet Guidebook, I managed to locate another route and doubled back along quieter suburban roads to my destination, the Tourist Dak Bungalow, near the Head Post Office.

I discovered a washing line in the garden and so ordered the usual bucket of hot water and rid myself, my clothes and my bike of the GT road grime. I had tea and chips and chatted to an English couple who had just flown here from Kashmir. I was surprised that foreigners could still go there. They told me that, if one is prepared to register with the police, it is possible to go by bus to Srinagar.

Varanasi, the oldest continuously inhabited city in the world, is also known as Benares. The name Varanasi comes from two tributaries of the Ganges that enclose the town, the Varun and the Asi.

There was an armed policeman sitting on a chair in the garden of the hostel, and I was told that he slept on the corridor floor, outside our rooms at night. After visiting the Post Office to send a fax, I went exploring on my bike and found the tourist office because I thought I'd better join an official tour of the riverside temples as there were so many of them, and it was easy to lose my way in the tiny alleyways, near the religious bathing ghats. There was a blackboard at the office saying that all tours were cancelled! I tried an international hotel, and they said I'd have to go on my own – still no reason given!

I found out that there had been a threat to destroy Varanasi's Hindu Golden Temple, because it was built on the site of a mosque – a repeat of the Ayodya problem of 1992. I had been in India then and trains had been attacked. I had found myself travelling on one with blood smeared and broken windows and had to spend a night on a station surrounded by armed police.

However, undaunted, I took the advice of the little man who brought my hot water, and took a certain rickshaw to see the Ghats and paid only 10 Rs rather than the 50 Rs the others wanted.

I was approached by a man who said he was "not a guide" but "worked for a government silk factory". I told him I didn't need his services, but he kept chattering and I kept telling him that I wasn't a tourist, but a pilgrim. He led me through narrow twisting alleys, with shops at pavement level and homes above. Cows wandered these 'Gali's' and young men rode motor scooters in and out of the pedestrians. There were police at every corner, with walkie-talkie radios in their hands, and riffles over their shoulders.

My 'guide' pointed out the Vishwanath Golden temple, the oldest Varanasi temple, prohibited to non-Hindus. Its huge silver doors stood open to the alleyway, and by standing in the doorway of the shop opposite, it was just possible to see the pointed temple roof sparkling in the sunshine. The Maharaja of Lahore had, in 1835, donated the three-quarters of a ton of gold to cover this elongated dome. The Vishwanath temple is dedicated to the god Shiva, as head of the Universe and has stood in Varanasi for over 1000 years. The original temple was destroyed in the 12th century, and replaced by a mosque under Aurangzeb, the son of Shah Jehan. It was rebuilt again in the 16th century and again destroyed. The present temple was built in 1777. This chequered history is the reason why the Muslim threat to destroy it again, is taken so seriously, coming as it does on the heels of the previous week's re-kindling of the trouble at the destroyed Ayodhya temple

My 'guide' took me to see the Raja Harishchandra ghat, which is particularly old. It is the most sacred cremation ghat, and he warned me not to take photos. We stood on some steps beside the jetty where large and small boats were unloading wood from the villages, for the cremation fires.

Bodies are cremated by Harijans, very low caste people, known as 'Chandel'.

The body is brought on a bamboo stretcher covered in a white cloth if it is a man, red or gold for a woman. The stretcher is first taken down the steps to the river for its final washing – water is thrown with the hands over the covered body, which is placed with its toes in the water. The oldest son, wearing a white dhoti and cream turban, which he gets from the ghat authorities, has to register the death with a government official and pay 5000 Rs. This' all-in price' includes the garments and the wood. Only the very rich or famous have sandalwood to make their fires. There were about twelve cremations going on at the same time while I was there.

The son must break the skull to release the soul of the dead person (I was told that it would burst with the heat of the fire if not broken). A son stood on the steps and watched while the other male relatives sat around above the ghat. The female relatives stay at home. They are not allowed to be present. A body takes about three hours to burn.

Behind the Ghat was a 'hostel for the dying' and my guide took me inside, up two floors, one for men, another for women. Each floor had an open balcony overlooking the cremation area. Old and sick people, and abandoned widows, come here to await death. My guide asked me to make a donation. I gave 10 Rs. on the way out.

We took a boat from the Harishchandra ghat to the Panchganga Ghat and Aurangzeb's Mosque, visited the Bharat Mata relief map temple, and had a look at the Cathedral where I found a statue of Jesus in a Buddha pose.

Having shown me the tourist sites, he now asked me to go to his "silk factory" which sells to "Harrods, Monsoon" etc. I agreed to have a look, having absolutely no intention of buying anything. He was obviously a tout on a commission basis but he'd been very knowledgeable and was easy to understand and if it made him happy!

Entering the silk showroom, off one of the many alleys, I had to take my shoes off and sit on a white covered mattress which completely covered the 10 x 10' floor. I was offered tea by two young men, and I asked for 'elailchi' – cardamom flavoured tea.

After this came the demonstration. Lengths of silk brocade, table runners or shawls I suppose, were deftly floated through the air with an expert flick of the wrist, to land shimmering at my feet. Colour followed colour, there must have been about twenty of them piled one upon the other, I explained that I wasn't a tourist but a 'yatri' and told them about my mission. They weren't at all put out that I wasn't buying. They were both bachelor's from Bihar State, so we talked about the problems of cycling in Bihar. I was enjoying myself but when two tourists came through the door, I made a hurried exit in case I spoiled their potential custom. I found myself in the alley of the Golden Temple, so I knew the direction to take to get back to the chowk area, where I would be able to get a rickshaw.

It was the beginning of the evening shopping time, so I wandered along the streets, finding little hidden markets, behind the bigger shops. The flower market was a riot of colour. Men sat in the entrance with baskets and piles of flower heads, strung together for use as garlands and hair decorations. Red hibiscus buds, blue iris, white jasmine and tuberose. Golden marigolds were the most abundant item for sale. The next day was a religious holiday so garlands would be bought to decorate the altars and home, friends, visitors, the doorways, cars, bikes, rickshaws, the cows, almost everything gets decorated for one reason or another.

Wedding cars can be covered in a net of white flowers so that you wonder how the people get in and out. Failing flowers, strands of tinsel are used, especially in the streets to make awnings and decorate roundabouts and lorry cabs.

There were some lovely old houses with pierced marble veranda screens, but they were often in a bad state of repair, with flaking paint and festooned with electric cables in lieu of telegraph poles.

I hired a rickshaw, but he didn't know the way to the Dak Bungalow. I told him it was near the TV/Radio Tower landmark. It was dark when I co-opted a student of "science and maths, college, intermediate" and he guided us to my hostel. We had come four or five kilometres, so I gave him 12 Rs when he had asked for 10 Rs.

At supper in the hostel, I met a French couple, and they asked me how they could change their money. I warned them of the slowness of the banks from my Lucknow experience, but said that Varanasi was much more tourist orientated and getting money should be easier for them.

November 24, 1994

Sarnath

The next morning, I went to visit Sarnath on my bike, once again it was a pleasure to ride without my heavy luggage and, after stopping at an STD booth to phone Ramesh, I was soon at the Buddhist pilgrimage centre

The founder of the Buddhist religion, Prince Siddarth, came to Sarnath in 525 BC after he had, like St. Paul on the road to Damascus, been enlightened and renounced his princely status. The Buddha, as he was known, gave his first sermon under the Bodhi tree (a pipal tree) in a large deer park at Sarnath in about 528BC. Since then, the site has been revered and from that time onwards it is regarded as a holy place by his followers When Chinese travellers (Fatien in the 5th century and Huien Tsang in 640 AD) came to Sarnath, Buddhism was at its peak. There were 1500 priests living in the monasteries here, a stupa nearly 100 metres high, Ashoka's mighty stone pillar and many other features.

The Emperor Ashoka was converted to Buddhism, and he marked the site of Buddha's first sermon with the Dhamekh 'stupa', which today still dominates the parkland at Sarnath. The Dhamekh Stupa was built in the 3 BC to contain relics of The Buddha. It was destroyed in 1794 by the chief minister of the Maharaja of Benares, when a green marble casket containing human bones and pearls was found. The British Resident at the court of the Maharaja of Banaras, published an account of this discovery, thereby drawing the attention of scholars to the site.

The stupa, an octagonal 28 metre diameter and 30-metre-high cylindrical tower is probably unfinished. The stupa dates from Ashoka's Mauryan Empire but has been added to and rebuilt at least six times. Niches in the octagonal faces probably contained representations of the Buddha and saints, as many were found around the monument. The central part has elaborate decorations of birds, flowers and geometric designs of the later Gupta period. Relics from the stupa are taken in procession at a huge fair in May, marking the birth of Buddha, a festival known as 'Buddha Purnima'.

Ashoka's pillar at Sarnath, was one of many erected by Ashoka to promulgate the faith, and as a message to the monks not to create schisms, and to spread the word. Sarnath was a centre of religious activity, learning and art continuously from the 4th century BC until its abandonment in the 9th century AD. Muslim armies devastated the region in 1197. Today, thanks to the excavations of buildings by the British in 1836, Sarnath has regained some of its past glory. Today there are modern temples, as well as Tibetan, Japanese, Thai, Chinese and Burmese monasteries around the complex. The Buddha believed that Salvation, the state of Nirvana, was possible for all, irrespective of caste. He preached a message of the Holy Eightfold Path. Its essential elements were the attainment of perfect wisdom, morality and meditation, by rejecting greed, lust and desire. Buddhism developed rapidly, both in India and in other lands and had thousands of learned followers, monks and nuns.

Hinduism revived after 1197. Buddhism had failed to gain the support of the ordinary people and it became absorbed into Hinduism. It is more a philosophy of life than a religion. In Hinduism today, the Buddha is a thought of as an incarnation of Vishnu.

The Mahabodhi Society is responsible for the upkeep of Sarnath and Bodh Gaya and has a modern temple with frescoes by a Japanese artist depicting the life of Buddha.

I was surprised to learn that the Emperor Ashoka (272 – 232 BC) occupied more of India than any other ruler than the British

Chapter 7

Leprosy Still Exists!

November 25, 1994

<u>Benares to Bhabua</u> 95 km/ 49 miles

I was excited to be going to the Lepra centre in Bhabua and left Varanasi after a banana-water breakfast. I knew the back roads to the bridge over the Ganges, near the ancient mosque, and was soon in the company of early morning cycle traffic, with only the occasional lorry. There was a mist over the river, which just allowed a glimpse of the ghats as they were swallowed up in the greyness.

My route took me to Moghul Serai, on the outskirts of which, was a huge lorry repair area, for the traffic using the GT road. There wasn't any order in the vehicle parking. Huge trucks in various states of dilapidation, battered and rusting oil tankers and private vehicles, were scattered over a vast area of blackened and oil-soaked earth. Clustered around the edges of the parking area were repairmen and spare parts dealers. Vehicles were being cut up and put together again. Welding torches were used without eye protection. Lorries and buses were being rebuilt with parts from broken wrecks, rather than with new parts. In one way this is a tribute to the ingenuity of the typical

Indian mechanic. It explains why so many of the old Ambassador cars, which are based on the 1956 Morris, were still being driven nearly twenty years later. However, on the downside, the number of accidents and breakdowns involving lorries and buses makes one wonder if the mechanics of the vehicles are of sufficiently high standard.

Many times, on my journeys across many Indian states. I came across branches of trees and bushes, and a few large stones, spread across one lane of a road, in a rectangular pattern. They are the Indian version of the red triangle! Broken down vehicles would be surrounded by a few stones or rocks, and/or greenery as a last-minute warning to other road users. When the vehicle was removed, perhaps by towing, the warning signs were invariably left in situ!

Another 'speciality' of road accidents, usually mentioned in newspapers, was that the 'driver absconded! I suppose many drivers did not have insurance or proper documents, and would not be able to pay for damage if caught, or could face a long time in jail before charging. Many times, I would see burnt out, or long rusted shells of vehicles, embedded in trees, or at the bottom of slopes, looking as if they had been there for years.

The best maintained, and newest vehicles, belong to the fraternity of National Carriers. They ply across state boundaries and are the only vehicles which more or less keep to the 40 kmph. speed limit, imposed on all lorries. They seem to run in convoys and are usually recently made by Tata, the biggest motor industrialist in India. Fleets of new bright orange or blue Tata lorry-chassis are also driven up the GT road from the Calcutta end, on their way to customers. The Public Carrier lorries, which are licensed for only one or two states, were often ramshackle specimens.

I became quite friendly with a string of tractor drivers on their shiny red machines, who would sometimes stop at the same dhabas as me and we would spend the day overtaking and passing each other as they took much longer breaks than I did. The east bound traffic, going towards Calcutta, occupied both sides of the road so that it would take ages to clear a way for the west bound traffic, which was stopped on the Bihar side of the border. I didn't see any obvious border signposts, just large villages with narrow bridges that created bottlenecks.

For ten miles I cycled through a huge traffic jam. I was too busy concentrating, and trying to get past the parked lorries without losing my head, as people jumped in and out of cab doors, or car doors, or left them open. Thirty-six kilometres after leaving Varanasi, I crossed over the State boundary from Uttar Pradesh into Bihar. Only bikes and motorbikes could weave their way through the stationary vehicles, lorries, tankers, buses and private cars. Vendors from local villages walked up and down selling tea and snacks. Some drivers had made fires on the road to cook their meals. Others played cards in the shade cast by their vehicles, they seemed resigned for a long stay. I learned the next day that someone left Bhabua on the 4 p.m. bus and it arrived at Varanasi fourteen hours later. The journey should have taken six hours.

Once I reached the head of the traffic jam queue, it was very satisfying to have an open road. Without traffic, I could choose the best bits of road surface, sometimes in the middle of the road, to cycle on. In Bihar the surface of the GT road became noticeably worse. The crevasses in the tarmac were more widespread, and the potholes deeper and more frequent. I was often reduced to riding on the first six inches of tarmac, next to the soft shoulder, because that was the only place that was least worn. It required quite a balancing act on my part. I was between the devil and the deep blue sea.

Bridges had more sections of concrete balustrade missing. Whether they had been taken away when a vehicle crashed through them, or just rotted and collapsed on their own accord, I didn't know. It certainly gave an unprotected feeling as I bumped across the raised concrete of the bridge surface.

At Mohania I turned off Shah Jehan's Grand Trunk Road, now officially National Highway 2, onto a single-track road between trees and hedges. I followed a tractor and trailer nearly all the way into Bhabua. Sometimes cyclists hold on to the sides of trailers; while freewheeling on their bikes and I would have loved a tow, but it was obviously dangerous as the trailers bumped and wobbled across potholes in the road. I passed the court, schools, newish concrete roller-blind-shuttered shops, a petrol station, and branches of banks. before entering the old part of the town, the Chowk, with its narrow streets, open drains and a shrine, relaying Hindu hymns.

Bhabua's Leprosy Project

On reaching this old centre of Bhabua I stopped to show the letter I had had from the Lepra Centre Administrator, to a bystander. Luckily, I had chosen someone who could read, and he told me to take ' the road to the river'. The road had been divided by metal railings into two lanes, consequently the sandy roadside edges had become part of the road, making it very dusty and difficult to cycle on. I passed a police station and a hospital. Some traffic was on the wrong side of the road where the surface was better, not heeding the oncoming traffic. I decided to copy my road users and wove from one side of the railings to the other, depending on the state of the road. There were not many cars to worry about, and they could only do 20 miles per hour, because of the terrible surface.

After I left the built-up area of Bhabua I passed a temple by the river Suwara, blaring religious music to acres of fields. I could see a green shuttered building down a sandy track but couldn't read the sign in Hindi script, so I went over the bridge for a kilometre or two, until I met some people to ask for help.

They pointed to the green shuttered building, so I doubled back and rode gingerly along the rough track to the two storied building surrounded by fields. It was very quiet so I called out 'Hello' and made my way to the back of the building, where I could see a parked jeep, with the name Lepra on it.

A little boy appeared, followed by a man I took to be his father. He told me that as it was a Friday the centre was closed, and we must go in the jeep to the administrator's house in another village.

We took the road back towards Bhabua, but turned left at the first crossroads, passing a school before turning onto a brick road to the village of Anklaspur. We passed more primary schools and stopped at the first house in the village.

The Lepra Project Administrator, Lakshmi Singh, came out to welcome me. He was pleased to see me, but sorry that I had not told him the exact time I would be arriving! He took me into his house and introduced me to his wife, Savitri, who offered me the traditional welcoming glass of water, followed by biscuits. Lakshmi Singh explained that the centre closed every Friday because they used to have a Muslim worker and instead, they held special clinics on Sundays, when most people could attend.

Like many homes I was to visit, his house had just the bare essentials, with very little attachment to personal possessions or decoration.

Lakshmi Singh and his son, Barun, asked me where I would like to stay and as I didn't mind, so long as I wasn't a burden, it was decided that I should stay at the 'hospital'. I couldn't follow their discussions and found out later that the hospital had recently been broken into and they, Barun and his wife, Shouba, and little girl, Puja, would move there with me to look after me.

GKNP Hospital

The 'hospital' consisted of two abandoned wards with rusting beds, a laboratory, a physiotherapy room, storerooms, a guest room and meeting rooms on the ground floor, and the office and family living quarters on the upper floor. It was built by Lakshmi Singh in 1960 to cater for leprosy patients and treat them with, the then only available treatment, Dapsone. Used alone Dapsone was not able to prevent deformity, and patients could become Dapsone resistant. The Bihar State government provided funds to the centre, which were supplemented by the sale of produce from the land, and by asking for funds from better-off people.

I was told that the institute GKNP, dedicated to Gandhi, just about managed to survive despite political and economic crises. GKNP stands for Gandhi Kusth Nivaran Pratisthan, roughly translated as Gandhi's Leprosy Society. We went back to the 'hospital' and Lakshmi Singh came too. I was shown into an anteroom to the office on the top floor, one of several rooms off a large hall. A table in one corner of the hall served as a dining room. Shouba, Barun's wife and Lakshmi Singh's daughter in law, arranged for my room to be made ready while he told me about his work.

Lakshmi Singh had been one of those Indians who wanted political independence in the 1940's, and engaged in various acts of sabotage against the British authorities – locally and loosely termed a 'Freedom Fighter' or as I saw in a book, 'independence nationalist'. As a follower of Gandhi, he became disillusioned with politics, and turned to social work. In 1947 he founded Kasturba Gandhi Hospital for mothers and children, in his village. At the height of its success the local landlord created political problems and, to avoid harming the institution, he gave him the hospital. It wasn't run properly and closed in 1962.

Meanwhile, he started this 'hospital' for leprosy patients using the then only available drug, Dapsone. During my visit to Bhabua I was invited to the old Kasturba hospital, now a private school for 450 children of 1st to 7th standard. There are 12 teachers and the school charges 10 Rs. To 13 Rs. a month for tuition.

It was Lakshmi Singh's unstinting thirty years of work for leprosy patients that created such a good atmosphere regarding leprosy in the Bhabua area. He is respected, and his family and staff are trusted.

Patients come for advice, even from outside the area. Despite economic and political problems, he kept his GKNP Leprosy Centre going. The Bihar state government provided him with two jeeps, but with the economic collapse of the State, the funds to run the centre dried up. The jeeps broke down and the authorities wouldn't sanction their repair, wages for staff and for running the centre were not forthcoming, and after years of hand to mouth existence, the centre was forced to close in November 1989

In 1989 Lakshmi Singh filed a test case against the Government of Bihar in Patna High Court, 'GKNP v. The State' for the release or reimbursement of money to institutions. GKNP is asking for £20,000' but many similar institutions were owed huge amounts of money. The case was admitted onto a list for hearing in 1990. But nearly five years later no date had been fixed. If Lakshmi Singh would pay 500 Rs (£10 in those days) to the man managing the case list, he could be put on the computer for a hearing. Lakshmi Singh refuses to resort to bribery, as a matter of principle, and so, five years later, they are still waiting for a hearing.

Bhabua's New Leprosy Treatment Centre

In January 1993 the British NGO Lepra came to the rescue by sponsoring an MDT (multi-drug therapy) project at GKNP Bhabua. They provided 557000 Rs. on a yearly contract to cover staff wages, electricity, and office bills, petrol and travelling expenses, as well as providing a jeep and a motorbike.

The multi-therapy drugs, chlophazamine, rifampicin and dapsone were provided by the Nippon Foundation of Japan to the World Health Organisation and distributed to GKNP by Lepra. Barun and his wife, Shouba, run the office at GKNP. Some of the book-keeping sections overspend, and Lakshmi Singh has to get permission from Lepra, to transfer funds from one section to another. These overspends must not exceed 25000 Rs. When the jeep needed new tyres, the old tyres were sold for scrap and three new ones bought - even this transaction needed Lepra's permission.

GKNP owns five acres of land which grow rice, vegetables, wheat and pulses. The vegetables are sold directly to wholesalers. They are sold to raise money to feed the hospitalised patients, those with complications, who are kept in the ward for a week or two, where they are provided with steroid drugs and physiotherapy to prevent deformity.

The eldest of Lakshmi Singh's three sons, Arun, had left at 3 am in the jeep, to net fish in a small lake he had started as a 'fish farm', with 3000 fish. The fish will be sold in the market at 7 am. Arun plans to enlarge and deepen the lake over the next year. (90% of local people eat fish). Fish curry and rice is cheaper than vegetables, dal and rice. His second son, Tarun is the project medical officer.

A Rapid Survey done by Lepra in 1993 established the extent of leprosy in the project area. There were 166 cases of multibacillary leprosy (MB), a more widespread infection that required 36 months of treatment, and 877 cases of pauci-bacillary (PB) infection, that can be cured in just six months. The deformity rate was 4.4% and children accounted for 19.8% of the patients. The male female infection ratio was 58 men to 42 females, reflecting the reticence of women to come forward and be examined by male staff.

The new Lepra project catchment area of 200,000 persons was divided into eight sectors, each with a population of about 25000. Each PMW (para medical worker) was responsible for his sector and he usually moved into rooms or rented a house in his sector, for his office and homebase. Each sector has about 12 schools of roughly 150 children. In addition to the eight PMW's there were 2 supervisors, 1 doctor, 1 physiotherapy technician and 1 laboratory assistant. The GKNP area covered 219 villages plus the town of Bhabua.

Five hundred and one new patients were found in the first year of Lepra support, 157 came from outside the project area but in Bhabua District, 15 came from outside Bhabua District.

The PMW's spend their time either at their allotted 'Drug Distribution Points' (DDP's or clinics), or conducting surveys in villages or in schools, motivating people to come for treatment, and tracing absentees from the DDP clinics in his sector.

The supervisors attend all DDP's and are responsible for loading the jeep at the GKNP hospital base, with the necessary equipment for the clinics, organising the village surveys, and making sure that the record cards and registers are up to date.

A large village with about 5000 people, or four or five smaller villages grouped together, is called a panchayat. A 'mukia' is the head of a village and each panchayat has a judiciary section whose headman is called a 'sarpanch'.

Some village roads are wide enough to take a tractor, car or horse and cart. Only the largest, richest houses have an interior water or sewage system using septic tanks and bore wells. Many village houses are arranged higgledy-piggledy in alleyways with a few stepping stones between them. Often there is a channel for waste water in the middle of the lane from the houses, which attracts mosquitoes and becomes mud in the rainy season. The government provides water hand pumps in the village, and this is where the people wash themselves and do their clothes and pots washing. If there is a large pond in the village that too becomes the bathroom and laundry area.

Toilets in houses are rare, and most villagers have to go and seek a place on the edge of the village, by a canal or wood, to defecate. Ladies go very early in the morning and last thing at night. Men have more flexible timings. You can see them walking purposely to distant places or to the sides of fields, carrying pots of water, or these days plastic bottles of water, to clean themselves. This kind of toilet is referred to as an 'open toilet'. In towns there are urinals for men (without doors), but women are rarely catered for!

The working month at GKNP is divided into making 'Surveys' finding patients, and on 'DDP's,' delivering the medicines to patients in places near, or in, their villages. There is one day each month for record keeping, which doubles as pay day. DDP's occupy 23 days with 103 clinics for the 219 plus villages and four areas in Bhabua town itself.

For Drug Delivery Point visits, the Lepra jeep would leave the hospital base at 6 am, and return at around 2 pm, though earlier in summer to avoid the hottest part of the day. The jeep goes to a large village, or a spot convenient to several smaller villages, and stops under a shady tree, in a farmyard, at a temple or anywhere where people can gather, and wait for the paramedical workers to arrive, usually with the doctor and physiotherapist. Staff unload the patient record cards and drugs, plastic stools and a table, and will stay for about one and a half, or wait two hours for stragglers to arrive.

Patients queue for their medicines, and are observed by the physiotherapist and staff, for any kind of muscle weakness or new problem. Those being treated for neuritis are given their steroid drugs at the appropriate dose, depending on how many nerves are damaged, and how they are responding to treatment, assessed by way of muscle tests. The physiotherapist will teach them exercises and observe their performance.

The doctor's job is to prescribe medicines, and so he should sign the record card, and decide the dose, for patients needing steroids. In practice he has little to do, as the steroid dose is calculated by the physiotherapist, who knows how many nerves are affected, by his examination of the patient.

Everything is then repacked, and the jeep moves on to the next DDP of the day.

The team holds three or four DDP clinics a day, in villages two to three kilometres apart. Travel between the villages is very slow as most village roads are made of brick and those that are metalled have not been repaired since 1992 and are in poor condition. In remote areas the routes between villages are mud tracks, deeply rutted in the dry season and a quagmire in the monsoon season. On the days that I went to village clinics the jeep bumped along at an average of 15 mph.

On Surveys the PMW's and supervisors visit houses in the selected villages from 7am to 12pm, hoping to catch as many people at home as possible. They usually camp in the village overnight, having spent a day or two visiting workers in the fields, and in remote places, broadcasting their message with a megaphone. The survey team will leave a message that leprosy is curable and if you conceal it the leprosy will spread. The PMW's write the date of the survey on the walls of each house visited, and tell the inhabitants that treatment is free.

Multibacillary leprosy cases (MB), with many bacilli, and needing longer treatment, often have tell-signs of missing eyebrows, depressed nose, many patches of lighter coloured skin and possibly deformity on face, legs and hands. MB cases may develop complications and deformity many years after they first caught leprosy. PB cases show deformity after two or three years, such as clawed hands, drop foot, numb extremities and inflamed nerves.

All patients are examined for neuritis (nerve inflammation) by palpating certain nerves. Resting the limb in a plaster cast is a good treatment for neuritis, together with exercise and steroid treatment. When I accompanied the team, they found four or five new patients. They will be referred to the main hospital base at GKNP for further tests and physiotherapy assessment if necessary.

When Nathuni, the Laboratory technician, goes on Surveys he takes the smears, samples of the clear fluid that comes out of a shallow wound before the blood. It is wiped onto a glass slide for examination under a microscope. back in the laboratory. The cut is made using pieces of razor blade broken into small pieces, to save money on buying scalpel blades. The little pieces are held with forceps to make shallow cuts in ear lobe, eyebrow, forehead, cheek or from the lesion itself.

Back in the laboratory the slides will be stained with a chemical called methylene blue, to show the leprosy bacteria (mycobacterium leprae) in pink. It takes 45 minutes from smear, through stain and sulphuric acid wash and drying, to be ready for reading, using a microscope. A positive result confirms the person has Leprosy and the number of bacilli indicates whether it is PB (Paucibacillary with fewer bacilli) or MB (multibacillary with many bacilli). Nathuni sends every tenth slide to the Lepra labs in Hyderabad for checking

Many children drop out of school around the age of 10 or 12 because they are more useful working in the fields, in the house or minding siblings. Young girls mind younger siblings while mothers work in the fields. Only 16% of women and children have had an education beyond the 5th standard.

Schools are surveyed and, if a case with a single lesion is found, it is kept under observation for three to six months, as there is a possibility that it could be vitamin deficiency, or have another cause. If there are two signs, where there is a single lesion, treatment is started right away, for three to six months, in case it is self-healing. Five percent of single lesion cases are self-healing.

Leprosy is curable, but it has to be accepted by the patient, his family and the general community, as cured, and non-infectious. This can lessen the stigma and fear attached to the disease.

Ex-patients need to be seen working in the community, as earning family members. Running tea shops or selling eggs from wooden kiosks, could provide occupations for the weaker sections of society, including deformed leprosy patients.

Patients with anaesthetic feet cannot work in fields because they may get cuts, and infections, as they have no warning feeling in their feet. Special footwear, to safeguard the feet and align them correctly, was being provided by Kabir, the GKNP shoemaker, under the direction of Rajni, the Physiotherapist.

Rehabilitation opportunities are needed, but finding the money to finance such projects is very difficult. Bihar is a poor State with, at that time, 90 million people. It had very few natural resources, and an inefficient government. People can be seen riding on top of buses and trains to avoid paying a fare.

Shouba had prepared a room for me on the north side of the building on the second floor. Two metal hospital beds stood together, joined by a hand-embroidered cover. Barun, her husband, arranged a double- size mosquito net above the beds by tying the corners to nails in the walls. Each time I got out of bed I had to remember to duck under these strings, which were at neck height!

My room had two sets of shuttered, unglazed, windows but 90% of them were kept closed to keep the room cool. In the far corner was a cubicle with a squat loo and a tap. Under the window there was a small washbasin. There were two sets of concrete shelves built into the walls, complete with candles and matches, for there wasn't any electric light in the hospital building. My view was across fields.

Immediately below my window was a partially completed brick building, and its walled garden, Barun told me that it was being built 'as and when' donations came from the W H Smith school in Benares. The building would become a mother and child centre for the poorest people. Barun's idea was to teach the mothers 'arts and crafts' and to educate the children at the same time. Meanwhile, he keeps black and white pigs there.

Oil lamps were lit at night in the dining area, and in the little sitting room off the main hall. At dusk mosquitoes invaded the sitting room, and I put repellent on my arms, hands and face while Lakshmi Singh arranged for some mosquito coils to be placed on the window sill.

Two old men came to look at me and were given the customary tea, while Lakshmi told them about me. Lakshmi Singh had been ill recently, so he went back to his house, and Barun took me to my room. When I had unpacked my belongings Barun called me for dinner, which we ate alone, Shouba doing the cooking and eating later, as was the custom.

November 26, 1994

Joining a Survey Team and Visiting a DDP

Shouba made a special breakfast for me called 'halva'. It was made of ground wheat, sugar, ghee and water boiled together - delicious! There was also a thermos flask of tea.

Lakshmi Singh had made a programme for me, which included visits to village clinics, to the special Sunday clinic, to see the District Magistrate, meet the local press, talk to the Bar Association and visit a school in Benares which supported the Bhabua centre, by giving donations and buying chalk made at GKNP.

After filtering some water for my flask, we set off by jeep to visit the village of Bekass, where the survey team were working. The jeep bumped along at about 15 mph. Bekass village had a population of approximately 2000 in 175 households. The farmer we visited for a cup of tea, wasn't a headman, but he had the best 2 storey house in the village, and he had a TV! The survey team had stayed in one of his barns for several days. Four or five new cases of leprosy had been found in the house-to-house survey. I saw the dates of this survey and a previous survey written on the walls of houses, 30/3/93 and 17/11/94.

The medical team stood in the lanes between the houses, and placing a resident in a good light, in full sunlight, they examined them for any of the signs or symptoms of leprosy. Those with patches of light-coloured skin are classified according to the number of patches they have, and this will be confirmed by smear tests. MB have more patches than PB patients. Making an exact map of these areas is very important. PMW's draw the patches on an outline figure in the record card. I volunteered to draw some patients' patches because I found it easy – it was just like drawing a map, and I had a degree in Geography!

The physiotherapist tested the nerves passing through the wrists, ankles and neck, to see if there was any enlargement or thickening, where the nerves pass through the joints. There are special tests for finding individual muscle weakness.

The PMW's and supervisor (NMS- a non-medical supervisor) looked for six signs of leprosy, including, patches of skin that were lighter colour than normal skin, that had no hair and were anaesthetic. They performed 'feeling' tests. The patches were touched with differing thicknesses of plastic 'wire' and then with a wisp of cotton wool, made cold with ether, all tests done with the patients' eyes closed and asking if they felt a touch. Feet were tested in several places and weak hands were gripped to test muscle strength. All prospective patients were examined by the physiotherapist for neuritis (nerve inflammation) by palpating certain nerves in arms, legs and on the face – places affected by leprosy.

'Smears' are taken on glass slides by the Survey team supervisors, from people who are suspected leprosy cases, and they are sent to be examined at GKNP hospital by Nathuni, the lab technician.

Every month 103 DDP clinics are held, spread over 23 days. To deliver leprosy medicines to existing patients at the 'Drug Delivery Points', the jeep leaves the hospital base at 6 am and returns around 2 pm. The Lepra jeep goes to a large village, or a spot convenient to several smaller villages, and stops under a shady tree, in a farmyard, at a temple or anywhere where people can gather, and wait for the jeep, bringing the drugs, record cards, doctor, physiotherapist and a supervisor. The sector PMW is at the Drug Delivery point first, as he lives nearby.

The 26th November in Bihar was cold enough for me to need an anorak, yet there were some little children waiting at the DDP village we visited, shivering in thin nylon dresses, with broken zips, their breath visible in the cold air.

The DDP team holds three or four of these clinics a day in villages two to three kilometres apart. Travel between the villages is very slow, as most village roads are made of brick and those that are metalled have not been repaired since 1992, and are in poor condition. In remote areas the routes between villages are mud tracks, deeply rutted in the dry season and deep mud in the monsoon season.

Lepra staff don't work on Fridays, because at one time there was a Muslim PMW. Instead, there is a Sunday clinic at the GKNP hospital base in Bhabua, to which out-patients, and those with problems, can come from any village and from outside the catchment area.

Bihar is a very traditional and conservative state, often regarded as backward in some of its customs and behaviour. Women will usually cover their faces in front of men, hiding behind their saris, and may not even open a door to a man. In the survey they may face the wall and only show their backs between the sari blouse and the waist plus their lower legs to the PMW. They are shown cards with diagnostic pictures. I noticed that these had English words on them. If these cards were in Hindi they could be passed around among daughters, sisters and other females, and helped by those who could read. Women will rarely consult a doctor because most doctors are men and they only seek medical help as a last resort.

Leprosy is spread through droplet infection like coughing, sneezing and spitting. It is not very contagious, unlike its cousin TB. However, schools and 'healthy contacts' of patients are examined regularly

We visited the house of the paramedical worker who lived in Bekass and I asked him if the village had had any European visitors before. He told me that during the 1966/7 famine many Europeans, from Oxfam, the Catholic Church and others provided wells for irrigation in this area.

Meeting the District Magistrate

In the evening Lakshmi Singh took me to meet the District Magistrate. In India a District Magistrate, abbreviated DM, is an

145

Indian Administrative Service officer (also called District Commissioners in some states) who is in charge of a district, the basic unit of administration in India, of which there are about 750 in the whole country. They are a hangover from the days of British Raj when they were Collectors and were more concerned with revenue and judicial matters.

The DM had his residence and office next to the police station and the hospital. We passed several security guards and were shown into his office. He was on the telephone when we arrived, but we were motioned to take a seat, in the rows of chairs arranged before his desk. His secretary, an old man, hovered with a pile of files for his attention. The DM read the notes attached to the files and signed here and there, while we waited in silence.

The DM was about 35 years old, getting plump and dressed in an immaculate cream embroidered silk kurta. He had not been long in Bhabua, and this was the first time that he and Lakshmi Singh were to meet. A few more signings and a phone call or two and we were allowed to speak.

The Bhabua DM had firm views about the GKNP leprosy project. He was doubtful about the records kept, believing patients didn't take their medicine because they moved away from the area. He said that the government centres have 100% take-up. Lakshmi Singh pointed out that this was because they can't fill in bad figures in their reports! Lakshmi Singh quoted cases where government staff don't turn up at clinics. He told of one observer who found only 5% of patients were receiving treatment. He informed the DM that in the Bhabua Sector, 24 of the 48 villages now had no cases of leprosy. The DM agreed to come to the hospital and meet the staff on the following Wednesday and give me an 'official' send-off. I didn't know of this arrangement, not being able to follow the language well enough. I couldn't follow much of the conversation about leprosy either, however, Lakshmi Singh must have made a good impression on the DM because he agreed to visit GKNP.

November 27, 1994

I was sitting on an old hospital bed on the flat roof of the GKNP building, because resting in my room was too cold. My room had such thick walls and such heavily shuttered windows that I had been cold in the night despite a woollen blanket. I was sufficiently awake to feel cold but not enough to untuck the mosquito net, get out of bed, avoid strangling myself on the strings securing the net, just to find my jumper.

There was quite a breeze up there on the roof too. I had morning tea and at 7 am went on a motorbike with Barun to Dr Mishra's father-in-law's house. He was a retired lawyer, standing for the lower house in Bihar's parliament as a BJP representative. He would arrange for me to speak to the local Bar Association. We had breakfast of omelette, toast and rasgullas. Two other lawyers came to see me!

I was taken to see the new dining room and kitchen extension in the courtyard, and to the roof for a view of other houses and 'our lane' This house had two concrete storeys, whereas the one next door had three. The lane was just mud and grass! We were in the Bhabua town area and it was littered with plastic bags – the curse of modern India, according to me. They had replaced the hand-made paper bags made of old school exercise books and printed books, which pigs, cows and other animals, who wandered freely around the streets, could eat.

The streets of Bhabua were quite bad. A previous District Magistrate had the idea of making a two-way system, but the roads were not wide enough, so it's just jeep wide on each side, reduced further by the sand which spills over the road, from the sides

The Sunday Clinic

The Out-Patient clinic on Sundays was for people from outside the Multi Drug Therapy project area. These people came long distances and at great expense, because they have heard of the excellence of the Bhabua centre.

A ten-year-old boy had come 40 km with two small patches on his thigh, which he had had for 6 months. His mother had thought they would go away, but father had heard about GKNP, and they had travelled since 6 o'clock and walked 9 km.!

The physiotherapist was watching Durga Kumari, aged 14, walk across the floor. She had come 23 kms and has been treated for foot drop since 6/2/94. She has had her foot in plaster and now she is walking normally. I asked if she went to school. Her father said he would like her to, but she had only been to school for 4 or 5 days in her life, because she didn't want to go, and had cried. Most children who go to school leave at the age of 10 – when they are useful in the fields or the house. In every village it is common to see girls carrying young children around on their hips. Their mothers work from 10 am to 4 pm in the fields, especially at planting and harvesting times.

A boy relative of Durga's came with a patch on his thigh. He was asked why he had come if the patch gave him no trouble. This was to see if he knew about leprosy. His bus fares were twelve rupees each way, and he would need to come for six months. A nephew of the same family knew the lesions on his arm were leprosy, but not the light patches on his chest.

Two ladies from Uttar Pradesh, had come 45 km. They didn't mind that there were no female workers but would only show the midriff. One had had four months treatment and had a new lesion, but it may not be leprosy. She will have a smear test taken from the new lesion. Her old lesion was still anaesthetic and as she had been told 'if you have no feeling it is leprosy' she thought she had not been cured. After cure there may also be no feeling! The second lady had not got leprosy, she had been brought here by the first lady, she had dermatitis.

Little children often have wispy golden hair, it is a sign of vitamin deficiency, especially A and D. Calcium deficiency is also common.

Some families own a buffalo, but only the owner and his family will drink pure milk. The surplus is sold in the market for 8 rupees a litre - watered down to boost profit.

Adulteration, adding another product to increase the weight of the original item, is common in India. The idea behind adulteration is to increase the weight of the goods, and hence the profit for the person doing the adulteration. Before cooking, rice has to be carefully sorted, grain by grain to remove little stones from it.

I later helped my Calcutta friends do this daily chore. We sat around the dining room table with a plate in front of us onto which a cupful of rice was placed. Each of us, including the 7-year-old, pushed the rice grains to one side and the stones to the other part of the plate, repeating cupful after cupful– an opportunity for family conversation! My plate had 20 small pieces of grit on it at the end of the operation.

Flour may have powdered chalk added, Bisleri water and pop bottles are often filled with plain water, sugar may have glass added.

About 20% of villagers in this part of Bihar own cattle. Children here are breast fed for a year, and for the next year will be given milk from various sources. The majority of people only drink water. Tea drinking has only recently become popular. Anklaspur, a large village of 10,000 people now has ten tea stalls. They are used mainly by men, using the stall like a club, or a pub! Lakshmi Singh is thinking of introducing tea stalls for cured leprosy patients so that they become integrated into society, gain self-respect and possibly a small income. He would place them outside schools and colleges, and outside the court buildings and other public places where the general public might learn to accept ex-patients as fellow human beings. Each stall would cost £10 and ideally should be portable so that it could be taken home at night. I had noticed a sweet stall outside one school.

To westerners it seems a pittance, but finances are so strained in GKNP, that the money required is a fortune to find. Lakshmi Singh has applied for a government sponsored loan, with GKNP standing as guarantor for the repayment The society will make its decision about granting this loan in December 1994. Local banks were asked for a loan, but they didn't take much notice, and wanted to charge 12% interest. A private loan would be at 4%. Even at 4% the stalls wouldn't make a profit, but they would give employment to ex-patients and encourage suspected leprosy cases to come forward.

MB cases mix freely in the general population because deformity and evidence of infection come late, often ten years, after the onset of the disease. For this reason, contacting relatives and people who have been in close contact with the patient is very necessary.

The largest number of deformed people begging in tourist areas are lepers. The old, deformed, beggars are not looked after by their families and have to resort to begging. There are not any beggars in the Bhabua area. Three or four years ago there was stigma attached to leprosy, now this has come down in the area, through the work of GKNP and Lepra.

Arun had asked me, the previous night, whether I'd like chicken or fish for supper the next evening. Fearing that chicken would be expensive I opted for fish, thinking it might even be Arun's home farmed fish. Unfortunately, it was full of tiny bones and very difficult to eat. I noticed that Barun abandoned his fish curry too. I had obviously made a bad choice.

We sat and talked by the light of a hurricane lamp. Later we joined Shouba in their room, where she was sitting on the bed, reading a women's magazine. She asked me whether it was true that Prince Charles and 'Lady' Diana were getting divorced – a very popular topic of conversation, though not one about which I was very knowledgeable, having been in India for the last month without access to the British press. We went on to discuss marriage, birth control and HIV/Aids instead. We were talking for ages and got on very well, despite the age difference. Barun had asked me when I first arrived, what he should call me. He didn't like to use my first name, so he and all the people at GKNP called me 'aunty' following his example. I asked him for another blanket and hoped that they had not taken one of their own for me. By the end of my visit, I was known as 'cyclewali!'

A Visit to Darauli Village

I slept comfortably that night and woke for my second morning to bhajans being relayed over loudspeakers, from the little temple, on the metalled road by the river. Barun knocked on my door to wake me up, and I joined him for morning tea at the dining table in the large hall, off which the bedrooms, office, storeroom and sitting room were arranged. The hall led onto a roof terrace above the front porch. Shouba did her washing -up and cooking there, and Barun sat at a hospital bed, using it as a table, shaving with a cut-throat razor.

We were to visit a Drug Distribution Point in Darauli Village, and had been invited to lunch at the family home of the physiotherapist, Rajni Kant Singh.

We travelled on a metalled road and then turned onto a brick road for one kilometre, which in turn, gave way to a mud road in the village centre. Darauli lies on the edge of the project area, against the Uttar Pradesh State border. On the way I noticed a dead cow next to a pond and wondered if the water might get contaminated. The carcass was covered with vultures, not a space could be seen between them. When we came back along the same route two hours later, there was just a skeleton!

We left the jeep and walked to a grassy knoll, next to a little whitewashed village temple. The Lepra staff were distributing drugs and examining patients. There were eighteen MB cases and four PB cases in this village. Two new cases, both babies, were detected that morning.

Some villagers brought tea for us, and I was asked if I would like to visit the local school. I was delighted to have the opportunity, and was taken across a field, to the single storey concrete shell of a building. The children were sitting on small pieces of waterproof cloth, on the ground in front of the school. There was no sign of a teacher, yet they sat in silence, their books, slates and chalk beside them. It was 11 am. and he should have arrived by then. The children were sitting in groups, the boys separated from the girls, in parallel lines facing each other. I asked some of the older boys to read to me. They opened their books and read aloud, in chorus. I had noticed that much of the education in India is by rote-learning.

With great effort, linguistically, I asked them to read individually. The first reader's place was to be taken by the boy next to him, taking over from one another when I said – 'agle', next! The best reader would follow the text and correct any mistakes made by his fellow student. They stood up to do this reading for me. When it was in full swing, I wandered over to the little children, whom I asked to write on their slates. I was fascinated watching the children hanging their letters from a solid line, them rubbing out the spaces between the words. It made writing easier but would only apply when using chalk or pencil.

The village headman came over and introduced himself, and we returned to our host's house. It was a traditional, joint family home, built around a central courtyard, for parents, their two sons, their wives and children. The brothers were twins, the only ones in the village. Father was a 'landowner' having seventy-five acres. He owns a tractor, trailer, harrow and drill and they grow rice and gram (a pulse of the pea family). They also have cows and bullocks. Their harvesting is done by combine harvester, hired by the day from firms in Uttar Pradesh or Haryana States. I sat at a table with Barun and Rajni – an honorary man again!

Before I left, I went over to the kitchen, to thank the ladies of the household. They were squatting on the floor, surrounded by shining stainless steel bowls and plates. A small stove stood in the corner of the room, supplementing the traditional clay stove in the courtyard. A large bowl of dahi (yoghurt) was being set in the warmth of the now extinguished fire

Rajni took me to see the rooms of the family, which were grouped around the courtyard. The house was quite old, and the doors of some rooms were richly carved. An aunt wanted to see me and I was taken to her home across a farmyard, with an awning for the buffalo, and stacks of straw and grain.

We were due to go to the courts to meet the members of the legal profession, and I was anxious not to be late. I made the hands-together greeting and said 'namaste', and was invited in to take tea. I asked Rajni to explain that we had to get back to Bhabua, and hoped that she wouldn't be offended. She appeared with a dish of home-made sweetmeats. I accepted a sweet and waved to her, as we walked back to the jeep. She didn't come outside her house, she just peeked around the door, dressed in a pink sari, pulled over her head. as a sign of modesty!

The Bar Association

Lakshmi Singh took me to the Bar Association meeting. A long open veranda-ed building, stood in a huge compound. Solicitor's clerks were squatting in front of clients, on the veranda, talking in excited high-pitched voices. Lawyers in suits, or shirts and trousers, could be identified by the white tabs pinned to their collars, like nonconformist ministers. Some of the suits and jackets were very ragged and torn, obviously not a well-paid profession here in rural Bihar! There seemed to be two rival Bar Associations, and I was greeted by the Presidents of each.

Solicitors and barristers crowded into the large room in the middle of the building for the meeting. The doors remained open for ventilation, and the non-stop babble of noise percolated the building. A long table, seating perhaps fifty lawyers, filled the room and I had trouble making myself heard against the background noise. I was asked to give my impressions of India and about Charles and Diana again! I told them about my yatra and leprosy. English is the language in which most of them were trained, and most of them understood it. One gentleman composed a poem for me, calling me a Mata Devi – a mother goddess! He seemed to be admired for his effort and was not given the sort of bawdy reception he might have received in the UK.

Poetry plays quite a large part in the cultural life of Indian people. Their religious texts are, after all, long poems. Millions of people know these writings, being able to recite them, having learnt them in childhood. The Presidents said a few words and made a donation on behalf of their members to LS, to help with his rehabilitation work.

When we got back to the hospital there was a staff meeting going on. I sat with them for a time, during which we were served tea. The tea was taken with much slurping, rather like wine tasters use, appreciation I suppose, but it sounds awful to some-one brought up to the British way of tea drinking, with quiet sips!

November 29, 1994

W H Smith School Visit.

Lacksmi Singh, Barun, Dr Ajay and I left for Varanasi at 6.45 am. I was put in the front passenger seat of the jeep, and Lacksmi Singh sat on a temporary seat, made of a block of foam and a blanket, placed so that he could lean back on to the spare wheel, wedged between the front seats. We both suffer from vibration through the vehicle from the rough roads. I wore my neck collar, to protect myself from pinched nerves which give me dead hands and pins and needles, among other nuisances.

We took the back roads, sandy tracks for the most part, alongside a canal. Our intention was to avoid the usual traffic jam at the State border, between Uttar Pradesh and Bihar, on the GT road. The journey was uneventful, although I did see a beautifully marked brown bird, its wings and tail edged in an iridescent blue-green. We reached

Ramnagar Fort, approaching along its main street, vibrant with the colours of the fruits and vegetables, laid out in the markets at the side of the road. The fort, its imposing red sandstone gateway fronting the town, was lit by the early morning sun.

We drove down a sandy slope and queued for permission to cross the pontoon bridge over the Ganges. The traffic flows are controlled by a man with a whistle, sitting in a kiosk before the bridge. The pontoons are hollow tanks, pointed at each end, which are joined together as they float on the water. Metal duckboards are placed across the tanks to make a roadway. There are wooden fences to keep pedestrians and traffic from wandering off the bridge into the Ganges. There is only room for one lane of traffic, and so the waiting vehicles form a queue on each bank waiting for their turn to cross. Passengers take the opportunity to have a wash in the river, and visit the tea stalls nearby for refreshments.

When we got into Varanasi, we stopped near the Durga Temple, and tea was brought to us in the jeep, by Tarun's wife Usha. She is studying for her Ph.D. in Organic Chemistry, at the Hindu University in Varanasi, and living with her parents, and young son. Her father came to chat to Lakshmi Singh, through the open window of the jeep. He had a most interesting face, close cropped hair and lovely eyes, I would have liked to take a photo of the two men as they talked together, but I was too close and if I had got out of the jeep, they would have noticed and been self-conscious.

Lakshmi Singh told me that he refused dowry from Usha's parents, as being a follower of Gandhi, he doesn't believe in the system. Varun had also told me that none was asked for Shouba either. In Bhabua rich people pay five or six lakhs of rupees, about £10,000, while poor people give saris and shirts. Money will be offered in the wedding of the first son, and maybe some jewellery, but a second son will give less, and so on down the line. Lakshmi Singh said that people in the Bhabua area don't borrow from money lenders to pay for weddings.

155

We said goodbye to Usha's family and drove to the home of Dr Ajay Mishre's father-in-law, in a new block of flats. He showed me the handprints on the wall, near the front door - the traditional way of wishing the family well in their new home. We had breakfast and LS changed into a clean dhoti, for our visit to the W H Smith Memorial School.

When we arrived at the gates of the school, the jeep had to stop, because the huge playground was occupied by children. Two lines of clapping children made a formal guard of honour to the assembly hall on the far side. As I entered the gates, with Lakshmi Singh, Dr Mishra and Barun, I was welcomed by the head boy and head girl, as they placed three huge garlands of orange marigold flowers round my neck.

I was led to meet the Principal of this 6000-pupil secondary school, Mrs Anita Das, and her mother Pauline, who was the Deputy Head. The school is named after Pauline's uncle, it's founder. The Principal, wearing a pink sari, was a bubbly, overweight, enthusiastic teacher of Anglo-India origin. She seemed to have a good approach to her pupils, teachers and parents. This became evident to me during our conversations before and after lunch, and in the conduct and attitude of the children I came into contact with.

We took our seats in the reserved front row, Mrs Das, her mother Pauline, Lakshmi Singh, Dr Ajay Mishre, Barun and me. Behind us a hall filled with navy uniformed children of, I should say, the lower secondary grades, perhaps twelve-to-fourteen-year-olds. A concert had been arranged for me, and it began with a choir of senior girls singing a hymn in English, one which W H Smith had particularly liked, and. coincidentally one of my favourites too! ('God Is Love, His The Care'). They then sang an Indian hymn in Hindi.

The choir was followed by several groups of children, boys and girls, performing traditional dances from various parts of northern India. Two girls gracefully interpreted Dawn in the classical Bharatanatyam style, using their eyes as well as their bodies, in this centuries old style of dance. A Bengali seed sowing dance followed, the children wearing costumes they had made themselves, from their own hand-woven cloth, called 'Khadi'. Next was an exuberant performance of a Punjabi dance, improvised by eight older boys. This was very well received and obviously very popular with the young audience behind us.

Mrs Das addressed the children from the stage, and I was invited to do likewise. I told them why I had chosen to help the fight against leprosy, not only by collecting money but by raising awareness about the disease. I said I had decided to cycle along the Ganges, following the ancient pilgrim route, so that I could spread the facts about leprosy to the people I met in the towns and villages. Having told them about my typical cycling day, I concluded with a message for them. In essence, this was that as the future professionals, they will be leaders of men and can greatly influence attitudes in society. I told them that I knew that they, as individuals, and collectively as a school, already made donations to the GKNP centre at Bhabua for the rehabilitation projects, and were helping to build a mother and child centre, for the poorest people in the villages. I urged them to tell as many people as possible, their relations, friends, and servants, that leprosy is caused by a germ and is curable. They can be the messengers of the truth about leprosy and by persuading those that they tell; to pass on the same message, they are creating a powerful chain reaction. This dynamic force can be used to encourage sufferers to come forward for treatment and lead to their acceptance in the community.

After this nerve-wracking episode, I was taken to the staff room, where 100 teachers were seated in rows facing the table where Lakshmi Singh and I were installed. We spoke to our audience in a similar vein though this time I let Lakshmi Singh do most of the talking. I think he repeated himself quite a few times, as we all do in old age, but as age is respected in India, as in China, I was able to be lazy and leave most of the talking to Lakshmi Singh.

We took lunch in the Principal's house; her mother was supervising the servants, who were preparing the meal. Anita Das amused me with her description of pan-chewing fathers. Pan is a mixture of betel nut, spices and lime paste, wrapped in an edible leaf. Pan sellers will make different varieties to suit individual customers. Mrs Das refuses to talk to fathers who are chewing pan. She mimicked their garbled speech and described their drooling mouth-fulls of red juice, and the obnoxious spitting, used to get rid of the excess scarlet saliva. I had only seen my Bombay friends take pan on leaving a wedding, and on being invited to try some, I had swallowed the package after a few chews.

After lunch I signed some autograph books for girls who came to the principal's room, and politely asked for my signature. As we left, we passed the donation box on the veranda, decorated with the Lepra logo of a hand and the words, 'see me, hear me, heal me, touch me'. There were also some samples of the candles that the ex-patients make for Christmas and Diwali.

After thanking Mrs. Das we took Lakshmi Singh to rest at Dr Mishre's home and Barun, Dr Ajay and I went to see his friend, the Sports Editor, at the Daily Jagran newspaper.

The part of the building which I saw was truly amazing. It was so unlike any newspaper office I had ever seen. We entered an old building at street level, through iron-grill gates, past a huge reel of newsprint, and were taken into a warren of dark concrete tunnel-like corridors. The Sports Editor's office was two feet wider than his desk, and about twice its length. A battered manual typewriter, a couple of phones, a television and a fax machine were the only pieces of equipment, in the windowless room.

I gave the editor my press release and he read it and asked me some questions before phoning through to, I presume, the News Editorial office. Someone was sent to make a Hindi translation of the details the sports editor had selected from our conversation, and the Yatra account.

I was highly amused at the unexpected demonstration of the very habit of pan chewing, that Anita Das had so recently been telling me about. The upward tilt of the head, to stop the juices dribbling down the chin. The spitting streams of surplus juice when the mouth became overloaded – in this case into the waste paper bin. The plum in the mouth, or the hot potato in the mouth, effect of talking with a full mouth. I could see how she felt annoyed by the habit – especially as most people don't care where they spit! However, my story was published in the Daily Jagran, along with a photo of the principal and me. Barun bought me a copy of the article a few days later, when I was in Patna. He told me that it would have appeared in several syndicated newspapers around Uttar Pradesh and Bihar.

We collected LS and Usha on our way back. This time we took the GT road and got stuck in the traffic. However, Shouba had supper ready for us when we arrived back at the hospital at 9 pm.

I needed an early night to prepare for my return to cycling so I went to bed as soon as I could after supper

Chapter 8

On The Road Again!

November 30, 1994

Bhabua to Sasaram 50 km/31 miles

I got up at 6.45 am, put on my clean Lepra tee-shirt and leggings, packed my panniers, and prepared the bike, before having an omelette and toast breakfast, with Barun. Lakshmi Singh arrived and so did several other people I didn't recognise.

There was a great deal of activity, some school children arrived, along with their teachers, Dr Mishre's father, and several GKNP staff. I didn't know that anything special had been arranged so I was surprised when I went downstairs to the clinic room and found it filled with chairs, facing a long table covered with a white cloth and bearing several vases of marigold flowers from the garden.

I was seated at the table. Lakshmi Singh took a seat in the 'audience'. Some school children sang a song, and one did a little dance to fill in time before the 'proceedings', whatever they were to be! Judging by the milling around of the staff, something was about to happen. It did! The District Magistrate arrived, and he came to join me at the table. Apparently, he was late, hence the impromptu

160

entertainment. We were all given tea and biscuits, and Lakshmi Singh spoke about Leprosy. Speeches were made to thank me for coming to Bhabua, for showing that outsiders cared, and wishing me a safe journey to the Bay of Bengal at the mouth of the river Ganges at Ganga Sagar.

I was led outside and Lepra workers and young men crowded round me, and put garlands of marigolds around my neck. I was presented with an envelope, which I still keep, bearing the words "from the staff at GKNP". These badly paid leprosy workers had given me 300 rupees to give to Lepra India. I nearly cried! Rajni saved my embarrassment by wheeling my bike out to me. He was beaming, for the bike had a large, hand painted, notice attached to the front handlebar bag, which said in Hindi,

'Gandhi Leprosy Institute, Mrs. Manya Norris, Cycle Yatra, Gangotri to Ganga Sagar'

It was a brilliant piece of publicity and proved so useful that I had it replaced by one in Bangla Script when I reached the state of Bengal.

Barun had written an explanation about me and my mission in Hindi, on some notepaper, which I used to hand around when I stopped at dhabas. The District Magistrate waved me off with a green flag, like the ones used by guards at railway stations.

Several GKNP staff, who had bicycles, lined up behind me. I hoped that I wouldn't fall off on the bumpy grass track, as I pedalled away in front of my fellow cyclists. I dare not take my hands off the handlebars to wave to Lacksmi Singh, and my well-wishers left behind at the hospital. I couldn't even look behind me, in case I ran into some obstacle on the track I hoped fervently that I could get up the slope to the metalled road. After four days of not cycling my legs felt like jelly. Barun kept just behind me and said we were going to take a shortcut, a good road, to the GT road. There must have been about fourteen of us on bikes when we reached the older, narrower part of Bhabua town. Barun told me to go slow, because of the traffic, however, it was mainly carts and pedestrians, so I was able to ride it easily, hands ready on brake and bell. Leaving Bhabua chowk the 'good road' proved to be one of the most pot-holed I'd seen. The craters were often two feet across, and I had to weave my way between them on curving strips of the original surface, often only six inches wide.

It was like cycling around the edges of a piece of jigsaw puzzle. Barun kept shouting 'Aunty, not so fast!'. The entourage were laughing and calling out to one another, but I couldn't make out much of what they said. I asked them if they would like to come with me to Calcutta and they giggled and laughed. After seven kilometres we were waved down in a little village where I recognised the doctor and some GKNP staff. They would like to come with me to Calcutta and they giggled and laughed.

After seven kilometres we were waved down in a little village where I recognised the doctor and some GKNP staff. They had arranged a tea stop for us while they were taking a clinic. Crowds of villagers gathered round us, reading the notice on my bike, shaking my hand, and generally enjoying the spectacle of the cycling send-off team. Twenty minutes later we were on our way again. The road would typically improve for a few kilometres and just as I was becoming complacent about its improvement, it would deteriorate again.

After 18 kilometres we reached the GT road. I crossed it and was just wondering how far my escorts would come, when I was overtaken by one of our lads, who signalled for me to stop, with a wave of his hand. Waving his left hand from the wrist, while the extended arm points to the ground, seems to be the Indian version of "I am going to stop". It was such a minimal movement, that it could easily be missed, or mistaken for someone relaxing his wrist! Barun introduced me to his uncle and we were given more cups of tea. My escorts were now leaving me and returning to Bhabua, so I thanked them again and said goodbye. Barun made me promise to phone him when I reached Patna in about five-days-time, adding that he would combine a business trip with renewing our acquaintance.

The journey to Sasaram, where my first stop was to be the Tourist Bungalow, took less than four hours. I kept a lookout for signs of the hostel, but when I reached the far side of town, I began to think I had missed it. I stopped to ask a group of rickshaw drivers, who were resting under a tree, and they directed me one kilometre back the way I had come. I retraced my route and still had no success, everyone whom I asked looked either doubtful, or vaguely mentioned one or two kilometres. I bought some fruit at the main crossroads and decided to visit the Muslim tomb of Sher Shah, to which I had seen a sign. Perhaps the tourist bungalow was near the tomb?

A most impressive tomb stood in the middle of a huge rectangular tank, or lake. The banks of the half-kilometre square lake were laid out with grassy terraces and flower beds. The whole area is separated from the perimeter road by iron railings like those once common around English parks. On the eastern side, a pair of gates, the only entrance to the gardens, led down to a long shady colonnade, with steps going down into the lake. There was no one about, it was early afternoon, so I sat in the welcome shade of the pavilion, enjoying the peace and quiet, looking at the magnificent sixteenth century building in the middle of the shimmering lake.

The Afghan, Sher Shah Suri, was the Ruler of the present-day Bengal and Bihar area, for the Sultan in Delhi. He was responsible for rebuilding the Grand Trunk Road from Delhi to Calcutta. Like the Great Wall of China, it is reputed to be visible from space, being some 2000 miles long. If he could see it today, he would turn in his grave, bullock carts and pilgrims have given way to a 'suicide alley of ramshackle vehicles and neglected maintenance'.

Sher Shah commissioned his architect to build a tomb for his father, Hasan, at Sasaram. He was obviously pleased with the result because he ordered one to be built for himself and another for his son.

Sher Shah died in 1545 and was buried in this unusual tomb just off the Grand Trunk Road.

The tomb rests on a square plinth in the middle of the lake. The dome is not onion-shaped like the Taj Mahal but is shallow, reminding me of the breast-shaped haystacks I'd seen on a previous visit to Rajasthan. The four corners are decorated with domed pavilions from which steps lead down into the lake. The whole cleverly combines square, octagonal and circular shapes with a series of arches, pavilions, and colonnades. The stone is a sandstone from Chunar, near Varanasi, and although the domes looked grey, the walls and plinth took on a rosy hue in the afternoon sunlight. The dome used to be painted white and the mini-spire was covered in gold. Cycling around the perimeter road the tomb looked fine from every angle, its reflection in the waters of the lake added a symmetrical dimension.

Looking around, above the trees, I could see the domes of other Muslim tombs in the area, but I was content with this unique building in its unusual setting so I made no attempt to see them at close quarters. At the far side of the lake, local villagers had bent the railings to gain access to the water in the tank and were busy washing clothes and themselves. The intrusion was not obvious to tourists and was tolerated by the authorities. In a country without washing machines and a village without a river, the local tank was the place to wash.

I found an Archaeological Survey of India building, and went into the garden to ask if they could direct me to the Tourist hostel. At last, I was given clear instructions and this time I managed to find the elusive place. The building looked like a factory, in grey concrete, a concrete yard, and a stubble of neglected grass. There was a tea stall at the metal gate and the building was euphemistically called the Sher Shah Hotel! There was no food, and hot water was only available in the middle of the day. There wasn't any electricity but "the generator would come on at ten o'clock". It didn't, probably because I was the only customer, and not worth the kerosene needed to start it. I couldn't be bothered to go out looking for a hot meal, and I didn't fancy a walk in the dark. It would be about a kilometre to places providing food so I ate some fruit and had an early night. I managed to get an omelette and a three-cup-pot of ready-made tea from the stall by the gate at 7 am and left soon afterward. I was not too impressed by the standard of this example Bihar State Tourist accommodation.

December 1, 1994

<u>Sasaram to Aurangabad</u> 48 km/ 30 miles

I was heading for Patna, but was undecided about which route to take. The most direct road would involve 99 km. to the first chance of overnight accommodation. An alternative was to cross the river Son by the 'longest bridge in India' at Dehri and stay at Aurangabad, both on the dreaded GT road but only 47 km, and sure to have some hotels. I would then have a reasonable distance for the following day to get to Bodh Gaya, the Buddhist pilgrimage centre, and from there 100 km. to Patna. I chose that route. The 'longest bridge' marked as a tourist highlight on my map no longer holds this record. It had been surpassed in Bihar since 1983 by the Mahatma Gandhi Bridge at Patna – a massive 5.7 km crossing to the east of the city – making it one of the world's longest bridges. I took the bypass from the GT road into Aurangabad, whose long main road straddled one of the minor Ganges tributaries.

I had no information about the town, and it didn't feature in any guidebook, so I had to look around and ask for hotels. I found one, but it was built on top of a parade of shops, and would have meant carrying my bike up the narrow staircase, so I asked again and was given a couple of names. They both seemed to be closed and I was trying to get some help from a pharmacist, as they often speak English, when a man on a scooter stopped beside me and said severely, "This is Aurangabad, go to the Police station!" He was the first English speaker I'd come across in Aurangabad. There seemed to be a majority of Muslims in the area, judging by the mosques and the shop signs written in Urdu script. I began to wonder if the head shaking, I had encountered was because of a religious aversion to a woman, alone, on the street, not in purdah.

At the police station, recognised by its diagonal blue and red sign, I asked if there was a Dak bungalow nearby. A police constable was assigned to take me to what turned out to be a Circuit House. I knew that these establishments were meant for the use of judges, and high government officials while travelling about the country on official duty. Many of them were built in the days of British rule in India and were usually superior to accommodation provided for the public works and irrigation department personnel, and lesser government officials. The hierarchy was Circuit House, Dak bungalow, and PWD/Irrigation bungalow. Over the three months, I managed to sample each of them. As I expected the manager told me I would need to get the District Magistrate's permission to stay at a Circuit House. I had come to India prepared for such an eventuality. The policeman took my South Cambs. security pass, a letter from the manager with my signature on it, and departed for the DM's office for official authorisation for me to stay at the Circuit House.

Meanwhile, I was introduced to Rajendra, my room servant, and he arranged for the shower and loo to be washed, and ran me a bucket of cold water for my shower. I was pleased that the bed had a mosquito net, folded over wooden supports. When tapped to dislodge any mosquitoes which might be trapped in the bed-side of the net, it deposited vast amounts of dust over the bedding. My right heel had some lovely new bites, which had become blisters where my trainers rubbed them. I kept putting antiseptic cream on them whenever I felt the urge to scratch, and at night I took an antihistamine tablet to relieve the itching and enable me to sleep. In Sasaram I had been too hot with one blanket which just shows how cool the hospital building at Bhabua was.

A dignitary arrived to stay in room three, a red light flashing on his car, and an escort of police or army, I couldn't distinguish their uniforms. The official seemed to have so many visitors that I was surprised when a rickshaw disgorged a visitor for me. A gentleman introduced himself and said he wanted to see the 'honoured guest', meaning me. I showed him the usual pictures and leaflets about leprosy and he offered some money as he left. I felt shy accepting it so he left it on the seat when he went away.

My next visitors were a press reporter and a photographer. I thought they had come to see the Minister, but apparently, news had got around of my arrival in Aurangabad, and it was me they had come to interview. We sat on the veranda outside my room and talked about my pilgrimage to increase awareness about leprosy. I gave the reporter my printed information to use in his story, which he hoped would be in the December 4th edition of the local paper. They told me that the official in room three was the Minister for Goals and Rehabilitation. As Indian goals have a terrible reputation for keeping remand prisoners for as long as ten years before charging them, and as there are so many deaths in prison, I didn't think the 'Rehabilitation' part of his title could provide him with much of a workload. The photographer was called Akhouri Pramod. He said he had to go to a football match but would come back later to take a photo of me on my bike.

I spent the rest of the afternoon reading, wearing my one and only best dress, and sitting in the sunshine in a basket chair, everything else having been washed, and laid out to dry on the grass at the back of the bungalow. As sunset approached, I gathered up my washing and changed into long trousers and my long-sleeved, polo-necked black woollen jumper – my most useful article of clothing, it provided plenty of cover to protect me from mosquitoes and was just the right amount of warmth for north Indian winter evenings, teamed with long, cream and black skirt of Indian origin, in the then current, fashionable 'crinkle' cotton. This meant that it could be rolled up for packing and screwed up and tied in a knot after washing, to maintain the fine pleating. My usual evening dress was, therefore, a jumper, skirt, and flat gold sandals plus mosquito repellent if I wasn't wearing socks. My jumper also had enough warmth when worn over a tee-shirt, for chilly early morning starts. The huge polo neck could be pulled over my hair to keep my ears warm and was useful as a head covering for temple visits.

I put some leggings on for the bike photo and we made sure that Rajni's Hindi notice was prominently displayed in the picture. I received a copy of the photo, made into a Christmas card, from Akhouri when I reached Bombay for my flight home. After the photo session, taken against a background of the sunset sky and palm trees, he invited me to visit his family.

He lived on an estate, called a colony in India, of concrete bungalows just a few hundred yards away, down an unlit road from the Circuit House. We sat with his three student children in a small room that had twin beds and turquoise-painted walls, adorned with photographs. I was offered 'churra' and one of the girls went to make it – a spicy snack of fried puffed rice in a ball, which can have peanuts and strips of dried coconut added to it. It was like a savoury version of Rice Krispies. The children spoke very good English, like their father, and they were all doing advanced studies in science subjects. Rupesh, the 22-year-old son, was in his third year studying Chemistry, Shaleeni was in her first year of BSc, and Moilineeni, aged 16, was taking the equivalent of A levels and hoping to go to university. They were not at all shy. When their father asked them to play their musical instruments for me, they gave a most enjoyable impromptu concert. The son played his 'tabla' – a pair of small drums that are played, one hand on each, the wrist resting on the rim of the instrument. I liked the rhythms and counter-rhythms and was amazed at the speed of his fingers. I often saw men drumming at an imaginary tabla when they were relaxing. The youngest daughter played the small Indian harmonium, opening and closing a flap of wood on the back of the instrument. We both took photos with the children to record my visit. The older daughter played a stringed instrument and sang songs for me. They gave a lovely concert of Bihari folk songs and at my request, some in Muslim style called Ghazals.

Akhouri had dozens of photo albums, and he showed me some of his favourite pictures. Akhouri suddenly asked me if I liked 'poached eggs Indian style'. As I had ordered dinner at the Circuit House I had to decline his offer, but he explained that hard-boiled and poached eggs can be bought from the Indian equivalent of barrow boys, in markets by day, and sometimes around the houses by night. This discovery provided a new dimension to my diet from Aurangabad onwards. Whenever I saw a barrow boy with a stack of eggs, and a bulbous metal pot, I knew that cooked eggs were available. I would buy four hard boiled eggs for eight rupees. Safe from contamination in their shells and just boiled they were as bug-proof as my bananas. Just before I left the Akhouri house his friend called to ask me if I would call at his house, "just two minutes away!", "His family would like to meet me!".

He was an engineer working for the Irrigation Department and he was able to show me a map of the Inspection Bungalows where I might be able to get accommodation. The power went off while I was at his house, but a neon tube rechargeable hand lamp was produced and I was introduced to his wife and daughters. His youngest child, a boy, was asleep in an adjoining room. I talked to them for a while and took a photo of the smiling ladies, all wearing red salwar-kameez.

My host walked me back to the Circuit House, taking a shortcut, up some steps which led over the wall into the Circuit House garden. It was pitch dark in the street, but there was electricity in the Circuit house, perhaps they had their own generator. I wasn't aware of the humming sound of an engine, but there was a fair amount of residual noise coming from the dining room. The manager appeared and asked me not to enter the lounge, but to stay in my room and have dinner there! My meal of chips, salad, chapatis, and vegetables was brought to me by Rajendra. I sat at the dressing table, the only surface in the bedroom, and had a brainwave. I decided I could use some of my filtered water in my spare enamel mug, to wash the salad and afterward the onion and tomato salad. I also dipped the over-spiced vegetables in the water to rinse off the chilli sauce

I performed this ritual whenever I had spicy food served to me in the privacy of my room. Traditionally dahi is served, to temper the hotness of Indian food, but it was not available in the places where I stayed, only in family homes. The custom of eating food in hotel rooms is quite common in the non-western type of hotels in which I stayed. Tourist hostels and government accommodation, however, usually had dining rooms for guests. A mother I spoke to at Haridwar said the guests at Tourist hotels usually ate out, because the standard of food and service was so bad.

December 2, 1994

Aurangabad to Bodh Gaya 76 km/47 miles

I paid my bill and was amazed that I was charged only 7 Rs 50 paise for the bed element. When registering I had not known what the column headings said, and used my initiative to follow those who had stayed before me. One column always seemed to be filled in with the word 'Official'. I didn't know whether this was a description of the visitor, or the purpose of the visit. I just followed suit and wrote 'official'. Later, I found out from a newspaper article that people on government work were heavily subsidised. Indeed, when I once wrote 'yatri' – pilgrim. I was charged 50 Rs. for the night, after that, I was 'official' in government accommodation.

The chowkidar had woken me at 5.50 am., but I had been aware of noises outside on the veranda, and temple music since 4 am. I returned to the GT road, which was fairly good to begin with, and I covered 28 km, in the first hour. After one banana and two water stops, signalled by the hourly bleeping of my watch, I reached Shergati. The road surface became horrendous and there were lots of parked vehicles. It was impossible to cycle. The road surface had completely disintegrated. Cinder-like pieces of broken tarmac and changes in level, up a few inches, down several inches. I couldn't maintain a safe direction alongside the huge lorries and, fearing an accident, or at the very least a puncture, I got off my well-laden bike. When the road became its normal self again, I remounted.

I had missed the turning-off point for Gaya, it was somewhere in the chaos of Shergati, but I wasn't worried because I could see from my map, that there was an alternative route, just eleven kilometres down the road. Shergati must have been the lorry drivers 'lunch stop, because the volume of traffic decreased. I took advantage of the relative peace and rode on until I came to a wide, grassy valley, backed by groves of broad-leaved evergreen trees. Its river was a thin band of silver, winding between golden sandbanks, braided with more silver streams. In the distance, a family was crossing the sandbanks and going towards the woodland, the woman with a basket on her head, the children running about alongside the adults.

I also saw a new method of getting water from brick wells. A tripod of sapling trees supported another tree trunk, a sacking bundle containing large rocks, which was tied to one end of the fourth sapling which was supported by the tripod. The stone acted as a counterweight to raise the buckets of water from the well. I had just finished my snack when the enjoyable new experience of not having an audience was shattered. as a group of secondary school-age boys stopped to ask questions. The crowd grew as each passer-by, from either direction, stopped to see what the attraction could be. Not wishing to antagonise any youths this time, I got out my photos and the Hindi leprosy letter from Bhabua. On this sobering note, I said goodbye to them and was soon on one of the best roads I was to encounter on the whole journey.

The road from the GT junction at Dobbi, to Gaya, was originally a single-track road. but it had been widened by three feet on each side. A thin covering of trees gave shelter from the sun. Every now and again I could hear giggles, and cracking noises, coming from the trees. Girls climbed the trees to break off branches, while women were gathering dead leaves from the ground. I saw them using baskets with clever extensions which enabled the basket to hold a much greater volume of leaves. They had inserted sticks into the woven cane of the basket's circumference and wrapped sacking around these projections. It was the only example of this ingenuity that I saw, and I wished I'd stopped to take a photo. The missed shots always irked me – knowing that I might not get the opportunity again, but hoping that a better setting or better light would present itself. Rarely does the opportunity re-present itself! If I had an infinite supply of camera film then I could have afforded to take more pictures, but my thirty reels of film had to reach the end of the journey at Ganga Sagar. This applied even more so to the film for the Polaroid camera, for which I had enough for only thirty exposures.

I was gaily bowling along the road, which might have been a country lane in rural Cambridgeshire, when I was surprised to see a sign announcing a 'Dr. Anse, Physician and Surgeon', almost in the middle of nowhere. I stopped and went back to confirm the writing, proclaiming that his degrees had been obtained in Patna and London. Here, I thought, was an opportunity to ask about leprosy in this area. After a little wait, I was shown into the small room where Dr. Anse sat behind a table. I spoke in English. It was soon obvious that he had difficulty understanding me. He managed to say when I mentioned his London degree, "correspondence course". When I told an English doctor, working in India, of this encounter, he said that even in Patna doctors are trained in English. The physician and surgeon on the way to Bodh Gaya was probably a 'quack' and not qualified in western medicine at all.

A few kilometres before Gaya I stopped at a little tea stall. I was amazed to see how the little boy, of eleven years or so, made the tea in the western style, by pouring hot water over a red cloth containing tea leaves. The cloth was then screwed up tight in his hand, by twisting it, to release the brown, obviously not very hot, liquid, and I hoped that his hands were clean! I think the boil-everything-together way the anything can be regarded as hygienic in India!

I checked my position, and found that I was directly opposite the road to Bodh Gaya. Indeed, there was a circular Buddhist-style brick gateway built right over the road. I cycled under this arch, and was soon at two government hostels simply called Tourist Hostel 1 and Tourist Hostel 2. These wanted over the usual rate of 200 Rs a night. I had become accustomed to paying less than this, so I decided to try somewhere else. I met a young man who asked if I could stay at a pilgrim centre attached to a monastery. The monk in charge took one look at me and said they were full! My guidebook had warned of westerners abusing the hospitality of ashrams, by not refraining from tea, coffee, cigarettes, and drugs.

The Dak bungalow was full, and there was a doctors' conference going on, but I made contact with a local doctor, who could find someone to tell me about the incidence of leprosy in the area. I then went to look for an Indian hotel. I found a guest house at the very end of town. It was newly built, with half-a-dozen en-suite rooms on the first floor. I was invited to put my bicycle in the basement garage, which meant that it wouldn't be getting the usual clean that night. It might seem pernickety to wash and clean a bike every day, but the road sides were, more often than not, pure sand, which is blown around by the aerodynamics of the vehicles, if not by the real wind, and acted as a grindstone on the chain and gear teeth.

There was also vehicle exhaust, from the diesel lorries and buses, which covered me in a black film, made the corners of my eyes have black specs in them, and coated the insides of my ears and nose like the old-fashioned London smog of my childhood. I would be so grimy when I arrived at my accommodation that I had to use specially moistened tissues to clean my face and hands before I dared present myself to anyone official! I also used these wipes to clean my hands before I ate my picnics and for cooling down generally.

I ordered a tray-tea and had a bucket shower, the first time I'd had hot water since I'd left Varanasi, nine days previously. Unfortunately, I knocked my glasses off when I was changing and the lenses shattered when they hit the terrazzo floor.

However, I had some spare specs with me, of an older prescription and not photochromatic, but they would be better than nothing, as my distance sight was poor. I hung out my washing on a balcony at the end of the corridor, overlooking the recently ploughed rice -paddy fields – there was no garden. The front of the hotel overlooked a large park beside the river Phalgu. A small fair was established on part of the area and I wondered if it would be playing music late into the night, however, I had my wax earplugs, which I always take on my travels, and they do help to shut out a fair proportion of the local noise.

It wasn't until 1836 that a Scotsman, Major General Alexander Cunningham, a retired engineer, who had served with the army in India since he was a young man, identified Bodh Gaya as the ancient centre of the Buddhist religion. He found extensive ruins, including the pyramidal temple. Statues of Buddhas were scattered over a fifteen-mile radius and were objects of worship to the local Hindus. Even the temple was in charge of the Brahmins. Every now and then strange foreigners would come to Bodh Gaya to tour the overgrown ruins with books in their hands. One such visitor claimed the place was the residence of Gautama, and that the temple was built by Ashoka, king of Pataliputra. Ashoka and Pataliputra meant nothing to Cunningham, but he knew Gautama was the Buddha. In the same year, two eyewitness accounts of Buddhist India were translated, they were the travelogues of Fa Hsien and Hsuan Tsang, who travelled extensively in India visiting monasteries, and collecting Buddhist manuscripts in the 5th and 7th centuries. Their accounts had been acquired by French orientalists, translated in Paris, and found their way to friends of Cunningham's at Oxford. At last, there was reliable evidence to date and source Buddhism's foundation in India. The present-day Bodh Gaya is the epicentre from which the world's major religion radiated out to Tibet, China, Japan, Sri Lanka, and Southeast Asia.

The Bo tree in the Mahabodhi temple precinct is not the original, but is a cutting from the tree taken by Ashoks's son to Sri Lanka, when

Buddhism was established there. The 50 -metre pyramidal spire of the Mahabodhi temple houses a large gilded image of the Buddha. The original 3rd Century temple of Ashoka was restored in the 11th, 14th, and 19th centuries.

The Mahabodhi temple courtyard has hundreds of small and mini-sized stupas erected over the centuries by visiting pilgrims. The paved and terraced surrounds of the temple were the praying, meditating, and exercising places for the many maroon-clothed monks, male and female, as well as ordinary pilgrims, both Buddhist and Hindu, who flock to Bodh Gaya. Some monks walked clockwise, around and around, the paved terrace which surrounds the sunken gardens, with the lotus pool where the Buddha is thought to have bathed, the stupas, and the main shrine.

Under the holy Bo Tree, men and women were performing a salutation and obeisance, on wooden boards, to prostrate their bodies to the ground. The action was almost hypnotic to watch. Hands are folded together as in the Indian greeting sign, then raised over the head, brought down to the hips as the practitioner kneels, his hands spread before him on the wooden board. He straightens his knees and slides forward on a folded blanket, does a press-up and stands up, ready to begin again. I saw men and women doing this form of adoration, young and old. The wooden boards, which allowed a good sliding action for the blanket, were worn to a mirror-like shine. I don't know how long these adorations went on for, but I was watching for over half an hour and no one stopped in that time.

Other groups of monks, and lay pilgrims, sat in groups reading scriptures or chanting. Some revolved hand-held prayer wheels, looking like spinning tin cans on a stick. Large trays of candle night-lights were being prepared for the evening ceremonies. I sat and absorbed the smells of incense, of marigolds, the ringing of bells, and the murmur of prayers in this holy place. Three ragged children kept climbing over one of the gates in the perimeter fence. They were gently shooed away by monks. A few minutes later they would be climbing the gate again, walking cheekily down the steps, into the temple gardens, only to be scolded and made to climb out of the garden again.

I went to look at the pretty, pagoda-shaped, Thai temple which I had passed on my way into town. The Buddha was clearly visible from the path leading up to the temple. The building was about to close, as it was beginning to get dark, so I contented myself with photographing some of the decorations on the outside of the temple. I sauntered back past the stalls where the Tibetan refugees sell woollens, other clothes and crafts, to the many tourists who come to Bodh Gaya. Tibet is one of the countries where Buddhism flourished until recently outlawed when the Chinese annexed the country between 1959 and 1965.

A mud road led between dozens of large canvas tents, which provided accommodation and restaurants, for the thousands of Tibetan pilgrims who flock to Bodh Gaya every January, when the Dalai Lama takes up residence there. They were not serving food until eight o'clock, much too late for me, so I walked back to my hotel and asked about food. The young man's mother offered to give me some of their meal "if I could eat Indian food!". I was pleased to accept their offer.

While I was waiting for my supper, I went to get my washing in, and found some things had blown off the balcony, presumably into the rice field. I was discovered trying to get around the house and wasn't allowed to go looking for my undies. The young man insisted on wading through the muddy field to retrieve them - most embarrassing! After that, I was shown a washing line in the garage! My supper was brought on a tray, two parathas, dal and vegetables. I had nearly finished when there was a knock on the door, to ask me to have some more. They couldn't believe that I had had enough to eat and it took a lot of convincing them. When I paid my bill the next morning, I found that I hadn't been charged for the meal – very kind of them.

December 3, 1994

Bodh Gaya to Jehanabad 65 km/41 miles

I went to look for some breakfast near the hospital, as I wanted to call there later. I was directed to the "Hotel Shiva". A hotel is. traditionally, a cafe type of restaurant, and not a hotel with accommodation as we understand the term. This one was run by Mr. Sunil, and was the only 'hotel' catering for westerners in Bodh Gaya. He proudly told me how it was started by his father twenty years previously. He offered American breakfast, (two eggs with toast), grilled cheese and tomato sandwiches, and toast with almost everything, including peanut butter, honey, 'French' and 'buttered'. I chose his muesli with curd, but could have had semolina, rice pudding, all kinds of eggs, carrots, and apple juice). It was hard to choose. Sunil translated my order to the cook's boy, who disappeared into a dark corridor. A glass of tea and the peanut toast arrived first, followed by the cheese sandwich, the marmalade toast, and a few minutes later by the muesli. I was surrounded by steel plates. I might have been having an Indonesian meal! The muesli was served on a gleaming dish with red cherries and grated coconut sprinkled over the surface of the curd. The main ingredient was not oats but rice, mixed with pieces of apple and banana. Wanting something else to drink, I asked for apple juice and Sunil had to go into the street to buy the apples, which he prepared in his Yamaha juicer. They either don't have many power cuts here, or they have a generator! I had overestimated my appetite and sandwiched the toast together for my lunch.

The doctor's surgery in a small white-washed building, was just around the corner, in the grounds of the hospital. I waited on a bench with four patients. A teenage girl was reading an English reading book so I spoke to her. When she didn't reply her father came over to me, and said that she didn't know English. He explained that the children read their books, pronouncing the words, but not understanding them! This probably explains why, despite numerous advertisements for English Medium education, the majority of under 15-year-old's I'd spoken to, could only say, "What is your good name?" and "What country?". The sixteen-plus age group, who are at college, can learn English to a reasonable standard, but they are a very small minority of the school population. Moreover, the numbers attending school in Bihar are also minimal. The literacy rate in Bihar was very low, only 28%, and as low as 3% among some castes.

The doctor gave me the address of a leprosy worker, Bhupendra Kumar, and I went to find him. He was listening to cricket on his radio when I arrived, – Indians are very keen on cricket. He told me that he works in a Government Centre, but that they don't use MDT, they just treat patients with Dapsone and multivitamins. Occasionally they give Rifampicin' All his MB cases are sent to a hospital in Gaya, and PB cases are treated for six months. They also did not do any charting or keep individual records, because this is only the required practice when MDT treatment is given. I asked him how many people had received treatment in the last year. He didn't know off hand and got up to look in a book and counted the names – 32 cases!

This man works one day a week but the rural population is very similar to the poor agricultural scene around Bhabua. He thought the government might be starting MDT treatment after March 1995. If that were the case, he would earn three to five hundred rupees extra, above his present government salary. He knew some centres where MDT was offered. He had trained at Ranchi, as a non-medical worker. Despite my intrusion into his home, he was very pleasant, and I was offered tea, which he made himself, and he gave me a sweetmeat called 'tilcot' which is made from sesame seeds. I thanked him and made my way towards Patna, intending to stop overnight at Jehanabad, 52 kilometres away, another short run, but it was already half-past-ten.

After an hour I reached Gaya. The town is on slightly raised ground, and there are burning ghats along the holy Phalgu river, which flows here from Bodh Gaya. Gaya's temples are dedicated to Vishnu, who is thought to release the sins of those who are prayed for in the special puja ceremony, which includes bathing in the seasonal river Phalgu. The river dries up after the monsoon season so pilgrims are seasonal too. The town is on the main Calcutta-Delhi railway line and I was so occupied with asking for Patna at every intersection, that I didn't find the older part of Gaya, with the temples and the ghats, and soon found myself in open countryside again.

One new feature of this slightly hillier region was the abundance of stone-crushing plants. The road cut through northerly protruding ridges of the Deccan peninsular which occupies most of peninsular India. The mountains of Nepal were two hundred kilometres away to the north, across the narrowest part of the Ganges valley, so that I was 250 kilometres due south of Kathmandu. This was the narrowest part of the Ganges plain. The crushing and grading of rock were done in situ. Men and women carried the stone in cane baskets on their heads, and climbed brick-built ramps, to toss their loads into a wooden hopper. The stone was mechanically crushed and entered a belt-driven tumbling device, like a huge perforated rolling pin. Stones of varying sizes dropped through the graduated holes in the wire mesh of the drum, producing three separate heaps of stone in differing sizes. The completely crushed material was powdered limestone and cement powder.

The noise of the engine driving the belt, and the crashing of the stones in the metal drum, could be heard for quite a distance, like the roaring sound of distant motorway traffic. The grey stone dust covered the area like a fog. Every plant leaf was coated with a grey powder, as if some gigantic attack of mildew, had infected every piece of vegetation. The cement powder was being shovelled into lorries from the piles deposited from head baskets. There was no need for JCB's, or lifting machines, in a state where labour is so cheap and easily available. These were the lorries that were passing me, probably shuttling back and forth to Patna.

Some twenty kilometres north of Gaya I saw a sign to the 'Barabar caves'. I had read these were the caves on which EM Forster based his 'Marabar caves' in his book 'Passage to India'. To visit them would be a 15-kilometre diversion and, not knowing much about them, apart from the film's representation, I didn't rate them worth a visit. It was only later that I found out that they contained some of the earliest examples of rock-cut temples in these granite hills, older than those at Ajanta. Two of the caves had Ashoka inscriptions, some show Buddhist barrel-vaulted roofs, chambers of polished stone, and horse-shoe-shaped gables, thought to be the pattern for arches of Muslim architecture. Some caves were retreats for sects related to Jains, Ashoka was tolerant of all religions. I always try to do my homework before I visit a country but this time, I had come unstuck, assuming they would be like the caves in the film.

I had left my water bottle, which fitted on my bike frame, at my hotel in Bodh Gaya. I discovered the loss before I left the village, but didn't think it was worth going back for, as it had a lid which was hard to close. I could use a Bisleri bottle instead. Just for a change, there were no irrigation pumps spouting water on this route, and there were hardly any villages either. Consequently, when I saw a man washing himself under a pump in the front garden of a large house, I stopped and went up to ask him if I could have some water. He pumped the handle for me while I filled my water filter, and we were soon joined by an older man, who turned out to be the owner.

This was no ordinary house, but a small factory that made metal buckets, employing twenty-five workers. Although plastic buckets have become common in India, metal ones have their uses, one of which is for the serving of food, in ashrams and railway restaurants. I should imagine that this bucket factory was a welcome source of employment in such a remote rural area. I stopped a little way down the road and had my left-over breakfast, so-called marmalade (it is always sweet orange jam), and peanut butter toast.

It was shortly after this that I met a group of about twelve men trotting along the road towards Gaya, calling out some words that I couldn't understand. They were accompanied by a drummer and two other musicians. At first, I thought that they might be a political demonstration, but as I got nearer, I could see that they were carrying a bier, with a female corpse on it, evidenced by the red shroud.

Upon entering Jehanabad I passed the police station and decided to ask for their help in finding accommodation. It must have been siesta time for the doors were opened by a man in a singlet, who had plainly been woken up. I was taken to a 'Dak bungalow' which turned out to be another Circuit house. The caretaker and the policeman tried to get permission for me to stay by telephoning the DM's office, without success. However, I was able to leave my luggage in the store room, and my three- or four-kilometre journey, in the rush hour, to the other side of town, trying to remember the complicated instructions, was not too arduous.

The DM saw me almost immediately. He was much more approachable than the Bhabua DM. He talked about my 'mission' and praised my efforts. He said that his cook was at the Circuit House and I must order whatever I liked. This was the one and only time I was offered such a carte blanche.

A huge kettle of boiling water, an oil lamp, and a cup of tea without sugar - but regretfully not a pot of tea, awaited me. I had a shower and washed my hair. I got talking to a policeman who spoke English, about MDT, my family, and my pilgrimage. He introduced me to a doctor who had arrived to distribute equipment to handicapped people, white sticks to the blind, and tricycles to other disabled people. My policeman was called away when the Deputy Commissioner of Police arrived. Before he left, he complimented me on my knowledge of India and said "I salute you!" He told the chowkidar that he must give me "big tea, full to the brim" and he arranged that I would get an omelette and toast at 7 am.

The sunset was magnificent and the birds gave a beautiful evening chorus. By 6.05 pm. it was quite dark and there was only the sound of crickets rasping in the gardens surrounding the house. I sat in my bedroom, on a cane chair, with an oil lamp on the table, reading my book, Trotterama. I don't know whether it was the soporific effect of the warm air and the gentle glow of the lamp in the enveloping darkness, but I kept on yawning and would have gladly gone to bed, were it not for the fact that I needed to have my dinner. I didn't feel hungry but I knew that I must eat to refuel my body or I wouldn't get to the Bay of Bengal.

A nearby muezzin had called his faithful to the mosque and the ensuing singing was far enough away to sound pleasant. I got up and managed to fit my mosquito net over half the bed and to close the high-level windows, which were eighteen feet up on three sides of the room. My main doors led directly onto a veranda with its arrangement of chairs and low tables. The open sides of the veranda had iron grills for security. Across the lawn was another cream-painted bungalow, in better order and newer than this one. It was shut up, probably used only for VIPs.

My suite comprised a large bedroom, a dressing room-cum-lounge, and a large bathroom with one of everything! It had a urinal, a western loo with a broken seat, a squat loo, a washbasin, and a shower area. I had just finished bucketing myself, and the bike, when the electricity went off. Power cuts were very common in India, but they are fewer in winter because people don't use fans and air-conditioning units in cool weather.

I was called to the dining room for my dinner and sat at one end of a large refectory table, at which many eminent people, judges, ministers, administrators, and governors would have taken their places in the hundred years of its history. The DM's cook had indeed produced a meal of excellence for me, omitting chilli, but including other spices subtly for me. He gave me aloo-gobi, chunks of aubergine, rice, dal, and a salad. The only off-putting part of my meal was the presence of the chowkidar, standing to attention next to me, waiting for my comments or commands, just as his father doubtless had done in the days of British India. I had forgotten to bring my water in with me and he probably thought it strange that I didn't drink any of the water he poured for me. After dinner, he told me his father had indeed worked as a chowkidar at this Circuit House and lived until he was 125. I couldn't bring myself to believe this figure, I thought he was calculating on some other calendar or had made a mistake in the translation, but no doubt his father reached a venerable old age before dying in 1969. Whatever his father's longevity, his son had proved to be a very solicitous, caring, and capable individual.

December 4, 1994

Jehanabad to Patna 48 km/30 miles

My first stop at 9.10 was for mango juice, water and an orange. A man with some English said hello, and read the poster on my bike which Rajni had made for me. It said I was cycling from Gangotri to Ganga Sagar to help people with leprosy. He said he saluted me, and I gave him a card about leprosy in Hindi. He invited me to eat at his house in the market 'about a kilometre away'. I refused. The market was more like 2 kms! I had chai for one rupee. and bought biscuits which I stuffed into my jumper pockets and ate while going along

There was thick fog all the way and I couldn't wear my glasses as the fog condensed on them, as well as on my jumper – looking like snow! Visibility was about 30-40 feet. Patna was 48 km. on the N 22 highway.

I stopped again, because I had a headache, was feeling rather tired, and had a tight feeling in my head. I had a ten-minute rest, had half a pint of water, and ate a satsuma and some biscuits. I bought more bananas and oranges for 17 Rs. a kilogram. It may have been that I was concentrating too hard in the fog! The visibility improved to 40 or 50 feet, so I put my glasses on again. The road was rather bumpy and I had to ride on the centre strip. There were more buses and lorries now that the fog was lifting. The full sun was at 45 degrees to the road, like a silver moon. I reached Patna via the usual lorry the route, parking/repairing area, and a bypass.

It took me ages to find the Tourist Bungalow, like the one at Allahabad, it used a grandiose name, 'Hotel Kautilya' and in Hindi script too! It took half an hour to find a room but it was only 187/-. I sent eight things to the dhobi for washing, and phoned Dr. Ajeet Singh, the Bihar State Leprosy Officer. He came round with a Scotsman, called Richard, who is working here in Bihar, with a Netherlands leprosy NGO. He offered to take me to Rajgir and Nalanda the next day, or on Tuesday.

The cooking for the restaurant took place just below my second-floor window, in the open air, by men using bottled gas containers. I noticed that they washed their hands quite frequently, but used them too!

I decided to walk up the road and see what the Ashoka Pataliputra hotel charged, and post my letter, which I had "pasted" with glue at the tourist bungalow. Ready-gummed envelopes are not the norm in India. Post offices, and offices generally, have bottles of glue or gum, for DIY envelope sealing. Dinner at the Tourist hotel began at 7.45 pm, but snacks were available in the bar. There was no tonic water so I had canned orange juice and soda water with my gin! The measure of gin was generous, about one and a half inches in the glass!

I chose tomato soup and grilled fish for dinner. There was a wedding going on outside, with a cacophony of sounds, videos playing, and men dancing. My mix of gin, soda, and orange juice was OK! I chose pineapple and ice cream for dessert but apparently, only plain ice cream was available! Barun came at 7 pm and I went for a dosa with him. There was another wedding going on in the next-door hotel until 2 am. Someone rang my doorbell at 11 pm and someone started shouting in the corridor at 4 am.

Barun came again at 8 am. I spent the morning talking with Dr Richard de Soldenhoff, who has worked for the Netherlands Leprosy Relief Agency NGO for 5 years in Nepal, and ten years in Malawi (formerly Tanzania). He has come to Patna to coordinate with the State Leprosy Officer. He has been living in Patna for a month, paying 800 Rs for a three-bedroomed house.

We visited the excavated ruins of Pataliputra of the Chandragupta era, about 300 BC. It was underwater at the time, but we could see part of an Ashoka Pillar. The information centre had some relics without labels, and there were no books available about the site. We saw the sandal type of shoes of the last Sikh Guru, who was born in Patna in 1660 AD and visited his shrine, Har Mandir, one of the holiest religious Sikh sites in India, the other being the Golden Temple in Amritsar. There was a large complex for pilgrims and we had to cover our heads and remove shoes and socks.

The state of Bihar had a population of 90 million in 1991. It is administered by 55 District Magistrates and District Commissioners For medical purposes Bihar had 39 districts and is divided into Blocks with PHC's (Primary Health Care Centres), and Additional PHC's, in areas with large centres of population. Each PHC is supposed to have four to six doctors and a midwife, ADHC's should have 2 doctors and a midwife. Richard found that there were often only ruined rooms. At one PHC, the salaries of three doctors and 50 staff were on the payroll, and were being drawn. Seventeen patients and one doctor turned up when Richard visited the PHC.

The leprosy drugs themselves have to cope with the wetness of the monsoon, with high temperatures, mice, and with being stolen. Clophazamine sticks to the plastic and ruptures when handled. Rifampicin in bulk disappears or goes 'missing' as it is used to treat gonorrhoea and TB. Glass bottles would be too expensive so the best solution is to use blister packs. They look 'good' to the patients too!

Rajgir and Nalanda

Dr. Ajeet Singh took me to visit Rajgir and Nalanda. Rajgir, which translates as 'city of kings' was the capital of many kingdoms that evolved into the Mauryan Empire (321–185 BC) and extended over three-quarters of India. The Hindu epic the Mahabharata mentions its rulers. A huge 2500 years old wall once surrounded the city and Rajgir is itself surrounded by five hills, where many Jain temples are situated. Rajgir was the birthplace of the 20th Jain Guru, Mahavir. Mahavir and the Buddha both taught at Rajgir during the sixth and fifth centuries BC. The Buddha was at Rajgir for twelve years.

The nearby ancient university of Nalanda, said to be the world's first residential university, is thought to have had ten thousand Buddhist monks in the tenth century, housed on a thirty-acre site of brick-built temples, stupas, and cells. Other scholars think there were probably only 3000 residents. The monastery/university operated from the fifth century AD to 1197 AD promoting the arts, grammar, medicine, logic, and mathematics, with vast manuscript libraries and academics, especially in the fifth and sixth centuries of India's Golden Age. Surrounding villages supplied the monks with their daily rice, butter, and milk. Many Sanskrit texts were taken to China and influenced the spread of East Asian Buddhism. Nalanda was sacked and the monks were killed by the troops of Muhammed Bakhtiyar Khiliji. It was partly restored and continued to exist until 1400 AD.

A gleaming white Buddhist Temple or 'Peace Pagoda' stands atop Ratnagiri Hill, built by the Japanese. Buddhas face four directions. Its creator was inspired by Mohandas Gandhi's reaction to the atomic bombing of Japan. Prayers are conducted for universal peace.

Chapter 9

Flooding and Erosion

December 7, 1994

Patna to Baktiapur 51 km/ 32 miles

I left Patna at 6.45 am and knowing the route, past the Pataliputra archaeological site, I soon found my way over the flyover to the GT road's vast overnight halting area, where the trucks are parked. Men sleep in the lorries, so there is no need for accommodation. Sleepy figures wander around in the morning wearing shawls, woollen hats or balaclavas. Clearing throats for the morning or wandering around with toothbrushes of neem sticks, cleaning their teeth – a process that lasts a lot longer than the recommended time in the west. However, as the sugar content of the Indian diet is immense, this is just as well.

The neem tree twig is the traditional way of mouth hygiene in India, and accounts for some of the desecration of roadside trees, but it is a proven source of disinfectant. Ironically, a toothpaste has now been introduced that is called 'Neem'. In fact, the whole of the tree has traditionally been employed for its disinfectant qualities, for man, in animal husbandry, and in agriculture. Belatedly the native neem tree is being recognised for its value, and the government plantings of eucalyptus in the 60 's along so many roadsides, are now seen to be water guzzlers of little intrinsic value.

Having reached the open countryside by 7.20 am, I was ready for my second chai and an omelette. By the time I neared the village of Bahapur, on my way to Baktiapur, where Dr. Ajeet Singh had arranged for me to stay at a medical centre, it was noticeably colder. I could feel my ears hurting, but couldn't be bothered to stop and find my jumper.

I stopped at a dhaba that had a large frontage of three, partly built, shops that was only complete at one end. Ramakant Sharma, the shop owner, explained that, as there has been a bad harvest that year, the rendering has not been done, or the second storey built. There was a lot of unemployment in the area – of those gathered in the forecourt of the 'hotel' there was a mechanical engineer, and Mr. Sharma's brother, Murari, who worked as a night supervisor on the road mending team, the remainder were unemployed agricultural workers. There were two other Sharma's, one in the police CID, and another in the Finance Department in Patna. When I jokingly made a comment on police corruption, I was told that they were a Brahmin family and "so our family is not corrupt". He added that being a Brahmin today in Bihar is not easy. This was a polite way of saying that the Chief Minister of Bihar, Mr. Laloo Prasad, who is of the Backward Class, is very anti-Brahmin.

Traditionally, Mr. Sharma had the honorific title 'Shukla', but today they didn't use the title. and were just known as Sharma. Mr. Shreekant Sharma invited me to take tea. He didn't speak any English, but I showed him my family photos, and he told me about his family, and how he liked to meet people from other countries, because he cannot travel himself. He has a buffalo, two cows, and some land. Two of his children were away at college in Patna, and his twelve-year-old daughter with a red hairband said 'hello' to me, on her way to school.

Their old father, Valmiki, arrived to join our group – he was 75 and said that he learned English from the British and that, in his opinion, the government was better in the Raj times! He had been to Madras, and Delhi, as well as to Joshimath and other Himalayan pilgrimage places.

Mr. Ramakant Sharma wanted to know what my bike cost, and how much it costs to maintain. He wanted to know about my sons, and how much I earned. I learned from him that the field crop that I had thought was young papaya trees, was in fact an oil seed plant. On reflection, it did look a bit like the Ricinus species which we call the castor oil plant, but I was assured it was an edible oil and not medicinal. Other small grey-green oil-producing plants were there, as well as tomatoes, aubergines, onions, gram, and potatoes, and mustard oil plants in the fields alongside the road. A cloth bundle of green-podded plants was next to me on one charpoy. They told me it was fodder for the buffalo. Mr. R. Sharma and Mr. S Sharma owned the buffalo between them, and they said that the milk was sold for 6 Rs. a litre.

After an hour of this very enjoyable chatting, and passing around leprosy literature, I took my leave, having given them a polaroid photo, and proceeded at a leisurely pace, toward Baktiapur where I had been invited to stay with Sister Lucy and her nuns at the Public Health Mother and Child Centre.

I passed parts of the road on which wheat grains had been spread over half the road to dry in the sun, and village houses painted with red designs on whitewashed backgrounds. I noticed that storage bins were now circular, some were ten feet in diameter, with walls of reeds and conical thatched roofs. In one village I found a prettily decorated hut, with the family cows tethered outside.

Sister Lucy, whom I had met the day before, on my way by jeep to Rajgir, was out. Sister Angena was in the clinic when I arrived, and she left her post to sit with me, and give me lunch. She told me about their religious Order of Saint Vincent de Paul. It had its 'mother house' in the USA, while the main convent was at Mokama, a few miles down the road. There were five nuns. One sister visits the ten villages they cover, two work in the hospital, one in the 'Outpatients department', and one is the principal of the school.

Their priest had gone to Patna to get some exam papers from the printers, and if he returned in the evening, it would mean that I could go to Mass for the first time since leaving England.

The sisters wore ordinary saris, and yet everyone knew they were nuns, because they didn't wear the vermillion sindoor powder in their hair-parting, as married women do.

For the same reason, the school children called me 'sister' when they were going to mass the next morning, at a chilly 6.30 am. The nuns also do not wear bangles and wear only two rings - a plain silver signet ring, with the initials of their order, St Vincent de Paul on it and, something new to me, a silver ring with raised dots which is called a 'rosary ring'. The ten dots for the Hail Mary prayer and the bar for the 'Our Father' prayer.

Children, and young adults generally refer to older people, even if not related, as 'aunty' or 'uncle', or if very old as 'grandmother' or 'grandfather'. Adults of similar age call one another 'brother' or 'sister'. Cousins are often called 'brother' or 'sister'. To sort out the relationship I would ask if they meant 'cousin brother'. Respectfully I was called 'Manya Madam' or 'Manyaji'. More informally I was addressed as 'Manya Aunty' by younger people, and in Bhabua, where I was well known, I was referred to as 'cyclewali'. I noticed that in hospital the nurses were called 'nurse', and the ward orderlies were 'aunties'. One of my staff members used to call me 'Mummy' because I reminded him of his mother, after that it caught on, and as I was at least 20 years older than them, to this day I am still called 'Mummy' by the Indian ex-colleagues, of my physiotherapy days.

Sister Angena said the Primary and Kindergarten schoolchildren, where the children pay 2 rupees a week, but they "had few attendees", even at this low price because "the parents don't value education". However, the school had 300 pupils! The youngest children are boarders because it is too far for them to walk to their villages – two or three kilometres across the fields. There were twelve members of staff and 89 of the children are Christian, "though only nominally", "they are Hindu when it suits them", and for this reason, they do not have nativity plays at Christmas. It was exam time, and the children are tested in all subjects. As this was not a 'government assisted school' it set its own exams, and those of eight other convents, and did not offer the 'Delhi Board' or government exam papers.

I had been taken for a walk towards the remaining mainstream of the Ganges earlier in the afternoon, but time did not permit us to reach the villages lining the Ganges proper, some three kilometres distant across the sandy dried-up part of the riverbed. Sister Lily and Sister Angena had brought a bag of peanuts for us to eat as we walked along. The sisters were frequently stopped, by people returning to their homes, after the day's work. It was because these chats would be so numerous that we would not have time to reach the river. Children, some only about five or six years old, were also returning from school to these and more distant villages. One woman we met on our walk was carrying a large woven basket, now empty. I asked her what she had been selling. She said she had been selling cow-dung patties, - six for one rupee.

The fields were newly sown with winter wheat and oilseed plants. I recognized fennel and sweet potatoes that had been them planted in the dried up river bed by people who don't have any land of their own.

During the monsoon, the water comes right up into ditches that border the road. Floods are a regular feature of life.

Brickfields are a common site in the country areas, but are only able to function in the drier months of the year. The sisters told me that the landless labourers and the brick workers often only get a small part of their dues because the contractors extort money from them.

From mid-Bihar to its mouth, the Ganges suffers alternate flooding, silting, and erosion. The riverbanks are continually at the mercy of the effect of deforestation in the mountains, and from frequent cyclones in the Bay of Bengal. All further compounded by low water in the hot season, and too much water in the monsoon season, and from water restrictions at the Farruka Barrage Dam. The riverbanks are undercut and collapse into the river, taking away farmland and homes, people's livelihoods, schools and sometimes whole villages.

Sister Lucy asked me if I had ever seen a baby being born and as I hadn't, apart from my own, I was honoured to be given the chance to see this miracle of nature. The mother was with her own mother in a ward adjacent to the delivery room, in her own clothes and shawl. She didn't appear to have any pain at that moment, "if she does, she will be given an injection".

I asked how old she was, sister said they don't know their own ages around here, but that she was probably about 18. They stay at the hospital for a day, or if it was an evening birth they want to go home in the morning. Breastfeeding is encouraged because it is most nourishing and of good, clean quality. Powdered or cow's milk is often adulterated and is mixed with water, which is invariably itself contaminated. Sister Angena said a litre of milk costs 10 Rs. and goes up to 15 Rs. at Divali and other festival times, when it is in demand for sweet making. Whether or not the baby is breastfed depends on the caste of the girl, and the say-so of the Hindu pujari or priest. He is consulted about when and how long the babies are to be fed.

I was writing up my journal when Sister Lucy called me to say the birth was imminent and I hurried along to the delivery room. The mother, Laksmi, wasn't pushing correctly, according to sister Lucy, so she was allowed to alternate between lying on her back and being in a squatting position. It was dark, save for the light of the hurricane oil lamp, which I held. Eventually, the baby, a girl, was born but the little mite wouldn't breathe or cry. After an injection, chest massage, slaps to the feet while upside down, and much suction of the nose and mouth, an oxygen tube was pushed up its nose, and the baby opened its eyes but gave no cry. After more efforts by Sister Lucy, the baby gave a little whimper.

The baby wasn't given to the mother at all, but put into an incubator with a broken lid, and given oxygen. When I looked in after my visit to the chapel for evening prayers, the mother was back in the ward, and the baby was only making tiny noises. The baby wasn't weighed, or the birth time noted, or given to the mother to hold, which I felt was sad. Having since seen how even very young nurse their siblings, and how joint-family babies are almost common property, I suppose the mother-baby bonding isn't very necessary here in India.

Evening prayers in the chapel took the form of a bhajan (a hymn) and mediation on the doctrine of the Immaculate Conception - the feast day was the next day, December 8th. This was followed by personal intercessions from each nun. They prayed for lepers, the outcast and rejected, and for their perseverance in the long treatment; they prayed that women may have more say in their society, because in some castes they are very downtrodden. They prayed for victims of an accident, in which a body was being taken to be cremated by the Ganges, and had overturned, killing all the close relations. Intercessions were made for me, and my safety and perseverance, for other members of their community, for the forthcoming drama performance; for guidance and help for the children doing their exams. The prayers for me brought a lump to my throat. My eyes filled with tears – I was embarrassed and grateful at the same time.

Dinner consisted of mushroom soup, pumpkin with coconut, reflecting the sister's Keralan origins, and potato paratha. I was given two cups of coffee, but the sisters had only water. Sister Lucy, the Principal, asked to see my bike and I demonstrated the gears to her. I was given really hot water for a bucket shower and sat writing my journal before climbing into my mosquito-netted iron bed, with sheets on the top and bottom, and a quilt, in the Needlework Room at 8.45 pm.

December 8, 1994

Baktiapur to Lakiserai 85 km/ 53 miles

I woke the next morning to the sound of the sisters getting ready for Mass, which was held in the school hall at 6.30 am. I went over in time and saw the crocodiles of children, the girls with huge red bows on their plaits and bunches. The children removed their sandals before entering the carpeted hall, and sat cross-legged on the floor, wrapped in shawls of various colours, patterned and embroidered designs, worn by boys and girls. Mass was in Hindi, with hymn singing which went on for quite a long time and included a sermon by the saffron-shawled priest, on Mary and motherhood.

After replacing my trainers, I went over to the hospital for a breakfast of omelette, toast, marmalade, and coffee.

I left the sisters at 8 am and stopped to phone Dr. Ajeet but learned that he had left for the airport, so there was no way of finding out where I was to stay in Lakiserai.

At 10 o'clock I was overtaken by a large government jeep, and I was just wondering where it was going, when the driver waved me down, and Dr. Richard came to greet me. He was on his way to inspect a government medical centre at Madhapur and he gave me a message that Dr. Singh had tried to contact me before I left Benares – I had gone with Barun to get some dinner in his 'cheap dosa place'. Richard told me that I was to stay at the PWD bungalow, so I said goodbye and went on my way feeling glad that I had secure accommodation that night.

The road was good and had white lines to mark its centre, a rarity in rural India. I came upon a herd of a hundred camels and wondered where they could be going in an easterly direction. I was told later that they were very popular for transport in Nepal. This made sense as they were going towards the new bridge over the Ganges.

By 10.40 am. I was eleven kilometres from Mokama and stopped for a cup of chai. I thought that I had made a mistake in leaving the by-pass, and taking the cobbled main road of Mokama, but consoled myself that I might find the convent with the pilgrim shrine in front of it, that the sisters had told me about.

I didn't find the convent, and was feeling really fed up, when I saw a road sign saying that I was only 20 kilometres from Lakiserai! I stopped for a banana and then had to cope with about two kilometres of cobbles on Barhiya's main street. I was surrounded by a mob of schoolboys, one of whom was rude and objectionable, so I quickly set off again and found a little dhaba further up the road, where I ordered three cups of tea without sugar, and an omelette.

At village dhabas, the tea is usually pre-prepared, and near the heat source in its kettle or saucepan, ready for the next customer. Sugar has been added to the milk in its first boiling of the morning, and the tea leaves are strained into the mix, followed by a long time of boiling. My 'three cups of tea' order was because I had an enamel mug that could hold three times the usual volume of a glass of Indian tea. If I wanted sugarless tea, as opposed to sugar-less tea, it is only worthwhile to the stall holder if I order more than one cup of tea, hence the mug and three cups! Sugar-less in India means less sugar than normal, which as they have very sweet tea even the sugar-less is too sweet for me!

I got chatting to a young man and showed him some of my photos. He spoke some English and told me he was a graduate, but he couldn't find a job. The PWD bungalow was easy to find but there was some mistake, and I was given a room already occupied, judging by the suitcase and shawl on the bed.

I had a chai for 2 Rs. and went to the market where, with the help of a dear old man, I bought dates and cashew nuts. I couldn't make anyone understand 'dried apricots' – despite drawing one! After getting some hard-boiled eggs and the usual tomatoes and bananas and papaya, I made a lovely supper for myself because I didn't think there would be any food in the PWD. I hadn't even found a towel or clean sheet, only a blanket. I passed an STD phone on the way back and called Ramesh, but he was out until 5.30 pm and by then it will be too dark for me to come out again.

When I got back the lights were not working, not because of a power cut, but because the bulbs were broken. I asked the 'boy' to go and get a candle and thought I'd mention it to the chowkidar. The occupant of the other room arrived with an entourage. He turned out to be an Electoral Registration Officer who had responsibility for issuing Identity Cards to the voters of the Lakiserai district. Mr. Seshun, the Central Government Minister, had taken on the task of trying to prevent electoral irregularities, by issuing each voter with a photo card, and making electoral lists. He has also set down procedures to be followed, regarding the expenditure on electioneering, and setting a time schedule for the nominations, all in an attempt to get fair elections, and combat vote rigging, vote buying, booth capturing, and similar common crafty practices.

My neighbour invited me to have dinner with him, and suggested that I eat my hard-boiled eggs while he sent out to a hotel for some other food. We sat on the veranda with the mosquitoes, and he had several visitors – including a Congress Party man who belonged to a scheduled caste, and an entourage of photographers, who were part of the twenty who had been engaged to take photos for the ID cards. He asked me if I was comfortable in my room and I told him about the bulbs. He offered to pay for these, but I don't know if he did, however, he did pay for my lodging and dinner. He insisted on exchanging addresses, giving me his local Barhiya, as well as his Delhi one.

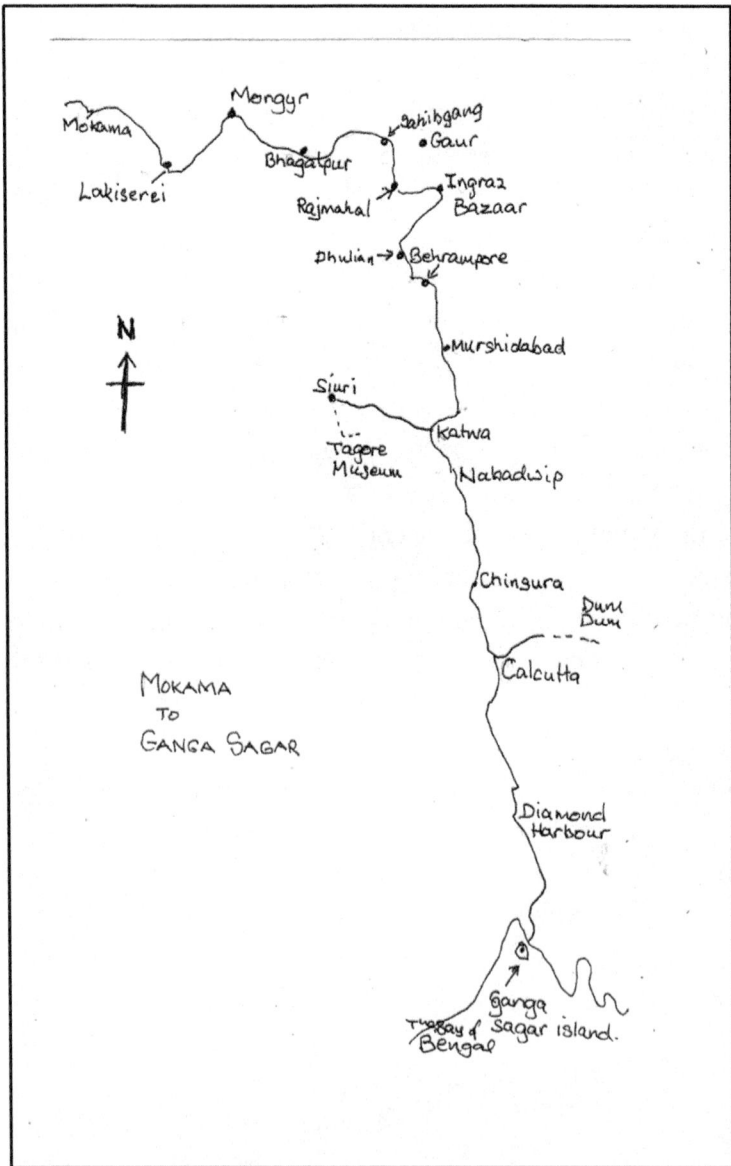

Mokama to Ganga Sagar

December 9, 1994

Lakiserai to Mongyr 60 km/ 37 miles

The road to Mongyr followed the Ganges in a northerly direction. I passed a potter making tall cylindrical pots with open ends. They were to be cut in half lengthwise and would be used as roofing tiles. Just as cow pats and storage-place designs varied across India, so too did the style of roofing tiles.

I was accompanied for the last few kilometres by a fourteen-year-old boy, riding a smart new bicycle. He spoke good, clear English and took me directly to the District Magistrates Office in the Courthouse building. When I asked to see the DM, (Indians are very fond of using initials instead of full words) I was told to come back at 4 pm.

It wasn't yet midday, so I asked for authorization to stay at the Circuit house, and was then shown into an office, where absolutely nothing was happening, workwise, that is! The room held three glass-topped wooden desks, the one at which I was seated wasn't occupied, a woman sat at another desk knitting, and at the third desk which was completely bare. Near the open door, which led onto the veranda of the courthouse, a man sat twiddling his fingers, looking quite contented. They had presumably been similarly occupied since the office opened at ten o'clock or thereabouts. At 11.45 a clerk came in with some files and placed them on the man's desk.

I was summoned by a very smartly dressed, uniformed person, so I didn't see whether the files were opened and attended to. One got the impression that they would be left to gather dust like Miss Havisham's wedding breakfast in Great Expectations.

I saw so many offices, including those in the High Court in Calcutta, which were piled high with untidily stacked folders, covered in dust. They were so faded and dirty that they might have been there since 1947. I saw only one office in a Court Building in Malda, West

Bengal, with a computer and that wasn't in use! Government offices were still using old manual typewriters, and I had yet to see a government office with a photocopier. This probably explains the proliferation of shops and booths offering xerox services in the towns and metropolitan cities of India. There is always the advisability of keeping copies of letters to the authorities whose filing systems seem to consist of stacking folders on the floor, on tops of cupboards, right up to the ceiling height, indeed on any available surface!

My escort, in a khaki shirt and trousers, with a broad stiff red and yellow sash, which he kept adjusting to make sure it was hanging just right, walked before me, to a building across the road. I was shown into an open-plan office where each desk occupant was hidden behind stacks of files between the desks. I think the gentleman who offered me tea, was probably the DM's assistant, but he could have been the boss, because he was reading the scrappy piece of paper which I had been given in the first office. I had written,

'Dear Sir, I would like to stay at your Circuit House for one night on my cycle yatra from Gangotri to Ganga Sagar'.

I had attached my South Cambridgeshire District Council security pass, which described me as a Government Officer. I imagined that they wanted to see my passport. I sipped the small, coffee-cup-sized, cup of tea, and waited for the man with the sash and a nine-inch oval brass badge to reappear.

Permission was granted, and I had to countersign my note. A peon was directed to take me to the Circuit House which was about a five-minute ride away. Set in open country, surrounded by trees and grass, the sparseness and parched look of the latter not meriting the title lawn. It was the usual pre-Independence building. I was given a large room, one of two, which opened off each side of the lounge.

This was the most well-furnished Circuit House that I encountered. Two four-seater sofas, and four armchairs, were grouped around a central coffee table, on which stood a large brass tray holding a vase with orange single marigolds, matching the orange carpet. There was a large, tiled fireplace, over which were pictures and newspaper reports of the effects of an earthquake that struck Mongyr in 1934.

It covered an area stretching from Nepal in the north, Dhanbad in the south as far away as Patna. Over 7000 deaths were reported, 142 in Patna, 3400 in Nepal, and 1400 in Mongyr.' The London Times reported, 'Artisans and craftspeople will have work in plenty at remunerative rates. Professional and middle classes have just escaped with their lives, for they have lost everything. The richer persons have reserves to fall back on, the shopkeepers too lost all – not one house in the streets of Mongyr is left standing'.

The lounge opened out onto a terrace, overlooking a large lake, that was partly filled with singara and duckweed. There were trees all around the lake but the pastoral view was spoiled by one new house, which had been started on the far side. Cows were lowing as they were being driven home along the lakeside and three little children appeared, one boy having a basket of cow dung patties on his head.

Rooms one and two opened off the dining room, and whoever was staying there, arrived with a jeep, full of armed policemen. Four of them were on the sofa outside my room, one was asleep in an armchair and the other four were on the veranda. The driver and his mate were tinkering with the official car, with its red light on the top, and washing the jeep.

I had bread, bananas, and tomatoes in my room, did some clothes washing, and ordered tray tea, which gave me four full cups! I walked down to the Ganges, to the ferry crossing point, from which an old paddle steamer, the SS. Benares took passengers to a temple devoted to Sita, on the north bank of the river. I then walked towards the walled gateway of this once-Muslim capital, and discovered, behind an earthen wall, a stone crucifix with INRI on it. The initials stand for the Latin inscription placed over Christ's head during the Crucifixion, meaning 'Jesus of Nazareth, King of the Jews'. It turned out to be part of a Church of North India addition to a late Victorian cemetery, which was now overgrown and inhabited by villagers, living in small shacks between ruined tombs, whose marble inscriptions were all missing. They had made little gardens between the graves. The main ghat by the river had a mark showing that the river was 36 feet high in 1976. I missed a photo opportunity of a man throwing a circular net into the water from a small boat.

There was a large Italianate building with a portico and balustrades that had been a victim of the earthquake. A famous Yoga Ashram, in the form of a mini skyscraper, overlooked the Ganges. People were greeting me with 'Hari Om' - they probably thought I was from the Ashram, being white-skinned.

Back at the Circuit House, I was given a single cup of tea, not the nice four-cup tray-tea as on my arrival. I took my washing in from the line, it was not dry but may dry off overnight in my room, or the bathroom. I fixed the mosquito net over half the double bed and ordered dinner for 7 o'clock – bindi, tomato and onion salad, chapati, and aloo-gobi. I remembered that I saw pat-gobi, cabbage, in the market for the first time. Dinner was moved to 8 o'clock, as the other residents seem to eat just before going to bed – that probably accounts for the paunches!

I have just finished half a jar of cashew nuts – lovely! My earache and sore throat are still with me, but maybe just about to 'break' into a cold. It hurts mainly at night and early morning.

I had passed small patches of tobacco plants after Baktiapur. They were like my garden Nicotiana, but had pale pink flowers and were two to three feet high. I saw some tobacco leaves for sale in the Mongyr market. I've seen a bee-eater, a blue kingfisher, and a bright green and brown bird. I must get a bird book to help me identify them.

December 10, 1994

Mongyr to Bhagalpur 61 km/ 38 miles

Breakfast was late so I wasn't away before 8 am. I'd washed the bike in my hot bucket-shower water, it was the first time I'd had hot water since leaving Jehanabad. The charge was 50 rupees plus the requested 10 rupees baksheesh (tip).

At 9 0 am. I was greeted with 'Chai pilo', "Drink tea!" from a little dhaba. They didn't speak any English but I gave them the press release Barun had written for me, and a leprosy leaflet. I showed them photos of my family. They wouldn't accept any money.

At 10.15 am. I was waved down by Srimati Mira Prasad, whose husband was ex-Indian Air Force., She was sitting in the garden of a house under construction. At one o'clock while refilling my water bottles and having a 3-cup chai stop at Makandpur, I met Rajiv Rangan, an unemployed Physics degree holder, with a first-class degree, who couldn't find a job, so he was working in the local brickfields for 4000 Rs. a month.

An hour later I entered the main street of Bhagalpur. I kept looking for the railway station, where Ramesh had told me to ask for Shyam Bijornia's house. I knew he was a textile merchant and when I found a Silk and Textile Institute, I asked for him and was directed back into the town, for half a kilometre, to a certain bank, near the railway station, up a small cobbled side street. They sent me back to the chowk – I walked this time, as it was so bumpy. I tried a textile shop 50 metres away, and they directed me to a tall house with a TV aerial. I was told that Shyam Bigornia and his son, Mitu, were at a wedding opposite, and was directed, shoes off, into the buying room, up some marble steps. Typically, the whole floor area was covered in a white mattress with pillows to lean on.

Shyamji and Mitu ordered tea and made me welcome. Mitu knows Ramesh's son Ravi. They had supplied him with silk to mix with polyester yarn for a year. They themselves spin tussah silk from local silkworms. Their mill is about 3 kilometres away in Bhagalpur.

I was offered a choice of soap and the servant was sent to buy Lux and shampoo for me. Mitu took me to my room – the promised bath was a bucket shower, but the water was lovely and hot. I washed my hair and left my dirty clothes on the floor! The bed was 1959 vintage - the wedding year of Shyam?

I went for a rest as suggested, 'because Mitu and father have to host the ladies at the wedding party for two or three hours more'. Mitu explained that this was because the man, the groom's father I suppose, was poor. I was asked what I'd like to eat and drink, the only requirement being that it was vegetarian. I refused whisky and said I'd have a beer at night as they didn't have gin

My chest feels peculiar, maybe it is pneumonia again. I became suspicious as I was cycling along in the morning, so maybe I'll ask for whisky and hot milk. I tried to sleep but the servant came and opened the door. I couldn't understand what he wanted. He said "aram se, shadi", which was 'take rest, wedding'. At 5.30 I got up and ordered a cup of tea, he hovered, and I gathered the wedding was upstairs, but he went away and I scurried back to my room to continue reading my Trotternama book and write my journal.

Mitu appeared briefly and apologised that the bathroom was simple village style, and not like the Toshniwals! Mitu said his family is in Bangalore, and that Ravi had gone to see his sister Kavita in Dubai. Mitu knew I was in Patna on the 5th of December, as he had a phone call from Ramesh, to read him the Times of India article about me.

It was now 7 pm and I didn't know what to do, or where to go. Mitu called in at 7.30 pm, "So you are up!". He said he thought I wouldn't like the wedding, which was next door in his house. He told me proudly that he had four houses, one in Bangalore, one here, one in Delhi, and one in Assam. It seems I was supposed to rest all afternoon and all night! He told me he has two sons, who are one and a half hours away, harvesting, but that they usually live here. Mitu and his father live alone with eight servants, "which are more than enough" so he lets the boys go to their land at harvest time!

I asked about a convent, and he said his driver will come at 7.30 am and take me to see the convent, and Mass if it is on! He informed me that my dinner would be ready in half an hour. Four bottles of mineral water arrived, and a small fridge with four beers. I opened one and it was so gassy that it spilled on the floor and the divan! Deepan the servant mopped it up.

I confessed to feeling poorly and will be taken to see a doctor tomorrow afternoon, after going to the convent, and "get thoroughly checked over!". Mitu has friends-cum-agents in Sahibganj and Rajmahal. He told me there is a ferry from Rajmahal to West Bengal, Malda, Gaur, and Ingraz Bazaar.

I decided to ask if there was a phone to contact Ramesh after dinner. I also asked for a blanket and Deepan nodded but one didn't appear. I showed him photos and postcards of Cambridge but he was not interested. I don't think Deepan can read Hindi. Mitu arrived with a friend carrying metal tiffin cans filled with food. I started the traditional way, seated on the floor, sandals removed (they are only allowed at a dining table, I was informed) at a nine-inch-high wooden table with a stainless steel (thali) plate. The meal started with a selection of sweets, rasgullas, (syrup-soaked white oval-shaped sweets), a cashew-nut flavoured diamond shape, covered with silver foil, and some gajar-halwa, - a sweet made by boiling carrots with sugar, butter, and milk. The next course to be served was vegetables, a pakora, and small bowls of potatoes and lentil cakes in dahi (yoghurt). The vegetables were too spicy-hot for me, apparently because they were from the 'five-hundred-person' wedding guest's menu. They were eaten with very thin parathas. When I commented on their thinness Mitu told me his would be thinner!

I couldn't find Deepan after supper to ask him about the phone.

My room had large iron hooks in the ceiling from which things could be suspended, with the help of solid three-foot-long bars, for example, an oil lamp. There was no glass in the windows, just fancy iron grills and wooden shutters, marble floors and walls to dado height, including window sills and inset shelves.

I went down to my bike, to sort out my daily malaria medicine tablets, and work out how many Chloroquine tablets I needed to buy for the Sundays of next month. I had been in India for seven weeks and two days. It didn't seem as long. Ramesh accused me of not ringing him for six days. I said I rang but got the maid, and he was away until the 5th. I arrived here in Bhagalpur on the tenth.!

I was in bed by 9.45 pm. under a rather low-slung mosquito net. There are poles for a double net, but Deepan didn't seem to know where they were. Deepan appeared at 7 am and I asked for tea. A driver was coming at 7.30 am to take me to a convent and hopefully, to Mass. Tea was served in a plastic cup with biscuits. Deepan may have feared that I would break a china cup on the marble floor after yesterday's beer-spilling episode!

Mitu's house, next door, is 70 years old, and above and behind his go-downs (warehouses) at street level, where the boiled silk cocoons are stored before being washed and unwound. Labour can be had for 10 rupees a day, or 5 rupees at times! He said there is a minimum wage but "who pays it when a man offers himself for less!!". He proudly stated that "he hasn't paid an electricity bill for nine years – 60% of the time it is off anyway". Then they use generators.

Apparently, I was in Nathnagar, an overgrown village, that has become a suburb of Bhagalpur. Silk weaving is the main industry. It is a cottage industry, worked in practically every house, on hand looms, and using child labour. Mitu said "Children won't go to school" Sixty percent of the population are Muslims. Mitu says he doesn't like them, he says they should have been sent to Pakistan, and that India should be a Hindu state. He boasted that he could show me the "filth and squalor" of the "uneducated people ". I suggested it was more a case of dharma and karma. He agreed it was 'Kismet' – fate!

I met his grandfather who was 75. He was an RSS supporter – he donated land to them and to an RSS school, which are being established all over India. The RSS is billed as the 'non-political wing' of the Bharat Janata Party. It is also described as described as 'a right-wing voluntary paramilitary organisation'. The RSS has more than 12000 schools in India.

His family numbers about a hundred relatives, uncles and aunts, cousins, cousin-brothers, and sisters all live around the house. "This is a small village, not like Bombay where people have no time".

December 11, 1994

Breakfast arrived, spinach and spring onions, rice, and dahl with one plain papad. The green vegetables were very nice and served less spicy-hot than they'd normally have been. We ate with our fingers. Mitu ate with his father and I was at a separate table next to the divan with a towel to act as a napkin. After eating, I was invited to take a rest again. At 7.30 am, we left to find the church at St Carmel School, where a sister directed us to St Benedict's Church. The priest didn't speak English, and the mass was in Hindi. I met a nun who was a doctor, now an administrator, at a mother-and-child hospital. She knew about leprosy, Dapsone, and Rifampicin, but not about Multi Drug Therapy. She had trained in Germany and for three months in London, at the Hospital for Tropical Diseases. There were 400 parishioners according to the priest, but I reckoned there were 400 at this Mass, and there is another mass at 4 pm.

December 12, 1994

It is claimed that Bhagalpur has the best mangoes, the Jalanga variety, whose scent fills a room. Papayas are available all year round. Tomatoes are cheap here – only 1 rupee a kilogram. I was told that after an hour I would be taken to see a village. Mitu and his father had left the house at 3 am, with much revving of the car engine and other noises, and went to a temple 134 kilometres away from Nathnagar, as it was his birthday. They arrived back at 11 am. and took me to see silk weaving and dying.

Silk weaving using two threads produces a thick silk fabric suitable for upholstery, wall coverings, and curtains. It is sold in London and in the USA. A weaver can produce four to five metres a day and gets 35 rupees a day (or less!). I saw one child worker and was told not to take his photo. The warp master gets more money, as it is a very important job, learned from childhood to the age of eighteen. They made twills, jacquard patterns, and checks. The designs are made by men in the design shop. One woman was making skeins from left-over bobbins; another was winding two threads together to make a thicker thread. Dying was done in large concrete tubs. The silk is first bleached and washed, then dyed. Later it may be printed.

Beaten silk is an old tradition and only Mitu Bigornia still does it. The workers sit with their legs in a pit in the earth so that they can operate wooden treadles which control the 'bats' that do the beating. Tussah silk is made only in this area – it is a very fine silk.

Mitu said that a woman may have 1000 saris in her wardrobe, her daughter will borrow some, and she will keep others unworn for say six years, and then bring them out. Mitu said that his wife had eighteen sets of gold necklaces, bangles, and earrings given by his father, for her wedding dowry.

Mitu was very anti-Muslim, He boasted of never paying doctors, not his father before him. It is OK if it is a friend, like the one we tried to find, but I felt very sorry for the little Muslim doctor opposite the Bigornia house, whom we visited. Mitu just marched in and stood, while I sat to wait my turn. The doctor got up, left his current patient, and came to see me. The doctor was told I had breathing difficulty. He applied a stethoscope to my chest over my jumper, at the back, and high on the front (nowhere near my breasts!) and said I had a throat infection – true!

He prescribed Salbutamol syrup and Benadryl and said I should take my penicillin. I can't remember now why I was on penicillin – maybe it was prescribed for me in Lucknow. He also took my blood pressure. I offered to pay but Mitu said, "no! don't pay."

I went to lie down. My head ached. Mitu arrived with the prescribed medicines and arranged for my lunch. I didn't see him or anyone again. I slept and woke up at 9 pm and asked Deepan for some hot milk, but he said he was busy preparing food, also that he hadn't any milk until morning. Mitu was at more weddings apparently. I felt miffed that no one enquired about me.

However, when I was having a cup of tea at 6.45 am., Mitu appeared and said I should have woken him and that he'd sent some silk to Bombay for me. I would rather have had a donation for Lepra!

December 13, 1994

Bhagalpur to Sahibganj 77 km/ 48 miles

At one time I saw a man walking on the far bank of the shallow river Ganges, with what looked like a canoe on his shoulders. Intrigued I kept watching him, and saw him pass another man with a canoe, but this was something altogether different.

The 'canoes' were hollowed tree trunks and served as an ingenious, easily portable, means of getting water from the low river into an irrigation ditch on the bank, almost a meter higher than the river level. The long scoop was raised and lowered by a tripod system, with a bundle of stones. or maybe bricks.

I was to stay with another connection of Ramesh's or Ravi's, in Sahibganj, a Mr. Chaudrey. He was chairman of the local Lion's Club and he had made a 500 Rs. bank draft donation for Lepra.

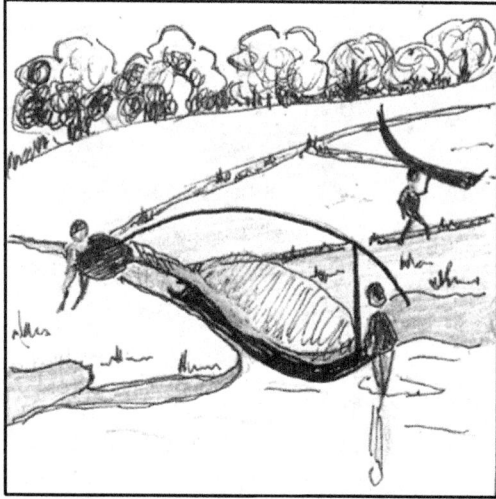

He showed me the Lions magazine with stories of all the charities they help, providing cataract operations, tree planting and immunisation campaigns - rather like the work of Rotary clubs. He too is a Marwari.

He has three daughters, two of them married, and one son. The girls all have degrees but they won't need to find work. They were doing embroidery when I arrived, a beautiful cross-stitch, which has taken two years so far, and all the background has still to be added. Their mother embroiders bed linen as a hobby. They were able to give me an address in Calcutta where I can enquire about buying canvas for Karen. One daughter also does oil painting, which she learned by attending a class in Uttar Pradesh.

Mr. Chaudrey has a stone-chipping business that is used in road making. His brother Harish has a flour mill which was started in 1935 by his grandfather. Mr. Chaudrey senior has twin sons aged 25, one has a steel rod factory here in Sahibganj and another son is in Delhi.

I was taken to visit 78 yr old Mr. Shital Chaudrey, his daughter Nilu, and grandson Rakesh. They gave me a special fruit called an amla. It is green in colour and looks like an unripe tomato, but has six radiating lighter green stripes on it. It is of religious significance and comes from a tree. The fruit can be pickled in lime water and then crystallised. A pujari arrived at the house carrying a brass holder with a lighted wick in it. Nilu placed her hands over the flame and touched her head with her hands. Grandfather and Rakesh did the same. Then prasad, of sugar and tulsi leaves, was given to everybody in the room. Prasad means, 'a gracious gift, that has been offered to a deity and then distributed in his or her name to followers, or others, with the deity's blessing residing in it.'

Nilu gave me pudina, adrak, senf, and masalas to taste - they were in order,   mint, ginger, fennel, and mixed spices. She also gave me a tray, with a selection of popcorn, lime pickle, a sweet sugary mixture, and flat hard biscuits. Rakesh phoned his school and asked me if I'd like to visit his school Principal – I suggested tomorrow, as it was only about 50 miles to Rajmahal, my next stop

Back at Mr. Chaudrey's house his daughter "fitted" a room for me, having sent a servant to make the bed up. I am now sitting on a settee, part of a three-piece suite, in the same room with an attached bathroom (the only disadvantage being there was no hot water). I was told that I will be given bed tea tomorrow between 6.30 am. and 7 am.

December 14, 1994

Sahibganj to Rajmahal 32 km/ 20 miles

I arrived in Rajmahal at 12.30 am. having taken only four and a half hours including two stops. Rajmahal was the capital of Bihar, Bengal, and Orissa in 1250. There is a government-funded Bird Reserve near the town. The main industries of the area are China clay kaolin works, silica, and quartz mining. Men smashed the boulders into fist-sized chunks with hammers, women were making them into smaller-sized pieces and carrying them in baskets on their heads to mechanical crushers, and more men were loading the resultant gravel into trucks, with shovels. It was hard and dusty work for a pittance. Everything was covered in grey dust, every leaf, every surface.

In Santhal society girls are given a dowry, in Hindu society boys are given a dowry. Santhals also have different rights of inheritance, between the sexes. In 1956 Hindu laws gave men and women equal rights.

I was staying with Arun and Sarita Chirania, and their two young children, Ruchi and Shonu. Grandmother also lived with them. There were a lot of cousins around including, Jyothi, Happy, Resmi, Mumtah and Maushmi. I'm not sure where they lived, but they took me to view the Ganges from the roof of another cousin's house. They said how beautiful it was, but didn't see the plastic bags, and rubbish, littering the lane to the river.

I hadn't changed or washed, but Sarita asked me about my programme and what I'd like to eat, through a lawyer friend of the family. He talked to me at lunchtime, around 1.40 pm, while everyone watched me and said how slowly I ate. I had been given a tray of fruits, banana, papaya, apple, and orange. I couldn't refuse them, so I hoped that they had been washed and that the knife that cut them up was clean. They said they ate at 2 pm and had dinner at 9 pm. I will eat at 8 and go to bed at 9 pm. I have been offered bed tea again. The first ferry is at 8.30 am so I will leave at 7.30 am. The whole family gave me a 105 rupees donation.

December 15, 1994

Rajmahal to Ingraz Bazaar 64 km/ 40 miles

Grandmother, 'Dadi,' woke me up at 6.30 am. and asked me to wash – I think a guest was supposed to be the first to use the bathroom. I couldn't face a cold shower so I made splashing noises and had a bucket wash. I then sat with the children for half an hour and was given breakfast in another bedroom. Apparently, there are four bedrooms in the house and I had been sleeping in the guest room, with the fridge. I was offered bananas, toast, and hot milk. Mr. A. Roy came to see me. He had a business called Ideal Tutors. He came to say goodbye and had written a poem, and a lengthy and verbose testimonial to me, which I read, while Sarita worried about my toast getting cold. I had the usual audience while I ate.

Mr. Arun and Ruchi came on a bike with me to the ferry – a diesel steamer that Arun said could take up to nine trucks. That morning there were four cars, a tractor, about 10 buffaloes, and a herd of cows, plus the usual sacks of produce and people. Mr. Arun paid my fare of 8 Rs. and it was 'Goodbye Bihar!'

I was a bit worried because one of the huge buffaloes had its back end to my bike. However, the crossing was accomplished without mishap, and with the usual crowd of bike viewers. I'd run out of toilet paper and hence didn't go this morning and I was dying to pass water but I couldn't stop, for fear of attracting a crowd. I must hang on until Malda.

There was a direct road from the ferry landing stage and I easily found the DM's office in the Court buildings. He was away or absent, referred to in India as 'out of station'. I waited for the Assistant DM, Mr. Taleen Kumar, and he phoned through to the Circuit House and gave me a letter 'to use if necessary'. He also offered me a car 'to see it all in two-and-a-half hours!' I thanked him but refused, with the excuse that on a bike I can keep stopping to take photos!

The Circuit House didn't have any food. I had a single bed with a mosquito net, a clean towel, and hot water. I did my washing, found a line in the garden, and then went to the market to look for a telephone and get some food. I forgot to take Ramesh's office number with me, but as it was Thursday Ramesh may be at the races. I bought 300 grams of pistachio nuts, almonds, and cashew nuts for 80 Rs. Bread and two sweet buns cost 15 Rs. Bananas, apples and oranges were 23 Rs.

There were a loudspeaker and a band outside the Circuit House – I thought it was probably some part of electioneering, and hoped it didn't go on late into the night. I couldn't find an egg man, tomatoes, or toilet paper! I would go to visit Pandua and English Bazaar the next day, and give myself a break from cycling with a load. I came across two beggars in the street today, one in the market and one outside the DM's office.

The Circuit House had two antique engraved panels on the terrace, and barrels of two 1920 canons, outside the main entrance. The garden was pleasant with shrubs, lawns, and lots of trees. It seems this Circuit House is officially called Ingraz Bazaar Circuit House, Malda! So maybe I am in Ingraz Bazaar already! I was hoping to find toilet paper if it was an ex-Anglo-Indian settlement. I was about 215 miles north of Calcutta.

The Chowkidar, Mohammed was very friendly and he made me a very good dinner of green vegetables, steamed (pressure-cooked) aubergines, rice, and dahl. I had told him I didn't like chilli, 'mirch', so it was all delicious.

Chapter 10

Ancient Capitals

December 16, 1994

Ingraz Bazaar, English Bazaar or Malda?

Mohammed brought me tea in bed at 7.30 and breakfast was ready at 8.15 am. This was omelette and toast, and instead of the offered tomato sauce, I had Marmite on my toast. As I was staying another night, I chose palak paneer, spinach and a bland cheese, from the menu, however, I was offered chicken instead. I'd seen chickens being sold in the market, chopped up on the ground and wiped with dirty clothes, but I said it was OK if it was pressure cooked, confident that the heat would kill any bugs.

Ingraz Bazaar Circuit House was about three hundred years old according to Mohammed, that would make it from roughly 1694. I haven't seen any Anglo-Indians on my visits to 'English market' town, but Ramesh said they do live there. An English factory was established here in 1671. Malda is seven kilometres up the road, but it is confusing because the district name is also Malda. The bank said

215

it was in Malda, and the police station was in Ingraz Bazaar. My German maps had the name Ingraz Bazaar, not Malda on them.

Mohammed told me that on Saturday they would be having the 'Departmental Picnic' and he invited me to go as his guest! He said there will be thirty people going in a truck. He twirled around and made happy signs with his fingers when he told me about it. I thought it would be a good experience and thanked him for his invitation and agreed to join him. I had only ten copies of my leaflet about Leprosy left. I gave one to the Circuit House, and thought about getting some photocopied, until I realised that most people here speak Bengali not Hindi, and some only read Urdu. Spoken Urdu is mainly the same as Hindi, but it is written in an Arabic script, as opposed to the Devanagari script, where characters hang from a line. Bengali script and spoken language are both different from Hindi.

At 9.20 am. the political loudspeakers got going again. They had stopped by 6 pm. when I went out to phone Ramesh – 189 Rs! Phone calls were my biggest expense. I would have to cash a Traveller's Cheque soon. I am going to ask at the local bank. I was waiting for the Post Office to open, most offices in India open at 10 am. I wanted to know if they had a fax machine so that I could send news to my family in England via Ramesh's office. They did not!

I found the State Bank of India, one of the Indian big five banks, to ask if, by any chance, they could cash my Traveller's Cheques. I met the CM, chief manager, and asked if he had a Foreign Exchange Permit. He spoke good English and was very helpful. He said that he was sure that there was FE at Berhampore, on my route along the Hooghly, famous as the first centre of the East India Company in India. I left reassured but when I got outside, I was hailed from a balcony and taken back to the CM. He said he had found out that there is no FE at Berhampore, only at Calcutta and Siliguri, each too far for me to go to at present. I was amazed that I was only able to change Travellers Cheques in major cities! I asked about receiving a Bank

Draft and he said the post was too unreliable and it would be best to use a courier company. I contacted Ramesh and he said he would send a Bank Draft for 1000 Rupees, by courier, drawn on the State Bank of India to the DM at Berhampore. Apparently, Rajmahal, where I had stayed, had a FE permit and my host worked at the bank! It was such a small town that I didn't even think to ask. Actually, Ramesh was first going to try and contact someone in Malda to see if they could lend me 1000 Rs. In English money it was about £20. I asked him to phone me back after 7 pm.

I was waiting to hear from the Assistant DM, Mr. T Kumar, about accommodation between Dhulian and Jangipur. The ADM phoned to say that Dhulian was "just a little village" There was a guest house, but it was full, so he was trying to get me accommodation at a bidi manufacturing company with a guest house, which Government Officers use. He had booked a trunk call (something else new to me) and will get confirmation and the address. He's going to ring me back. I was waiting for his call, it was 12.10 pm. Bidi's are traditional, very small hand-made cigars, usually smoked by older people. They go out very easily unlike cigarettes.

I had a headache and remembered that I had not taken my Salbutamol tablets every day and that my penicillin tablets were finished. Perhaps I should buy a strip of penicillin tablets, as well as some chloroquine, my Sunday antimalarial tablets. Mohammed came to ask if I had been to the museum, I said I was going later because I'd been talking to the ADM.

In Malda Museum I tried to get a guidebook in English, but none was available. I was taken round by the curator, who showed me sixth to tenth century sculptures of Hindu gods, and Buddhas mainly in a black basalt which comes from the Rajmahal Hills. He showed me artefacts from Pandua and Gaur, which were once capitals of this region when it was a Muslim stronghold in the thirteenth and fourteenth centuries. He said sculptures showed some influence of the Middle East. Some statues of Surya, the Sun God, had boots on, others were bare footed. Buddhist statues all had five mini Buddhas around

217

the top of them. He said some sandstone sculptures were more primitive, and from the sixth and fourth centuries BC. I wondered whether it could be through weathering, and the difficulty of working such coarse-grained stone. There was a four faced Brahma or Vishnu – usually there are three faces. Parvati was holding a mirror; Durga's had either eight or ten arms.

During the eighteenth-century Malda was the centre of prosperous silk and cotton industries. Today it is famous for mangoes and mulberries, used to feed silkworms. Jute, rice, legumes and oilseeds are widely grown. It is called 'Mango City' and, I found out, its old name was English Bazaar. The name was changed after Indian Independence. Malda is often referred to as the 'gateway to North Bengal'. My plan was to visit Pandua and nearby Gaur, however, I got 15 kilometres north of Ingraz Bazaar, but couldn't find the road to Pandua, and gave up the idea.

I cycled back through sparkling clean Adivasi villages. Houses had decorated doorways and arches. Some houses were tiled with flat tiles, others were thatched. Veranda extensions were thatched with arched openings. The earthen areas around the houses were swept clean and there were walled areas around the houses. I couldn't get near enough for photos without intruding. Split bamboo was woven in diagonal patterns and used for the walls of temporary shops and cattle houses A fencing of thin bamboo was often put around areas the cattle and sheep must avoid. As soon as I had crossed into West Bengal there were such protected fields of bright green – a second rice crop, I think! I saw skeins of wool hanging on rods to dry and wondered if it was another local industry.

North of Ingraz Bazaar there is a Development Zone in 'Rural Adivasi country'. Adivasi people are the tribes of the Indian subcontinent, they are the indigenous ethnic minorities who make up about 9% of India's population, numbering more than one million people. In this part of India, they are Santhals and have their own language and customs. The Bengali script is based on the Santali writing system. There was a cardboard and string factory, side by side with an aluminium factory, making pots with round bellies. I had often seen them being hawked around villages, suspended in net bags, by a man wearing a yoke. I stopped for tea at a neat looking lorry stop and met a man who had come from Sahibganj on the bus to bring silk screen materials. Silk screen printing is used to print labels for boxes. He offered to show me a factory, but I didn't have time as I had to get back for my evening appointment. There was the usual lorry and auto-repairing area, on the outskirts of Ingraz Bazaar, and a stream of effluent, almost like gel. Air and waste pollution laws either do not exist, or are not obeyed.

I popped into the police station and saw the Duty Officer, because the map the ADM had given me didn't show the way to the National Highway. They got a jeep to show me the way; it was under the flyover, which I had come into Ingraz Bazaar on from the Manichowk Ferry. The driver was quite oblivious of the fact that I had to try and keep up with him on a bike. However, we got to the NH junction, I drew up alongside the jeep and the driver hopped out and shook hands with me. I had suggested a sketch map of the route at the police station, but they couldn't manage to draw one. Mapwork obviously doesn't feature on the school syllabus.

When I got back to the Circuit House, I had a message that someone called Dilip Kumar was coming to see me at 5 pm to take me to meet his wife and three-year-old child at his house. I couldn't remember any connection, but he was probably a friend of Ravi Toshniwal. Ramesh also phoned and said that I was to see a Dr. Shiv Agarwal. He was a friend of Ravi's, and I think he said he was a relation of Prem's. He had a hospital in Malda and specialised in paediatrics. It turned out that Dilip Kumar was a friend of Dr. Shiv Agarwal, and he took me to meet him. He kindly lent me the 1000 Rs and let me speak to Ramesh on the phone from his residence. I mentioned my headache and previous ills to Dr Agarwal, and he suggested I get 15 tablets of penicillin, or I would get re-occurrence of my infection!

At Dilip Kumar's home I was welcomed by his wife and given coffee and a selection of sweetmeats and savouries, including rasgullas which are very popular in Bengal. Dilip Kumar had a salt factory. He imported the salt from Gujarat and Rajasthan. We had a discussion about salt and iodine. Iodine is often added to salt in India to enable the production of the thyroid hormone. Thyroid deficiency can lead to the enlargement of the thyroid, called 'goitre' and mental disability in the children of thyroid deficient mothers. It is estimated that approximately 30% of the world's population are at risk of being iodine deficient. The availability of iodine in food depends on one's diet, and must contain milk, cheese, eggs, shellfish and saltwater fish. A mainly vegetarian Indian diet can lead to a lack of iodine, and so iodine is added to salt, which is used daily by the majority of people. I took photos of Dilip, his wife Hema, and their young daughter. Dilip arranged for a new sign, in Bangla this time, to be made for my bike. Very useful indeed! According to Dilip Kumar, Mohammed 'needed watching with regards to money!' However, when I came to pay my bill for food was 146 Rs. and I recorded tips as 30 and 10 Rs – all perfectly normal.

Ingraz Bazaar CH was the best Circuit House I had stayed in regarding hot water, sheets and food. The geyser and shower actually worked, and I gave my bike a good clean. I discovered that 'baby-wipes' were excellent for degreasing and cleaning the chain and pulley. I laid my bike down to oil the chain on each side and wiped it with my piece of cotton cloth. One of the front spokes was a bit loose but I couldn't find my spoke key. I will have to find it after the picnic.

Mohammed will bring me tea at 7 am. and we are travelling in a truck – a large Indian truck in which I will have a seat. A bit different from the office Christmas party in Cambridge! I don't suppose anyone will speak English. He said we would be leaving for the picnic at 8 or 8.30 am. and that we will be back at 2.30 pm. The picnic will be breakfast and lunch. Such precise timings are unusual in India and I thought to myself that it would be a miracle if we kept to these timings, as Indian people are generally not good timekeepers.

December 17, 1994

The Departmental Picnic at Gaur

It was 8.40 am and the lorry hadn't yet come! At 9 30 am there was still no truck and Mohammed phoned the company. The truck arrived just before 10. I was seated in the cab, with the driver and six others, including the other 'special guest'. He was Mr Kumar Garam, who owned a country wine factory and came from Darjeeling. Country wine is distilled from sugar-cane, it is 25% spirit and 75% water. He said the government takes 50% of the shop price as tax, hence it is a big source of income for them. A bottle of country wine costs two rupees.

Approximately forty men and thirty children were standing in the back of the truck, along with two huge speakers for the sound system, to be run from the truck battery. All the cooking equipment, firewood, raw food and surprisingly, a folding chair and a china cup for me, were in the back of the lorry too. It was a male only party, men and boys.

The picnic site was a field at the ancient walled city of Gaur, once home to more than a million people and trading with China and Portugal. Gaur was created because of the Ganga but in 1575, after a three-month monsoon, the Ganga shifted several miles to the south. Its sandbanks and stagnant water became the breeding ground of mosquitoes and malaria. The 2000-year-old city was depopulated, thousands died, and the city was abandoned.

The lorry was unpacked, and the music started. Only one boy seemed to be dancing. The first job for the cooks, a team of about six, under Mohamed's supervision, was to break up the wooden crates they had brought with them for firewood. Mohamed produced a folding chair for me to sit on, under the shade of a tree. He then brought me a cup of tea in a lovely china cup and saucer with pretty flowers on it. It must have been from the Circuit House pre-Independence days.

A pit was dug for the fire and Mohammed, girded with a towel for an apron, and the other cooks, started preparing the vegetables, heating oil in large pans and frying the spices to release their flavours. When the rice was ready it was strained through muslin cloth. While the food was cooking, I went to explore the site as I could see lovely brickwork and blue glazed tiles on ruined buildings just a hundred yards away. There was a sign about a mosque written in Bangla and in English, but it had been erected on its side neatly secured with angle iron into a cement base. The workmen obviously could not read English or Bangla to place it in that position. The sign announced that the mosque was built by Sultan Hussain who lived between 1493 and 1519. It had been used as a prison and was later called the 'bat mosque' as it was infested with bats when it was cleared. There were extensive walls from the old city and other buildings dating from the 15th Century. Gaur was the capital of this region in pre-Muslim days. There were intricate pillars with semi-circular blue and white glazed tiles and dados patterned with alternating blue tiles.

Mohammed asked me if I would like some of the country liquor but I declined. I had read too many newspaper articles about people being ill or dying from drinking what they called 'Hooch' and I didn't know if it was the same thing, so it was best to abstain.

The children were fed first, meat and rice, sitting on the ground in a line with their leaf plates before them. We special guests were served at the same time as the children, I on my special chair. I think the meat was goat, boneless for convenience. The adults were fed next, served by Mohammed and by the special guest, Mr Kumar Garam. Mohammed came and asked me something. I thought he was asking if I wanted more food so I said no! I realised later that he was asking me to serve the cooks. I hope he didn't think I was rude. I didn't understand what he was asking me. The cooks, together with the driver, ate last and were joined by Mohammed, who had taken off his towel apron, and they were served, seated on a tarpaulin, by Mr Kumar Garam.

Some men played cards. One man got argumentative; they had obviously been sampling Mr. Garam's country liquor. Mohamed took him aside, and it seems he was told to behave in front of me! I hope the driver didn't drink!

Everything was cleared away, put back into the lorry and we went back to Ingraz Bazaar.

Two Circuit House boys appeared in my room and said, "No food, no tea". I wasn't expecting anything, I gathered Mohammed had gone to bed drunk. He had worked very hard all day. The boys wanted backsheesh, I gave one 10 rupees and told the other he would have to wait until I pay my bill. I shooed the boys out, as I wanted to write a fax to my family and was going to try and send it from Dhulian. I packed my bike for the morning. I was 650 miles from Calcutta, but I was making a detour to Bolpur. It was 140 miles from Calcutta to Ganga Sagar. A total of about 900 miles to go!

December 18, 1994

More Erosion and Lost Livelihoods

Ingraz Bazaar to Dhulian 52 km/ 32 miles

I woke up with the birds, but dozed off and didn't hear the alarm. I got up at 7 am and Mohammed appeared with tea. I said, "I'm late" and he said "13 minutes late!" Before I left, I took a photo of Mohammed, his wife and children with the Polaroid camera. I thanked Mohamed for his care and hospitality and told him I had really enjoyed the Departmental Picnic.

I crossed the Farakka Dam, a barrage across the Ganges-Bhagirathi River in Malda and Murshidabad districts of India, only 11 miles from the border with Bangladesh. A large sign informed me that it was started in 1962, inaugurated in 1971 and opened in 1972. It is 3 km long and in 1989 produced 11,000 MW of Hydro-electric and thermal power. It cost 208 million dollars! There were signs saying it should not be photographed! The barrage of openable gates had a road along it and a railway alongside it. Its purpose was to divert water from the Ganges to the Hooghly River to flush out sediment from Calcutta (Kolkata) harbour, without the need for regular mechanical dredging. However, it didn't provide enough water to do this, and it became responsible for land erosion and bank collapses, with huge displacements of population, loss of livelihoods and land, as water accumulated behind the barrage. There are also constant quarrels about the Indian authorities cutting off water to Bangladesh, and about how to share the water. There are reports of raised salinity levels, contaminated fisheries, hindered navigation, and threats to public health. Floods as far upstream as Bihar are blamed on the barrage, as well as the silting up of the Ganges.

I passed people using plastic sacks for gathering the leaves they were sweeping from roadside verges, probably for adding to cow dung. It made the verges look like manicured lawns. Sacks were usually made of jute. I watched men making bricks, using the sandy earth of the field, mixing it with some of a wetter pile of clay, gathering it into a roll and putting it into a mould, before sprinkling more sand on top and patting it down. Each mould took two minutes to fill. These moulds were then fired in kilns built in the field. The kilns varied in shape across different states but basically either oval or square and fired from below. The labourers and their families lived in terraces of small brick rooms around the brickfields.

Another first in this part of Bengal was to see silkworm cocoons laid out on the roadsides to dry in the sun. The yellow cocoons were spread on metal beds, inclined to the sun's rays, rather like banks of solar panels are these days. Wheat grains are often encountered spread on the tarmac all over India. There were also hanks of wool drying on sticks. I saw my first container lorries and an oil tanker from Bhutan. Public carriers, namely trucks with licences, were travelling between Calcutta and the mountainous state of Assam. I saw large white birds in the distance but couldn't make out whether they were cranes or storks. I knew that six-foot-tall Sarus cranes came to northern India from Siberia.

The surface of the Grand Trunk Road, officially named National Highway 2, was as bad in some places in Bengal as it had been in Bihar, and was being repaired piecemeal as usual. I stopped in Murshidabad district for lunch near a brickwork and attracted the usual crowd.

I turned off the main road before Dhulian and asked for the 'bidi factory' thinking there would be only one. After asking a few stall holders I was taken to Shree Bikash Chaldar, who lived alone in a very spartan cement house. He spoke English and had a telephone and was obviously the man my bank manager had contacted about my accommodation. He was the 'Government Branch Divisional Officer' and he phoned my 'night halt'. A young man arrived to take me through several villages, along a rough track for three kilometres. I was ushered into a 25 x 15-foot, twin-bedded room, with two lumpy looking mattresses and a blanket on each bed. The bathroom was next door - cold water only! I decided I had better get a new torch battery for the night but there were none available. I washed the grime off myself and changed, intending to sit outside in the sun, under a coconut tree. A huge pigeon was up the tree dropping messages, one onto my book and one on my shoe. I retreated inside.

The door from my room led to the buying area, with white covered mattresses to sit on. Mr Charu Chandra Shahar was sitting in front of a cash box. I didn't relish spending the next twenty hours cooped up in there!

Someone appeared who spoke English, and he seemed to think that I was from Switzerland. He was the second person to think that, and I haven't worked out why. He told me he was going to take a bath because he had just had a haircut!

A Mr Ajeet Kumar came and saved me. He had learned English at a college for six months but had had to leave because his family lost all their land, it was swept away by the river Ganges. He was currently employed as a social worker, taking people to hospitals in Malda or Behrampore. He said he regretted the loss of the English language, as he thought its use as a national language would have united India. He was also in favour of Sanskrit, on which Bangla is based. He complained about the weakness of government medical facilities and about government workers in particular, saying they had no work ethic, were working only for money and lining their pockets at the expense of millions of poor and sick people. He mentioned files stacked up in offices gathering dust and went on to praise the two-hundred years of British government, giving India laws, democracy and good administration. I asked him how to solve these problems, and he said, 'by education'.

Mr. Shahar's son, Sanjay, and his wife came to see me. He was in the bidi business too, as an agent of ITC, the Indian Tobacco Company which is a subsidiary of BAT, the British and American Tobacco Company. He had been married for ten months, and his wife was in the bidi business too. Bidis are made by men in 'factories' (meaning workplaces) but women make them in their own homes. Mr Shahar gave me tea and explained bidi making to me. He also gave me a ballpoint pen with Murshidabad written on it. The best bidis are made from the Shal leaves, which are imported from Orissa, where they are picked from the Kendu tree. Inferior bidis are made from leaves grown in forests in Bihar. The tobacco is imported from Gujarat. The leaf is cut, and granules of tobacco are placed in the leaf which is then rolled and folded. The finished product is about two inches long. A man can make 1000 bidis in four or five hours. He gets twenty rupees per thousand.

The bidi factories provide the much-needed employment in this area, where many people have been made homeless and landless and have lost agricultural work. Most of Dhulian is under water, because the Ganges moved. People had lost their houses three or four times. Old Dhulian was under the Ganges and people live in fear, in temporary shacks, and have no compensation. The Ganges was very calm when I saw it and Bangladesh was only five kilometres away across the river.

The residents of Dhulian want an embankment with a road on it, but the one proposed by the Irrigation Minister was estimated at 40,000,000 Rs and was not forthcoming. This year stone was dumped in the river to deflect the water. but the water came to within nine inches of the top sandbags.

Dhulian High School, founded in 1897, paid for by donations from the old Zamindar class landlords, and extended later by the government, has 1760 children. A ferry brings people to buy in the market and to work and children to attend school. A cinema, the only source of entertainment in Dhulian is threatened by erosion. The population of Dhulian was 30,000. Dhuli means dusty!

I was introduced to Mr. Vijay Kumar Jain who was secretary of the High School Association and Mr. Ajeet Kumar Jain, the President, who offered me 'Mithi Pan', a sweet pan to eat. He lived in a large, veranda-ed house. He said that those interested in education, and by implication, able to afford it, go to the English Medium school in Farakka. English 'Medium' means that lessons are taught in English.

There was also the Convent of Mary Immaculate, in Berhampore. Convents are reputed to have a good education and 'convent-ed girls', the fact that they have been convent-educated, is mentioned in the advertisements of 'brides available for marriage' columns of the Sunday newspapers. The Chief of Police was visiting and was also introduced to me. He told me that the local crime was mainly high-way robbery, in which thieves board buses and steal money and jewellery from passengers.

I found a Calcutta Sunday paper and there were several interesting articles. I noted that the temperature ranged from a maximum of 27.4 to a minimum of 13.4 degrees Centigrade. Relative humidity was 55% at 5 pm. Sunrise was at 6.12 am and the sunset at 4.55 pm. At Garden Reach the Hooghly River had a three-metre difference between high and low tide. A fire among 450 shanties in a slum area had made 2500 people homeless, and the place was a charred mess of plastic and burnt-out homes. There was also an article saying 113 postmortems had not been performed since 1989, as there was only one Medical Officer, and that 9000 postmortem reports were pending. A new morgue had been constructed in 1991 but was never used – there was only a façade existing. Electric cabling, cold storage units, doors and windows had been stolen The Raj Era morgue set up in the Police station ceased functioning in 1981, yet two employees were still drawing salaries. Viscera was lying around in jars in the compound. Apparently rape and molesting crimes are not filed in time, and are therefore useless.

Lunch and dinner were served to me at a coffee table in front of an upholstered settee. As a guest I was served first and watched while I ate. Lunch included sweet white syrupy rasgullas with not-too-hot food, that included one vegetable which looked like wooden sticks tied in bundles.

It got quite noisy after 4 am, and I was worried about oversleeping. I fell asleep and woke up again at 5 am. I finally got up at 6.10 am, had a cold shower and was ready by 6.30 am. I read a book about Rabindranath Tagore and then went to look for Mr Shahar, with a note I had written to him and Mr Ajeet Singh, thanking them for their hospitality. I left at 7. 05 am.

December 19, 1994

Dhulian to Behrampore 100 km/ 62 miles

The stone road signposts were only in Bangla, the numbers too, and they were not very frequent. Lalgola was about half way according to my map, but each village name was anonymous to me because they were written in Bangla script. I didn't have the satisfaction of knowing how far I'd come. and the road seemed endless.

On reaching Murshidabad, I passed the Katra mosque-cum-tomb, with five domes and two towers, dedicated to Newab Murshid Quli Khan, dating from 1723. Murshidabad was the capital of the area since 1705 having been moved there from Dacca. It had suffered extensively in the 1897 earthquake. I was told it was now a seminary for seven hundred students of the Koran.

At a crossroads I was given the 'news' that the Circuit House was 'to the right and about 2 kilometres' away. This turned out to be the sub-divisional office of Lalbagh, near the famous Palace of One-thousand-doors, the Huzardaura, and an Imambara. It was still 40 km or 24 miles, to my night halt at Berhampore Circuit House.

Newab Murshid Quli Khan. made Murshidabad the Mohammedan capital of Bengal in 1704. It was capital for seventy years, its jurisdiction covering modern day Bangladesh, west Bengal, Bihar and Orissa. Murshidabad was a cosmopolitan city of 10,000 in the 1750's. It was home to wealthy banking and merchant families from different parts of the Indian continent, and Eurasia, including the Armenians, the British East India company, French and Dutch companies. All conducted business and operated factories around the city. Silk was a major product.

Murshidabad was also a city of art and culture, including ivory sculptors, Hindustani classical music and the Mughal style of painting. The city's decline began with the defeat of the last Newab, Siraj-ud-Dulah, at the Battle of Plassey in 1757. He was demoted, and the British moved the treasury, courts and revenue offices to Calcutta.

When I found the Circuit House Berhampore, it took ages to get my accommodation confirmed. I spoke to the DM on the phone, and he only allowed me one night and advised me to go to the Tourist Lodge of West Bengal Tourist Corporation in Berhampore at ten am. the next day. Berhampore was a large town with a main road that goes on and on. The traffic from 4 pm to 5 pm was ninety percent bikes and rickshaws. According to an old man in the Circuit House office, Clive had his barracks here in Berhampore and stayed in the Circuit House. There were pretty arched windows with wrought iron security grills. I was offered tea on arrival and ordered hot water.

I'd fallen off my bike today. I had to go off the road onto the sandy side, several inches below the road surface, and couldn't get back onto the road because of jeeps and cows! I grazed my elbow and hit my head on the road. People were very nice and helped me up. I'd just been talking to some young men about my trip, and they were with me. I cycled more than a hundred kilometres today, from 7 am to 4.30 pm. with hardly any stops, only one to fill my bottles and one for breakfast.

When I went to get my second water bottle from my pannier, I discovered it had emptied itself! I'd had seven bananas, an omelette, two buns and two oranges! The Convent of Mary Immaculate was nearby and I thought about visiting the sisters, to enquire about Mass and a guest house! Otherwise, it would be the Tourist Bungalow tomorrow!

By seven o' clock I was settled in the Circuit House and had done all my washing, without hot water, and found out that I was to have dinner in the dining room at 9 pm. I ordered two cups of tea to tide me over. I am having vegetarian food with roti tonight. I don't like eating late and then having to sleep – it can't be good for one! I cleaned the bike frame and bags with baby wipes and planned to give the bike a shower, if the hot water arrived.

I discovered jute today. Most people in the UK know jute as sacking, but in India sacks are called 'gunny bags.' Jute fabric is made from the fibrous interior of a plant that grows eight to ten feet high. The stems are placed in water for a month to rot and make it easier to remove the fibre. I remembered from my school days that his process was called 'retting' when applied to flax, when making linen. People were squatting on the water's edge pulling long strands of fibre from the central core of the plant, which looked like bamboo canes, but without the joints. The strands were given a final fling in the water to align the fibres and then deftly made into a hank and thrown behind the person on the bank.

Cart loads of glossy fibre are collected and can be seen drying on racks. I had mistaken these hanks for wool when I saw them earlier. The stripped canes are used as fencing in West Bengal and also as thatching, in very neatly made tile-size widths. Some village house walls had criss-cross jute cane walls between them. I also saw cane boxes being made with jute canes

Another discovery was a beautifully made 'Prayer Hall'. A temporary structure made for travelling gurus to offer prayers, preach sermons and have hymn singing with local residents. These buildings are about thirty feet square and are constructed with jute-cane windows, and have three stories thatched with straw' They must be left in place for 100 days, for religious reasons

There was plenty of fishing activity today, mostly with seine nets. They hang vertically in the water, and surround the chosen fishing area, their bottom edge weighted, and the top edge fitted with floats.

On a deserted stretch of road, I noticed a bicycle with round cane baskets attached to it, and wondered what they contained. I parked my bike to get the camera out, to capture a view of the bicycle with two large cane baskets connected to its pannier rack. The baskets held fish!

A lungi-clad young man with a turban about his head, came running toward me, along the field boundaries. He was pleased that I wanted to photograph him and his bike panniers.

Near Mongyr I saw drag net fishing. Men stood on each bank of the river, with the net suspended in the water between them. as they walked slowly upstream.

Fields extended into the river with mud walls like tentacles, and were being ploughed and flooded ready for growing rice. I was told that the best and most fragrant Basmati rice comes from the Dehra Dun area. Round here the rice is called 'terri-cotton' rice, something to do with its polishing.

My bed charge was 50 Rs, and my breakfast omelette was 10 Rs.

December 20, 1994.

An Abandoned Garden

I checked in at the Tourist hostel and devoted the day to seeing the palaces, mosques, gardens and prominent places in Murshidabad

My first visit was to the palace of 1000 doors, Huzardaura. The palace was built for one of the six generations of Newabs in 1837, and was shared by the Newab, working at the behest of the East India Company, with the British authorities, on business and ceremonial occasions, and as offices and guest house for the top officials. The many doors were to fool an outsider and prevent entrance to the palace. Actually 100 of the thousand were fake.

The palace was built in Italianate style by a British architect on the banks of the Bhagirathi-Ganges River, for Nazim Hamuyan Jahia between 1829 and 1837 The museum has pictures depicting the fashions of the time and the jewellery that adorned the princes of the day. Princes in long velvet dresses with jewelled brimmed hats and turbans, jewel encrusted regalia and buckles. The Newabs of Oudh are also portrayed as they were friends and allies of the Newabs of Bengal. A picture of Clive receiving the Diwani of Bengal, bronzes of Napoleon and Nelson, portraits of Cornwallis and Bentinck in the British Gallery, silver sedan chairs, filigree marble candle stands fifteen feet tall, carved ivory figures, collections of miniature paintings, and ivories, all testifying to the culture and richness of the Newabs and Murshidabad. A Durbar room, a grand reception room, with a huge dome and doors at the cardinal points was used by the Newabs and the British for their ceremonial occasions. Crystal chandeliers and stucco plasterwork, Corinthian columns and marble floors abounded.

Outside, in the gardens, I found a café selling mint tea, which I had not tried before, and I really enjoyed it. I ventured next to the other sites and buildings. The Katra Masjid mosque dating from 1723. Nawab Murshid Quli was buried under the stairs. It had many domes and two towers with musketry loopholes and was once a caravanserai, built during the 18th century, when the area was a major trading hub of Eurasia. A caravan was a group of people travelling together. A caravanserai in the Islamic world was an inn with a courtyard to securely accommodate the travellers, their goods and their animals, often camels. They were very necessary, for safety, in desert regions.

The Khushbagh, 'Garden of Happiness', is where the later Newabs of Murshidabad were buried, and I also saw the Bacchawali Tope,' a large canon 'which induces childbirth', made between the 12th and 14th centuries, probably by the Muslim rulers of Gaur. A couldn't think how it would induce birth, unless by the noise it made!

There are lots of palaces in Murshidabad, built as residences for the wealthy Jain merchants and bankers from Rajasthan. I came across a palace house known as 'Jagat Seth'. It belonged to a Bengali Jain banking family, who had risen from being jewellers-cum-money lenders, to becoming bankers to the rulers of Bengal. The emperor gave the title 'Jagat Seth' to the banking family. They minted money, bought and sold gold, collected revenues, dealt with foreign traders, controlled exchange rates and lent to emperors and zamindars, like a central bank.

In 1994, when I discovered the Jagat Seth palace and garden, it was deserted, with only signs of perhaps a caretaker family, or squatters, because of the pots drying on a cast iron seat near the exit. There was some spindly bamboo scaffolding erected on the main façade, but no sign of any workmen.

The house, garden, temple, wells and beautiful marble statuary, veiled in mystery, were deserted. I wandered around enjoying the solitude and taking photographs. A step well, marble parterres, statues of people and animals, pierced marble screens and, in one corner of the garden, a Hindu temple. I wrote in my journal that I thought the palace garden would make a wonderful background for a fashion show.

I found out later that it was destined to become a museum and provide stabling for horses to take tourists around Murshidabad in carriages.

I went to Mass at the nearby convent and got back to the Tourist Lodge just before dark. I chatted to the manager. about my itinerary, and he told me that he was manager of Diamond Harbour tourist hotel before coming to Berhampore. He said that I will have to do the Ferry and Ganga Sagar in one day. It was 75 km, and he probably didn't think I regularly cycled that far in a day. He mentioned a government hostel as well as a religious ashram called a 'Dharamsala' at Ganga Sagar plus tented accommodation during the Mela. He found out that the Bolpur Tourist hostel was full, and suggested that I try a private hotel or Siuri Tourist hostel, when I told him I wanted to visit Shantiniketan, for its connections to Rabindranath Tagore, polymath and recipient of the 1913 Nobel Prize for Literature.

Wednesday December 21, 1994

Trouble at the Bank

I sat in the sunshine outside my room and wrote a fax to the children, to be sent via Ramesh's office. I sent it at 10 20 am. and was in the bank by 10 35 am. I wondered how long this bank would take to cash my Traveller's cheques. The bank refused to cash them! Then, as now, one cannot get Indian rupees outside India, it is a non-convertible currency. As there were no ATMs or cards at that time one had to use travellers' cheques, drawn on large banks, Thomas Cook or American Express. I went back to the Tourist hostel manager who said other people had succeeded in cashing cheques, so he sent someone with me, but again I was refused, - they only cash sterling or dollar Indian Travel Cheques!

We spoke to the Branch Manager who said it was possible to cash a Bank Draft in two days by fax, but the bank doesn't have a fax machine! I asked my Tourist hostel assistant if he knew any Marwari people and he took me to see a Mr. X. but he was away for two days! The next suggestion was that I go by the 1 pm bus to Calcutta, a four- or five-hour journey to Dum-Dum. This was risky as the bank might be closed by the time I arrived. I decided to go to Calcutta the next day, Thursday. I bought a ticket and a reservation for 53 Rs. and went back to the tourist hostel for a meal. The manager met me with the news that there was to be a 24 hour 'Bangla bandh', a strike, the next day, Thursday.

Thursday 22, December

I got up at 5 am and took a rickshaw to the station to catch the 5.30 am Lalgola Express to Calcutta.
My train had been detained by strikers at Lalgola and others were halted at Plassey.
After an hour, I was helped to get a refund after I gave my Hindi press release, that Barun had written for me in Bhabua, to a chap who could read Hindi.
I went back to the Tourist hostel for breakfast and decided to leave for Katwa, continuing my route by bike to Shantiniketan, Calcutta and Ganga Saga.

.

Chapter 11

Power Cuts and Strikes

December 22, 1994

Berhampore to Katwa 86 km/ 53 miles

There was no traffic. No lorries, buses, autos or taxis either. Benches had been placed across the road, and a banner and flag proclaimed a strike. Vehicles were parked at the side of the road, and I was able to ride down the centre of the N 34, where the road surface was best, avoiding potholes of course, to near Plassey where Clive defeated the Nawab of Bengal and the French in 1757.

On empty roads I covered fifty kilometres in three hours, including an egg stop, a tea stop, and an omelette stop. I overshot the road I wanted, because I couldn't read the Bangla signs. One kilometre after missing the sign to Debagram, I found the rough single-track road to Katwa Ghat Ferry. It was difficult to believe that it went to a ferry across the Ganges, because it was so deeply rutted.

I stopped to eat my four eggs and two bananas, with an audience, but they said nothing. I stopped again for tea just five kilometres from the ferry, where there was a government family-planning jeep parked beside the dhaba.

At Katwa ferry, sand was being off-loaded from a large wooden boat by a dozen men. Wearing scarves wrapped around their heads, enclosing a ring of twisted straw, to enable them to carry the shallow cane baskets, piled high with sand, from the boat, across a narrow, springy gang-plank, to add to a vast pile of sand on the river bank. The men were bare-chested and bare-footed.

I continued on towards the town of Katwa asking for directions to the Sub-Division Office. My accent was obviously not understood by many people I asked, but luckily, I was rescued by a young man, Rathindranath Sahar. He took me back along the road I'd come along, to an office next to the bank, on the second floor. By mistake, I had taken a road to the left after the bank, my misunderstanding, and my language problem, recognising only the word 'bank.' The office was next to a bank!

The Sub Divisional Officer, Mr. N. D. Kumar, was woken up, but refused to see me. A security man said he was sleeping, come back at 5 pm! They sent me to the Superintendent of Police, Mr. A Ghosh, and he was 'out of station', meaning not in, or away. It was very quiet, all the shops were closed, and there were just a few drunks, some people playing cards, and some young men lolling around – the strike had provided a holiday.

Rathindranath Sahar remembered that there was a Municipal Hostel in Katwa, and took me there. I was given a bed for the night and taken up to the roof by Rathindranath and Mr. Das, the chowkidar, to see the view over a lake. Man-made by the Municipality, it joined the 'Sangam', the confluence of the Ganga-Bhagirathi with the river Ajay. Refugees from Bangladesh lived in thatched huts behind the lake. Rabindranath came back just before 5 pm and told me we were going to get 'donations for leprosy people'. We went to pharmacies and his friend's shops asking for donations. Unfortunately, most places were closed because of the 'band', the strike, but in the hour of darkness we collected 113 rupees, mostly in two-rupee coins, but some ten-rupee coins. A few people said 'no!'.

We cycled around the town without lights on our bikes. I stuck close to Rabindranath. He took me to see the temples and the burning ghats, where a body was being cremated. I could see the lit bier and the body engulfed in flames, with twitching legs.

Later, when we were in a very old temple, there was a power cut -very scary! It was now pitch dark outside and we had to walk with our bikes. The stars were beautiful, but I was relieved when the lights came on again. Back at my lodging. Mr. Das asked me if I would 'do him the honour of taking dinner at his house', which was next door. His wife was very sweet; she had a BA. in English and Philosophy. Her husband came from a village near Calcutta; his wife was from Plassey. They had been married for three years but had no children. My attention was taken by a double, clay pottery, water-filter. It had sand in the bottom and a tap near the base. The top had a porous plug to allow water into the bottom chamber. It was very old. They gave me roti, sabzi, sweet vermicelli, and warm milk.

The milk may have been a mistake because I didn't know if it had been boiled. I had stomach rumbles in the night and felt a bit queasy the next morning. However, I had to go to Calcutta to cash my travellers' cheques. Their friend Mr. Shyamal Das said he'd help.

A Fine or Prison?

December 23, 1994

Katwa to Calcutta by train

I arrived at Katwa junction station in time to catch the 6.20 am. train, but the trains were not running according to schedule, because of the 'band' the day before. We eventually travelled on the delayed 5 am train!

Shyamal told me to get my ticket at counter number two, but to hurry, as the train was leaving. I had to give my rickshaw man ten rupees as I had no change and was planning to pay him after I got my ticket and change. The three-foot square mesh window of the ticket buying kiosk, had a tiny arched opening in the wire netting, for people to reach through. There were about fifty men pushing and shoving to be served. Shyamal was standing in the doorway of a train and shouted to me "come quickly". I ran towards him and he helped me jump up the large steps into the train. Out of breath I was relieved to be on the train to Calcutta but he immediately grabbed my arm, and steered me across the carriage, to the opposite door of the train. We had to jump down onto the track, and climb up into an adjacent train. That was the one to Howrah, the Calcutta terminus beside the Ganges, here called the Hooghly.

Shymal was going to work and getting off before Howrah. He told me that there were several ferries, but that I must take the Fairlie ferry, to Dalhousie Square, from outside the station, in order to cross to the area with banks, law courts and other Victorian capital city buildings. He advised me to get the 3 pm train back to Katwa.

Most of the people on the train were commuters, wearing trousers and shirts and holding briefcases. A minority carried dirty holdalls, wore winter scarves, shawls and balaclavas. I was acutely aware that I was travelling without a ticket, and imagined the newspaper headlines, about a tourist not buying a ticket, the certainty of a fine, maybe even a court case or prison! How was I to avoid the station ticket collectors, who stood next to narrow exits, with sliding metal gates. Shymal said 'just follow the crowd!' as he left the train, before the Calcutta terminus, to go to his office. The train reached Howrah at ten to ten. My carriage stopped short of the platform, so once again I had to jump down onto the track. Remembering Shyamal's words I followed the crowd. I really stood out from them as I was white and about a foot taller than my fellow passengers. Amazingly the crowd popped through a gateway marked 'no exit'. I was not stopped and was greatly relieved when I found myself outside the station.

I found the subway to Fairlie Place. The ticket queue notice said 'New Fare', the one-rupee ticket had gone up to 1 rp 20 paise. On the other side of the river, in sight of the famous Howrah Road and Rail Bridge, built in 1943, (without any piers to avoid causing silting) I crossed roads, dodging through the traffic, but it was not as bad as I had expected. There were some broken pavements with loose bricks and sandy holes to fall down, but the streets were not as crowded, or the traffic as heavy, as that of London.

Dalhousie Square was built in the village of Kali kata, which became British Calcutta, and finally Kolkata. It marked the centre of the 'White town' populated primarily by English merchants, officers and functionaries which was kept separate from 'black town,' populated by native landowners and business men. The Writers building is the predominant red brick heritage building, occupying one side of Dalhousie Square, in the administrative and business hub of Calcutta. Now it is the official secretariat building of the State Government of West Bengal, employing 6000 people. Built in 1777 it was the principal office of the writers (junior clerks) of the British East India Company. It was the first three story building in Calcutta and effectively became the headquarters of the entire British Raj in the Indian subcontinent. It started out as a rather plain building but over the years had various facelifts and extensions to beautify it, adding porticoes, statues and colonnades. At the back of the Writers' Building, the streets were lined with long zinc-topped tables where people sat having breakfast, or lunch, of rice and curries.

I went to the American Express office to cash my cheques, certain that it would be easier than using an Indian bank, based on my experience in Lucknow. I then found The Great Eastern Hotel for breakfast at 11 am, and a bit further on I visited the Oberoi Grand and treated myself to a gin and tonic by the pool, nibbling peanuts and being decadent. I washed in the ladies' cloakroom, removed my leggings, and pinched a toilet roll. I phoned High Court Judge Basu, whom I had met in Gangnani and he told me how to get to the High Court, at 1.30 pm. It was just ten minutes away.

The High Court building was enormous and I climbed several storeys and negotiated many corridors before I found the right room. I noticed that when I could see into an office, the desks, floors, and cupboards were piled high with files tied with ribbon and there was not a computer in sight. It was no wonder that cases could take ten years to come to court – as in Lakshmi Singh's case. The Honourable Justice D K Basu invited me to see a People's Court in action on the fourteenth of January but I told him that I had to be in Mumbai by then. He said he would try to fix my accommodation at Siuri for Christmas Eve and at Ganga Sagar, in government owned Tourist Hotels.

The three pm. return train to Katwa had standing room only but someone directed me to a Ladies' Compartment, where I did get a seat, but there was continual traffic of men, selling peanuts, chaat, hair slides, bangles, oranges, and bananas. Books were on sale too and I bought one which was an ABC in Hindi. What started out as a Lady's Compartment at Howrah station ended up being full of men smoking bidis and making a lot of noise. It was a four-hour journey. A fellow passenger bought me a coular (a small unfired clay cup) of tea, served through the train window when we stopped at a station. At another station I saw a man hanging onto the outside of the train door, picking up a coular of tea from a tea man who ran alongside the train pouring out the tea!

Rathindranath met me at Katwa station and got a rickshaw for me. He was on his bike but he stopped for me to have a coffee, the strongest and hottest that I had had so far. Back at the hostel dinner had to be ordered from outside. Rabindranath gave me four New Year cards and said that his grandfather and sister were very pleased with the polaroid photo I had given them. I killed time waiting for supper by learning Hindi from my new book. I promised to send some other photos from Bombay. The supper was small and stone cold when it arrived but it was only three rupees!

Mr. Das wanted to say goodbye so I was shown round to his house. He was in bed. I took a photo of his water filter and a polaroid photo of him.

Chapter 12

Christmas

December 24, 1994

Katwa to Siuri 74 km/ 46 miles

I left Katwa at 7.35 am on a very busy single-track road. Every lorry and bus seemed to be racing to get home for the Christmas holiday.

I fell off my bike when a bus was speeding at me, and my only option was to head into the pile of soft sand at the side of the road. The single-track road was for most of my 74 kilometres, and I had to keep stopping to go off the road onto the un-tarmac-ed side. I counted that I got on and off my bike 63 times! Sometimes the road was too high to ride off and back on again. I had to keep stopping. At other times it was very stony and I dare not risk punctures. Lorries were empty and rattling along at breakneck speeds on the dusty road, with a headwind for me all the way to Siuri.

Not only was my journey very slow but I had no food with me. I managed to buy buns, eggs, half a loaf of bread, oranges and for the first time, lemon squash. I had a peaceful picnic at 11.30 am. near a level crossing in the middle of nowhere, and wasn't surrounded by people for a change, only accompanied by a dog looking for food. I saw a man on a bike dragging a dead dog after him. I wondered if he was going to eat it. The Santal tribal people are very poor. I saw women with no blouses under their saris and children with no clothes and it was winter!

The man at the government Tourist Hostel wasn't very keen for me to stay but he didn't refuse me. I wondered if Justice Basu had been in touch with him. I was the only resident as far as I could tell and yet I was given a room on the third floor of his very large hostel. I knew that I would have to go out to look for food. I had tried to get a radio station that was playing carols, or perhaps a church service, on my little portable radio but realised that the batteries were probably flat, and that I should go out to look for some in the market area. I tried a few places but they didn't seem to understand the word 'batteries' which is the same in Hindi and Bangla as it is in English, but pronounced differently of course. I eventually. spotted some hanging up in a general store. When I got them back to the hostel, they only lasted an hour! I learned that they are referred to as 'cells' not batteries. My AA size ones are called 'pen cells' for some reason!

I ended up celebrating Christmas eve sitting on the floor, in front of my radio/tape recorder playing carols from Buckfast Abbey's school Christmas concert, in which my sons were singing. A lighted candle gave a nice soft light to the scene. As I sang along with the children I picnicked on remains of food from my day's shopping and went to bed.

December 25, 1994

Shantiniketan and the Mela

I found the area of the Shantiniketan 'university' amid woods of mango trees, with semi-circular benches for students, but being Christmas, the students were on holiday. The Viswa Bharati, a public university of, 'the communion of the world with India,' began as an ashram, where people from all walks of life, could come together to meditate. Rabindranath Tagore, a polymath, established a co-educational school inside the ashram in 1901. He believed in open-air education. He did not have a good opinion of western methods of education, introduced in India by the British. He believed that everybody is a genius, and that all students may not bloom at the same time, and should be given the chance to study until the teacher, and the student, are satisfied with their learning.

Art, dance, drama, music, ancient Indian history, culture and archaeology, languages, including Japanese, Chinese, modern European and Indian languages are taught, as well numerous branches of science and technology, environmental studies, agriculture and computer science, journalism and mass communication. All courses are available at under-graduate and postgraduate level. Whatever subject a student wishes to study, is made available. Nature is respected and teachers ride around on bicycles.

I made my way to the museum which was Rabindranath Tagore's house. I was somewhat disconcerted when told to leave my bag on the lawn that surrounded the house, not a very secure place for my money and passport, so my visit to the house was just a quick whiz around.

There was a Christmas fair, a non-religious mela, going on nearby. All kinds of rides for the young and not so young included a ferris wheel, swing boats, musical cars and aeroplane rides. Clothes and crafts were for sale, sweets and extra curly jellabies were available, and everybody was having a good time. I was particularly interested in a hand painted scroll of the Ramayana story being offered for sale by the artist – an old tradition being maintained

December 26th 1994

Siuri to Katwa again, 74 km / 46 miles

I was carrying my bags down three flights of stairs, when I heard the strains of a Scottish Folk tune coming from a clock along the corridor, where I suspected the de-luxe rooms were to be found. I had to smile at the incongruity of this relic of the Raj. I checked my watch and was surprised that it was only six am. Having the maiden name of Alexander, I decided the tune was to wish me a belated Happy Christmas or an early Happy New Year!

There weren't any stalls open yet-a-while, to find a breakfast, it was too early and, for want of anybody to check my route out of town with, I took a wrong turn and found myself on the road to Saintia. Eventually, I came across a young man sweeping out his tea-stall, who told me to take the bypass and turn left, warning me that it was a bad road. It wasn't a metalled road but the red sand was relatively free of potholes and I followed the compacted areas made by heavy traffic. In the wet monsoon season, it would be a quagmire, but at this time it was better than many of the Indian roads I'd been on.

It had been a long detour, and I had lost the advantage of my extra-early start, but it was pleasant to ride through the awakening Santal tribal villages. People sweeping their thresholds, collecting water, and preparing for another day. I regained the road to Katwa and recognised the double bridges which marked the outskirts of Siuri, a narrow old one alongside a newer, wider one. I chose the old bridge this time, along with a few pedestrians.

When I reached the railway line, at Ahmedpur, I stopped to buy supplies at a 'village bus-stop-shop-cum-tree.' Another first! There was actually a bus stop sign nailed to the tree! I spread my custom around, tea from the small thatched tea shop, bread from one of the wooden stalls on legs, bananas from another stall, biscuits, for want of anything useful available to me, from another wooden stall.

Pedalling on I passed the small woodland where I had stopped to photograph the tree with the buttress roots. I'd learned about them at school, but this was the first one I'd seen. The trunk was triangular like a paper dart on its broad end, the tapering part supporting the branch canopy well above the trunk. By 9.20 I was at my Christmas

Eve picnic spot. The pieces of egg shell were still scattered on the grass, but the orange peel had gone. I had my breakfast and worked out that I was approximately halfway between Siuri and Katwa. When I left Siuri I was wearing my woollen jumper over a long-sleeved, high-necked tee-shirt. There was a breeze, and a thin layer of cloud, which made it quite chilly when the sun went in, but I shed my jumper. While I was eating, a train went by. It was a real 'puffing billy' with three carriages. Now I had seen the am. and pm. trains, probably the only ones per day, that ran on this two-foot gauge line.

As I got nearer to Katwa the number of Adivasi tribal villages increased and the roof constructions were more rounded, having lost the long ridge. A lady in a sari, but without a blouse, holding a naked baby, started talking to me. Soon we were joined by half the village, so I got out the polaroid camera and arranged the children in front of the adults for a group photo. Their skin colour was a bit light but I expect they'd like that.

When I was fifteen kilometres from Katwa, having another picnic stop at the edge of the road, a teenager on a motorcycle stopped and spoke to me in English, saying he lived near the rice mill and the petrol station and would like me to come to his house. He had to visit someone in the direction from which I 'd come but he said he'd catch me up later. I didn't see him again, perhaps he was delayed. The wind was strong, especially in the afternoon, but luckily it was behind me. I was feeling tired. I hadn't had much sleep the previous night.

The rice fields are, like the rice itself, known as 'paddy'. Some fields had been left unploughed after harvesting and there were new sprouts of rice plants coming from the old stalk stumps. I asked if this was a cheap way of getting a third crop, and was told "yes" by one man, but "no" by another!

I was glad to reach the Katwa Municipal Hostel again and had just washed and changed when Shyamal K Das, the man who helped me catch the Calcutta train, arrived at 5.30 pm. to take me to visit his family. We walked along the main street and on passing a sweetshop, he asked me if I had had rasgullas. I told him that I had, but he went to the glass-fronted display and selected half a dozen different sweets. Indian sweets are basically made from boiled milk and sugar, to which other flavourings are added, like cardamom and pistachio.

We left with ten rupees worth, in a wax-paper lined cardboard box. It was quite dark when we arrived at his house, there was another power cut. We entered a small alley and the door was opened by his sister, carrying a torch. We followed her up the stairs, into a wide corridor with windows along the length of it on the street side, and doors to the main rooms on the other side. The corridor was really a glassed-in veranda, and the windows could be fully opened in the hot weather. Taking off my sandals, I was ushered into their living room. As if on cue, the power was restored, to reveal a large room, fresh blue paint on the walls, an upholstered three-piece suite, side tables and a huge TV at one end of the room. The grey suite had antimacassars, very UK 40 's and 50 's, embroidered with cream and maroon applique work. A double bed filled the other end of the room.

Shyamal Das introduced me to his sari-clad mother, a widow aged fifty-two, whose husband had died of colon cancer two years previously. His unmarried sister, aged 28, was wearing a coloured shift with short sleeves, what we might describe as a nightie. (It always struck me as odd that to be seen wearing a nightie is permitted, whereas to show more than a glimpse of midriff is de-rigueur. I've been introduced to perfect strangers in my pink satin nightie, yet told to not walk past the servants wearing a floor length petticoat and sari blouse!).

Shymal now has the responsibility of trying to find a husband for his sister, before he himself can choose a wife. He said it was difficult with so much unemployment – I assumed he had to find someone who was a working professional for his sister, and not in danger of being made redundant. He himself had been an engineer-airman in the Indian Airforce near the Chinese border, near Ladakh. Eight months of minus eighteen degrees C., tinned food, Eskimo furs and sleeping bags, put an end to his career and he became a clerk in an insurance company. He has worked for the company for three and a half years, but the conditions must be quite trying because he told me that the mosquitos are up to knee height in the morning and despite spraying with the 'Flit' gun, they are head high by afternoon.

I was asked if I'd like an omelette, and his sister went to make me one, which she served on a stainless-steel plate, together with sweets. These were traditional Bengali rasgullas, jamuns and 'santesh'. I was watched while I selected some and I tried to get my hosts to join me, without success, so I ate a few and left the others. We talked about employment opportunities in Katwa. Shymal told me that there were twelve rice mills which offered seasonal work, but none in the monsoon time – June to September. Shymal pointed out some English quotes on his walls, including a jokey verse about a good wife.

I asked if I could take some photos, and the ladies disappeared into his mother's room next to the lounge. His mother emerged, a few minutes later, wearing a white silk sari edged with gold – widows are supposed to wear white as a sign of their marital status. His sister had changed into an orange and gold sari, which she wore over an olive-green blouse. I took a polaroid picture for them to keep. Shyamal stood proudly between the two ladies, in his red striped shirt, open to reveal just a little of his hairy chest and white vest. He doesn't do any exercise these days and it is beginning to show around his waistline. Mrs Das was amazed that I was older than her, and that I was making such an adventurous journey alone. Losing our husbands when they were both 50, from cancer, also united us.

When the power was restored, the TV was playing hymns and classical music as a sign of respect on the day of National mourning for an ex-President of India. Shymal was at home in Katwa because he had been ill with a stomach complaint on the 26th, following his Christmas Bank Holiday, and he would be getting an early train the next day for Calcutta, with me!

Shymal took me back to the Srabani Hostel. I hadn't made any arrangements for dinner, and was not hungry after my omelette and sweets. I was just going up to my room, after settling my bill, when I was told that my dinner was ready. I didn't like to refuse, so went into the dining room. The food was cold as usual, chicken, roti, vegetables and matchstick-like slivers of potatoes. The tall thin kitchen man gave me two helpings of the 'chips' and offered me rice too. I think he was looking after me because, when I had arrived at 4 pm. he had brought a large glass of tea to my room, without my asking for it. My bed had been made up, unusual in India, with two sheets, one top and one bottom, and a hand towel was spread upon the pillow (an arrangement which I saw later when I visited an ashram)

Chapter 13

A Temple Stay

December 27, 1994

Katwa to Nabadwip. 39 km/ 35 miles

While I was having my tea-toast-omelette breakfast in the hostel foyer, a Mr. S. K. Day started talking to me. I told him I was going to Nabadwip but didn't know where I was staying. He promptly gave me a name and address where he said I could stay.

Three hours later I was weaving my way through a village street, full of potholes, pedestrians and cyclists, carts and cycle vans, when I found myself behind someone pushing his bike, who refused to let me pass, despite ringing my bell to warn him that I wanted to get by – perhaps he was deaf! However, I came to a virtual standstill and overbalanced. An old man picked me up and dusted me down and hoped my 'gari', my vehicle, wasn't damaged! Perhaps he didn't recognise my bike as a pedal cycle.

My fall depressed me and I felt more tired, though perhaps it was only my enthusiasm that had waned. Maybe it was because Ramesh and Prem were not coming to meet me in Calcutta – I wanted to see familiar faces at the end of my journey.

The address I had been given turned out to be the dharmsala of a Hindu temple. The 'name' I had been given was away for the day in Calcutta, so I was asked to return the next day. I pointed to the sign in Bangla on my bike and the penny dropped. An oldish, tall, English-speaking monk took me to his office to complete the formalities "for a very simple room". I sat on the only chair at the end of the desk, piled high with books and ledgers. His office doubled as his bedroom and it was one of the rooms which opened off a courtyard behind the temple. His clothes, once saffron, faded to various hues of pinkish-orange, hung over the head and footboard of his bed and on lines of string tied to the walls. After I had registered, I was given a rolled-up woven bamboo mat about six-foot by three, and taken to room 5, one of the rooms on the far side of the cloister. These rooms were for pilgrims and many of them were occupied by visiting families who were on a temple-tour. Having pre-booked they were provided with charpoy beds.

My room was absolutely bare, with shuttered, barred, glassless windows in the front and rear walls. I was told to padlock the green double doors whenever I left the room. The toilet facilities were at the end of the cloister, not too far from my room. They consisted of a couple of squat loos and two cubicles with taps. A collection of rusty milk powder tins stood on the ground. These were meant to be filled in the shower cubicle and used for flushing oneself and the loo, in the traditional manner. It was much harder to aim and pour from a tin than it is from a jug with a lip! I wouldn't have to go very far on my night sorties, but I decided I had better take a candle or buy a new torch. I couldn't get small 'A 3 'batteries for my pencil torch in rural India, one instance of my trying to save space and weight that wasn't successful.

The reception monk introduced me to a beautiful lady called Nupur. She adopted me for the whole of my stay and I am indebted to her for teaching me what to do and where to go. She didn't speak any English but we got along quite well. She would take my hand and lead me, like a mother leading a child. We must have looked very funny because she was very small and delicate and I was five foot nine inches tall, and not in the least delicate.

Having placed my woven mat on the cement floor I asked Nupur if I could have a mattress. It arrived with a sheet and pillow. I arranged my mosquito net above my sleeping area, hooking it to a convenient nail in the wall. When I asked her about a blanket, Nupur said it was coming. I couldn't work out why everything was coming in dribs and drabs. I began to imagine monks being asked to volunteer, to give up various items of their bedding! Two cotton quilts were brought to me by my tall monk. He had a pattern, drawn in sandalwood paste, but looking like gold, of two vertical, parallel lines down his forehead and nose, joined by a triangle at the bottom. All the monks had this sign, but the freehand drawing varied with the skill of the painter, and was also influenced by the individuals' nose shape. The design means that the monks are followers of the God Vishnu rather than Shiva.

I asked Nupur about meals and she told me that the evening meal would be served after the aarti ceremony. First the Gods' must be given their food. Just then a bell sounded, and we went over to the temple complex, to join about a hundred others, men, women, children and monks. Taking off my shoes I followed Nupur up an outside staircase to stand on a veranda surrounding a puja room. Through the grill doors, a picture of the guru (teacher) who founded this community was displayed. In front of his garlanded picture, dishes of food were arranged on the floor. I counted fourteen different offerings, including rasgullas. Prayers were said and water sprinkled over the assembled congregation. The ceremony ended with a flame being offered to each person so that they could cup their hands over it, before kneeling down to touch the floor with their foreheads. After this veneration we all returned to the ground floor, and went to the temple.

The monks and boys arranged themselves in rows on the pillared, open-sided platform facing a separate building, which contained the statues of various gods. They chanted, some beat drums, others clashed cymbals, occasionally prostrating themselves full length on the marble floor. A young boy stood at the front of the prayer hall, and rhythmically pulled on a rope connected with a bell on the roof. The women and young children, with Nupur still guiding me, stood before the murti (idols) which could be seen through the open doors of three adjacent altars, about three feet above the pavement. Painted images of Radha, Krishna, a pig-faced deity, and the guru founder, were clothed in silks and satin, trimmed with tinsel, and garlanded with real and plastic flowers.

Dressed in a white dhoti and white jumper, the 'priest' stood before each of the murtis, in each of the three sections. He waved a flame, fluttered white material, and waved a flower before each of the statues with a horizontal, circular motion of his hand. Water was sprinkled from a conch shell. Some of the women present made donations of coins before kneeling, forehead touching the ground. Fire was offered to the women and following Nupur's example I passed my hands over the flame, before touching them to my face, and then to my head. A silver, furry fly-whisk was waved at the women and they made high-pitched 'ooh' sounds, by wagging their tongues very rapidly from side to side. This high-pitched tongue trill is called ululation. I was to encounter it again years later when visiting a very sick friend and I found it most unnerving.

After a quick hand wash, Nupur took me to lunch. We sat cross-legged on little mats, on the concrete floor, under a large colonnaded veranda. There were two rows of mostly women, a few men and children. Monks in the palest saffron robes handed round wetted banana leaves. I noticed that some were rejected and returned for a better leaf. Two monks passed up and down the double lines of pilgrims, ladling rice onto the leaves from a zinc baby-bath. They were followed by others with vegetables of various kinds. All were edible for me because the monks do not use onions or chilli. There was a sweet, rolled-up rubbery item, kedgeree and a very runny dhal. I managed to eat everything, including the final sweet rice pudding, with my right hand only, according to the custom. I didn't get any more than my palm dirty and I managed to keep everything on my banana leaf. The hardest part was sitting cross-legged, and leaning over my leaf. I had to put my legs to the side after a while, so that I was over my leaf for mouth loading! At the end of the meal, I folded up my leaf, wiped my floor area and followed Nupur outside the courtyard, to a walled garbage area, where dogs were awaiting our discarded food. Then to the pump to wash the hand. Nupur took me to my room, told me to rest and said she would be coming back after three hours. I went outside, sat on the edge of the cloister, my back against a pillar and wrote up my journal.

I got talking to a lady from Chandanagore, near Calcutta. She told me the gates opened at four o' clock. I hadn't realised we were locked in! She said I should go to Mayapur to see a temple on the other side of the Ganges. The evening aarti prayers were at six pm so I had time to go out. I was so full from my lunch that I didn't need to eat again, but I was dying for a cup of tea. Unlike the dharmsala up in the Himalayas, where we had huge beakers of tea, these monks didn't permit stimulants like tea or coffee. I would have to get it outside the monastery. I would have liked to take some photos, but I didn't get round to asking permission – there just wasn't time.

I decided to walk to the ferry and it was further than I thought. However, I made a few little discoveries on my way along the network of small roads next to the Ganges, so I was glad that I didn't take the rickshaw that was waiting at the temple gates. The first of these discoveries was that the tea shop wouldn't serve me tea, having seen me come out of the temple gate. I don't know whether he was trying to save his soul or mine, by keeping me away from the 'drug'. There wasn't another tea shop to try, so I headed off towards the ferry. I could hear a click-clack sound as I passed various houses and yards, well screened by fences and vegetation. At the end of the road, I found the explanation - a weaving frame! A young man was sitting on a porch at the side of his house, weaving an emerald green length of cotton. He said it was for a lungi, the sarong-style cloth worn by men, either long to the ground, or tucked up to above-the-knee length. I now became aware of lots of these looms being used in back garden sheds, made of woven matting with trellis pattern and jute-cane windows, to let in the air and the light.

Nearer to the ferry I looked in at the door to a wooden shed, and found two or three men and a boy, making brass water pots. They didn't mind me taking a photo and I watched them make the pot in three sections, the little boy responsible for rounding the base by hammering it on a convex mould. The finished article was given a brilliant shining finish on a lathe. Everyone worked squatting on the floor and the whole process was hand produced.

Down by the ferry I bought a bottle of mineral water, and a small box of mango juice, to quench my thirst. The ferry was full of Indian tourists going to the 'Iskon' temple, part of the huge International Krishna Consciousness Complex. The temple was still being built, a huge white marble dome, and a lotus flower-shaped building, around a central tank (pond). On its lantern window on the roof, 'Hari Om' was written in white paint. The temple complex was spotlessly clean and covered several acres of land. On the way by rickshaw to the main gates, there was a feeding centre for poor people, and a medical centre according to the slogans painted on its white walls. In the grounds there were several hostel buildings, modern and architect designed, to house the national and international Krishna Consciousness followers, the people I used to see shaking tambourines, in London's Oxford Street, whom we referred to as "Hari Krishna people". The road to the new Iskon Temple had many traditional style temples, gilded and painted in pastel colours, and securely fenced ashrams, for pilgrims to this ancient centre of Sanskrit culture.

Nabadwip. 125 kms. north of Calcutta had been the capital of Bengal in the eleventh and twelfth centuries, and is revered as the birthplace of the Vaishnav mystic Chaitanya Mahaprabhu, who taught here in the 16th century. My temple was his foundation.

It was getting dark as I returned on the ferry, standing up in a fifteen-foot boat, with its gunwales only a few inches above the water. It did, however, have a diesel engine but I could visualise the horrendous newspaper reports of boats being overloaded with pilgrims, which so frequently capsize. The ferry cost 10 rupees.

I was back in the Ashram, in the middle of writing my journal, when Nupur came to call for me, with the English-speaking office monk. He invited me to see the aarti ceremony – the same as at lunchtime but to the continual ringing of the temple bell, accompanied by drums and gongs. The person performing the aarti ceremony rang a small bell very rapidly with his left hand whereas he did the incense, whisk, fire etc with his right hand. After the ceremony everyone walked four times around both shrines, of Gods and the Guru founder, and then had prasad – food from the gods, small pieces of apple and sweet rice pudding.

I washed my hands and Nupur sent me to get my sandals on, to go to her room. Her room had a large bed and blankets and pillows neatly piled up. There was a little kitchen, and a Puja altar. She gave me some tangerine and a little brown ball, which her nephew said was coconut. I went next door with her, to meet her brother, his wife and three children aged ten, eight, and six. They gave me an orange fizzy drink. We swapped addresses and I went back to my ashram-monastery bed. Music was going full blast.!

Chapter 14

A Calcutta Invitation

December 28, 1994

Nabadwip to Hooghly 73 km./40 miles

Approaching Calcutta from the north, I was beside the Hooghly River, as the Ganges is known there, in the area where the first European settlers of India, Portuguese, Dutch, Armenian, French, and British had established their trading bases.

The Catholic church at Bandal, with its statue of 'Our Lady of Happy Voyage' on the roof of the building, was founded in 1599 by the Portuguese. "Have a happy journey" is a common phrase used to travellers in India, it is even printed on railway tickets! Destroyed in the Mughul siege of 1632 a new church was endowed by Shah Jehan in 1663. A story is told of a priest, and a few thousand Christians, being condemned to death by Shah Jehan. They were to be trampled by the ferocious elephants. One elephant saved the priest and the emperor pardoned the Christians, and restored the church at Bandal. Jesuits (in 1870) and Salesian fathers (in 1929) founded a school, and later a seminary. In 1988 the Mother Teresa nuns opened a convent there and Pope John-Paul 11 declared the shrine a Basilica. The

Christian community was growing - it had virtually disappeared through poverty and disease.

The Bandal Church had been given a facelift in 1990. The stucco was replaced with pink marble and the altarpieces were painted blue and gold, typical Indian fondness for colour, or some might say gaudiness! Grottos for statues and an abundance of coloured lights were added in abundance. The corridors were lined with explanations of prayers, told the stories of Biblical miracles and temptations. The church is a popular pilgrimage site and there were rooms "for genuine pilgrims" but "no bedding provided"!

My booking was at Hooghly Circuit House. I had only just arrived when I was 'summoned' to meet my next-door neighbour, Mr. T K Adhikari, secretary of a district-level Zilla Parishad. An elected official, he told me he was concerned with the alleviation of poverty among weavers, fishermen, and milk producers by giving bank loans to buy seeds, nets, looms, and knitting and sewing machines. He told me they had provided drinking water and subsidised rations to a hundred leprosy families in 1990 in Durgapur. He offered me whisky but I said I didn't drink alcohol, and not feeling comfortable with him, I escaped back to my room as soon as possible.

I lightened my bike by removing the pannier bags and went out on a quest – to find the 'Dutch octagonal church' I had read about it in the Lonely Planet travel guide. The architecture of many old buildings showed European influences, Dutch, Portuguese, Danish, French, and British. They had also left behind their churches and cemeteries. The Dutch cemetery at Chinsura with its Victorian grave architecture of urns and obelisks, all very neatly maintained. was easy to find. Chinsura also had a Church of North India, an Anglican church. The Rector thought that his church was the Dutch Church, but shared my suspicion that it was from the twentieth century, and it was definitely not octagonal. He opened the church for me; tinsel was strung across the ceiling and a harmonium stood on the altar steps

On the way, I noticed a highly decorated building with a pretty doorway and three sides visible. A man said it was now 'doctor's rooms' with very nice marble floors, and that it had previously been a dance hall. I wished I could have seen the floors. I took a couple of photos. It was definitely not rectangular and had intricate carving on the roof line. I was sure it was the missing Dutch church.

Before it got dark, I rushed off to find the Armenian church, also in Chinsura. I found the Church of St John, dating from 1692. The caretaker explained that there were no parishioners at Chinsura anymore. People came for a picnic on the feast of St John the Baptist. The church was locked but I could squint through a crack in the door and it looked similar to a Greek orthodox church, with many gilded icons. There were gravestones on the ground around the outside of the church, early ones in Armenian script, and later ones in Armenian and English. The most recent one I found was from 1922. The Armenian pastor said he was sorry but the Dutch church had vanished under the Ganges about fifteen years ago, somewhere near the Muslim College.

Returning to the Raj Era Circuit House I persuaded a boy from the kitchen, to go and buy some powdered milk, while I provided the tea bags, and we used his gas ring to make tea. There wasn't any food available at the Circuit House, but 'Bannerjee's Cabin' was suggested for vegetarian food. I found a Public Call Office and phoned Mr. Chandak. He was at his factory, thirty -five kilometres east of Calcutta, but I was invited to stay with his son and nephew, near Park Circus in central Calcutta.

December 29 th 1994

The Marble Palace

I took a taxi, with a driver who didn't know the way, but eventually found the enormous nineteenth-century, neo-classical mansion, known as The Marble Palace.

It was reputed for its Italian marble floors and matching ceilings, its bronzes, and sculptures. It was owned, and was still occupied by, descendants of Raja Rajendra Malik, Bahadur, and his seven brothers, who had made their money in property.

It held paintings by Rubens, Sir Joshua Reynolds, Rembrandt, and other artists of international repute, Chinese and French porcelain, and Belgian mirrors in the ballroom that reflected more than twenty crystal chandeliers. It was poorly lit and badly arranged, a collection of artefacts and bric-a-brac, reflecting a surfeit of money, rather than good taste. The army 'guide' didn't know anything about the exhibits or their dates. He just intoned "Chinese vase", "bronze", and "mirror" as we were shepherded around. He wanted baksheesh at the end of the tour. When I gave him ten rupees, he said there were four of them! I told him that if I hadn't had a fellow Indian tourist doctor with me, who spoke English, I wouldn't have been able to understand him!

After the Marble Palace, I wandered back to the main road, passing a dead female body, laid out on a house veranda, the face exposed and ringed with flowers. I assumed the neighbours would come and pay their respects before the bier was loaded onto a jeep and taken to a burning ghat.

Yellow trams shared the rather narrow main road with the usual traffic and, with what was a specialty mode of transport in Calcutta – a rickshaw pulled by a man. Since 1919 Calcutta has been the only place in India, and one of the few in the world, where fleets of hand-pulled rickshaws still ply the streets. The word rickshaw originates from the Japanese 'jinrikisha' which translates as 'human-powered vehicle'. Immigrants from British colonies like Canton, Shanghai, and Hong Kong, hit by poverty during the nineteenth and early twentieth century, and fleeing from devastating famines and displacement in China, introduced the rickshaw to Calcutta. where the large migrant, unemployed, unskilled, and uneducated populations of Bihar and

Orissa, are the twentieth-century official and unofficial rickshaw 'walas'.

The hand-built rickshaws seat one or two people and despite being banned by the Communist State Government in 1949 have survived and become an unofficial icon of the metropolis. The hand-pulled rickshaw is the only form of transport that can navigate the narrow side lanes and streets, often flooded because of poor drainage and low-lying land. They rent their vehicles from rickshaw owners, live on the streets and many save every rupee to send to their families back home. Some turn to alcohol and marijuana, known in India as Ganja, as they suffer from various diseases and medical problems associated with old age, and the physical stress of the job.

December 29, 1994

Hooghly to The Chandaks' Home.

I stopped at 8 am for tea and omelette and at nine o'clock, to buy bananas. I passed a huge Rath-chariot used to transport the gods at festivals and stopped to photograph a line of five temple domes with Ashoka trees. However, the road surface was not good and required my concentration. The architecture of many old buildings showed European influences.

The Chandak's home was reached without much trouble, apart from potholes and pollution. I had also written the address as Circus Lane instead of Circus Range. At one time I cycled up a one-way street, at the suggestion of a policeman! Another policeman held up the traffic for me, to cross a busy lane of traffic when he saw I was stuck in the centre of the road.

The Chandaks were a 'joint' Indian Hindu family of several generations, four aunts and uncles, their grown-up children and grandchildren, including three young boys. I tried, unsuccessfully, to make a family tree of them and counted about sixteen members. Ramesh and I had met Mr. Vishwanath Chandak and his wife Shanti, in Hardwar. He also had a textile mill. They had invited me to visit them when I arrived in Calcutta. I was given tea and shown into a huge white en-suite bedroom, 'given up' for me by one of the family, and was presented with a bouquet of flowers by a lovely smiling seven-year-old boy. It was a traditional way to welcome guests. I had a really good scrub and washed my hair.

I found all the ladies of the household sitting on the floor in the kitchen. They were jointly engaged in making Rotis, a twice or three times-a-week chore. Shanti, Mr Chandak's wife, told me they make over a hundred at a time. Kneading, oiling, rolling into small balls, rolling out into thin circles, and placing them on baking paper before deftly flinging them, Frisby-style, into a floured sheet

The family invited me to see some more of Calcutta and provided transport for me to the Indian Museum of Archaeology and told me that I would be picked up between 5.15 and 5.30 pm. at the Asiatic Society. The 1994 Archaeological Museum had interesting collections of prehistoric tools, and early archaeological finds, clay figurines, pots, and sculptures of different dynastic periods and of medieval times. Between museums, I treated myself to tea in the Oberoi Hotel and bought a black tee shirt to replace my 'once-white' one.

The Asiatic Society was founded in 1784. It had among its exhibits the oldest palm-leaf script of the 7th-century Gupta period. Palm leaves were inscribed in the Indian sub-continent and south Asia as far back as the 5th Century BC, before paper was used. The script developed was round and cursive to not damage the leaf and is the basis of many Indian and south-east Asian scripts. (Hindi writing developed from cutting messages onto rock and is angular). There was a black-inked paper with gold writing on it from Tibet, an Armenian parchment account of the Miracles of Jesus, an eleventh-century history of Shah Jehan's reign, and of Genghis Khan's, from the 16th century. Pictures, jewellery, and ornaments of Akbar's reign and a 1724 Catechism of Christian doctrine in Portuguese. An extract from a 1786 letter of Joseph Banks referred to the 'recent' Granary in Bihar, the Patna Golghar – the grain store intended to prevent perpetual famine.

In the evening Sandeep, Swathi, and Abhishek took me to see Calcutta by night. We went over the new suspension bridge, the Vidya Sagar Setu, completed in 1990 by a consortium of engineers. The French said it wasn't ready to be used but others said it was OK. The approach road flyovers were on spindly supports and have fallen down twice. – a comforting thought!

The south end of the Maidan had been revamped and furnished with dancing fountains whose coloured lights changed with the music. They were playing old Hindi film music when we arrived and then changed to Rabindranath Tagore Bengali music. South of the Strand was the area where traditional snacks are sold, bhelpuri, chaats, and bhaji. Going out to walk along and eat such snacks seems to be the equivalent of going for fish and chips! Not particularly healthy but enjoyable! South of the Strand, was where the Hooghly fishing boats were moored, their oil lamps illuminating the arched awnings of split cane and making them very attractive. Further along, the path was not lighted, Sandeep said it was dark and that is where lovers go, "so we will not disturb them"!

We went in the car again, to where there was a floating restaurant and to Park Road, the main hotel and restaurant area, decorated with coloured lights, in the trees and on the facades of the buildings, including Christmas scenes. Sandeep said that at Diwali and Durga festivals the whole of Calcutta is lit up with moving lights. We saw the racecourse on the Maidan and Eden gardens sports stadium, well known as an international cricket venue. Sandeep said he was against horseracing and is also against drinking coffee and tea, as they become addictions. I didn't mention that I drank about twelve cups of tea a day in Cambridge!

December 30, 1994

The Victoria Memorial

I was asked if I'd like breakfast or lunch. Thinking I'd spend the day in Calcutta I said I'd have breakfast. Apparently, lunch is at 9 am – rice etc so I'm having tea and toast for breakfast.

My other 'must see' was the white marble palace, the 'Victoria Memorial', set on the Maidan, in central Calcutta, built between 1906 and 1921, and dedicated to the memory of Queen Victoria. She was Empress of India from 1876 to her death in 1901. It was built, like the Brighton's Pavilion in Indo-Saracenic style, housing thirty-five galleries of books and paintings. I bought some prints of early landscape and town-scape watercolours and brushed up on my history of Calcutta in the Calcutta Gallery.

Calcutta (Kolkata) is the capital of the Indian state of West Bengal, in eastern India on the east bank of the Bhagirathi-Hooghly-Ganga River. From the 14th to the 16th centuries Calcutta was under the rule of the Bengal sultanate, it was conquered by the Mughal Empire in 1576.

In 1757 the British East India Company had the monopoly on the production and export of opium in India. The company bought opium from local traders, and later directly from farmers, and sold it at auction in Calcutta, from there it was smuggled to Canton in China by foreign traders, eventually leading to the First Opium War (1839 - 1842). The city was thus a colonial city developed by the East India Company, administered by Job Charnock, and after 1772 by the British Empire. Calcutta was the capital of the British Indian Empire until 1911 when the capital was relocated to Delhi. Calcutta grew rapidly in the 19th century to become the second most important city of the British Indian Empire, uniting Indian philosophies with Victorian traditions. Noted for its modern revolutionary history, ranging from leftist Naxalite to trade union movements, it is known variously as the City of Palaces, the City of Joy, and the Cultural Capital of India

Chapter 15

The Last Leg

We were going to Mr. V N Chandak's factory near the border with Bangladesh to celebrate the New Year. I showered and had porridge, which was more like semolina, and tea. Shortly after nine o'clock, I had a second fruit, sweet and savoury breakfast with the family. We went by car to the factory and its house.

I was taken to Mr. Chandak's office at the mill and was waiting for his chief executive's son, Mr. Manu, who was going to take me round the nearby villages on his scooter. Mr. Chandak has the same kind of mill as Ramesh, built in 1966, with an architect-designed, recent extension.

The factory employs about two thousand people dying, spinning and weaving polyester and viscose cloth. His textile weaving machines are new German and Italian ones, not second-hand, because Mr. Chandak insists on a good quality product that can be exported. The Prime Minister reduced the levy on machinery from 75% to 25%, and if you export the product there was a further reduction to 15%. Mr. Chandak has Mr. Birla as his chairman and has a Birla Management Citation. The factory is used as a Birla Management Centre training centre. There are quotes around the factory and grounds "We are not afraid of competition, let competition be afraid of us".

He uses a five-star system of management that is Japanese in origin. Mr. Chandak also has factories in Thailand. He supplies polyester-viscose cloth to a British company that makes it into goods for Marks and Spencer. Forty to fifty percent of the produce is exported to most of the countries of Europe. The old part of the factory has whitewashed walls, with flowering shrubs and grass in bays, to keep people from touching the walls and making them dirty. There are flowers, waterfalls, and lawns outside and pot plants and fresh flowers in the house and office. There are lots of bins for waste saying, "Use me".

Most of the workers are Moslem refugees from Bangladesh, which is only seventeen kilometres away. The factory is in a village and the whole village has piped water. Normally villages rely on ponds of green water. Many of the village houses are made of brick, not mud, and the largest village had a school, a hospital, and a college. The people in this area are mostly of the Ghosh caste, owning milk-producing cows and bullocks.

A new venture is for villages to be used in film making – negotiations are made with the village headman and panchayat council. Bananas are grown, and some jute, as well as rice and papayas. There was also a 'Mother and Child Centre', a Hygiene Lecture Hall, a Pottery centre with a kiln, and a Craft Centre – the gift of a benefactor in Brazil. The poorest people have ration cards to use in Government ration shops, giving them reduced prices for essential staples like dahl, rice, sugar and oil. I was told that Bangladeshi people also come from over the border, and get ration cards illegally.

I was taken to see the brickworks where twenty lakhs, twenty thousand, bricks are fired at a time. The moulded bricks are dried in the sun for a couple of days and then stacked in a section of the oval kiln where vertical fires bake them for twenty hours. The coal is from

Calcutta's hinterland, and the clay is from local villages. Cattle are used to rotate the mixer where clay and water go in the top and the mix comes out of the bottom.

Mr Chandak arranged for me to visit a school, whose nuns take orphans, and have a vocational training centre, of the non-religious type! The nine teachers, six of whom are nuns, have fifty children from slum areas and broken homes from the Park Circus area of Calcutta, as boarders. They stay on-site for six months. The Primary school had two hundred children. I had tea, pastries, and rasgullas with the Principal, Sister Juliana, and met Sr Annie and Sr. Salome. Their kitchen had a stainless-steel cooking range that burned wood or coal. A priest comes from a seminary where there are ten priests in training. Mr Aluj Sharma, who took me to the school, is a Nepali speaker, who comes from Darjeeling. He has been working with Eastern Spinning for eight years.

The factory employs 1600 people, 204 of whom were staff, in three shifts, 7-3, 3-11, and 11-7 am. The factory was very clean, with mosaic floors and fluff-blowing and sucking machines to keep the area clean. There were some very long automated machines, marked 'Export'. The dying plant dyed the raw material, which comes from India, especially from Madhya Pradesh, and some from Taiwan, before fluffing it, rolling and twisting it onto 27000 spindles, (11000 in the new plant).

Mr. Chandak let me wish Ramesh and his family a Happy New Year. He also invited me to choose a sari from the three he had laid out on a coffee table in the office. There was a blue, a pink, and an orange one. I chose the orange one!

Ramesh rang after twelve and said he was not coming to Calcutta. I will go back to the UK on the fourteenth of January. I was sitting in the sun. I wished I could have lain down, I felt I could just go to sleep. I have not slept properly for three nights as I have been worried about my son Steven, and the non-arrival of my case from Patna, as it contains important document.

Mr. Chandak is flying to Bombay on 8th January. He will take some of my luggage. I hope Dr. Ajeet Singh will get my case to me by January 4th. Mr Chandak said I could stay in a flat he owns, and he would give me a servant, and I could take meals at his house. I said I'd stay at the YWCA, but he said I wouldn't get accommodation. I didn't tell him I'd made a provisional booking. I didn't want to intrude on his hospitality. He was giving Lepra 2010 rupees from the Lion's club. He introduced me to the President on New Year's Eve. He was going to get me up on the stage to tell everybody what I was doing, but I had gone to the house, with his sister-in-law to get more clothes on, as it was freezing in the half-built hall with no doors.

The New Year Cultural Programme organised by the staff, Savita and Swathi, Mr Chandak's daughters, will begin at seven o'clock. It includes dinner. Apparently, we will be going back to Calcutta when it finishes. The programme included dancing, singing, a quiz and sketches by children and young people. There were stick dances by older girls and solos by little children. The sketches were beyond me, being in Bangla. I was so tired that it was hard to keep awake! When the show finished, we went back to Calcutta in the car and I was in bed by 2 am.

January 1, 1995

Calcutta to Diamond Harbour 62 km/53 miles

Despite returning from the New Year celebrations in the early morning hours, I woke at 6.30 am.

After tea and slices of papaya, I left with Sandeep's translations of my journey, by 7.30 am. I was out of the centre of town by 8.30 am. The road to Diamond Harbour ran south from Calcutta, through villages with holiday complexes advertised as 'resorts', embryo apartments offered 'country homes', both cheek-by-jowl with factory compounds. In some places, the roadside ditches were used to grow seedling rice, densely packed patches of lime green, like newly sown grass. These would be removed later and transplanted roughly into newly ploughed fields by scrawny, stooping dhoti-clad men standing barefoot in the water. The final spacing is done by lines of women, bent double from the waist, moving in unison as they rhythmically plant the individual stalks in water, to the left, centre and right, a few inches apart, before moving backwards down the paddy field.

With the expected arrival of hundreds of thousands of pilgrims to the Ganga Sagar Mela, many separate sections of the road were being repaired, and even widened. Piecemeal repairs by gangs of dozen men, melting drums of tar in rusty bodies of what looked like steam engines, their cylindrical bodies reminding me of Stevenson's Rocket. Barefoot labourers carted molten tar and raked stones into it, half a road at a time so that it was still possible to get by, if you could brave the thick choking fumes of the burning tyres, that were being used, as well as wood from wayside trees, to fuel the fires.

Ganga Sagar island is part of the delta of the Ganges River, with its ever-shifting course, subject to monsoons and cyclones, silting and flooding. The island had to be approached by ferries. There was an unusual element to the traffic today, a continual stream of lorries, packed with young men and blaring film music, obviously going on a picnic on their New Year holiday. They would give me a cheer as they passed me on the tree-lined roads, between the water-filled ditches, and paddy fields. Herons and egrets stalked these watery spots and I marvelled at the thin bridges of sagging bamboo poles that connected the roadside with the village houses. There were no handrails to cling to! Crossing them for me would have been only a shade better than walking a tightrope.

After Kalpe the road divided and I was on my way to the ocean. Ganga Sagar means 'the end of the Ganges'. It is traditionally the site of a huge religious mela in the first half of January. The temple of

Kapil Muni, a pink, blue, and white confection, overlooks the shallow waters of the Bay of Bengal which laps the island. The island itself is called Sagar Island. The road from Kalpe was a pilgrim route from Calcutta. Buses, coaches, private cars, and even government cars, would soon be careering along it to the mela where pilgrims would occupy the dharmshalas, the tourist hotel, and the vast tented city that was being erected there, complete with electricity and the usual facilities. The crowds were something that I wanted to avoid, having read many reports of people killed in stampedes of pilgrims. I would get there before the mela began. and leave the next day.

Hundreds of buses and trucks were going to New Year picnic places, with loudspeaker systems blaring, and vacuum horns wailing. Most of them were staying around Diamond Harbour but others went on – I wondered where? Diamond Harbour is half-way between Calcutta and the Bay of Bengal.

At the Diamond Harbour Tourist Hostel, I ordered toast and omelette for my breakfast. The toast didn't come, just bread and another omelette. I sent the bread back to be toasted! There were no hot drinks so I went across the road for cigarettes, bananas, and a bottle of juice. I had to take the bottle back later!

I then sat in the sun on my balcony, facing the Hooghly, watching country boats, with lateen sails, taking people for trips. The boats were steered from the rear with one oar. Fleets of sampans were lying midstream – a reminder of the trade with China in the opium days. Snack stalls, coconut sellers, and hat and bag vendors were assembled outside the front of the tourist hostel, known as Hotel Sagarika. Rickshaws were offering trips to a lighthouse. I noticed that there were security guards in front of the hotel. There were flatbed cycles to ferry larger groups of people around. It was quite pleasant when the picnic trucks were not passing through, and much quieter! I decided that it was the noise that I disliked, lorries, bus horns, bells ringing, vendors and people shouting!

I went for a little walk along the prom and found the lorry picnic sites and more fishing boats. I ordered a lager once back in the hotel, and was told it would come in half an hour – it didn't. I went to find it after an hour, and took the opportunity to order my dinner, vegetable-rice, and chicken chow-mein. Rice and chow-mein were 'off' the menu, and when my food arrived it was cold chicken and potatoes, for 65 rupees, washed down with a lager beer for 45 rupees. I went to pay my room charge and got a discount for being a single person.

January 2nd 1995

Diamond Harbour to Ganga Sagar 75 km/ 47 miles

Up and ready by 6.15 am, I was given a cup of tea by the manager.

I was 40 kilometres from the Kakdwip ferry. Some of the signs were in Hindi again. At Harwood Point by 10 am. I stopped for tea, bananas, and bread twists and bought two eggs. On the first of several ferries, I met a nice man and we got along well in Hindi. I overshot the turn-off for the next ferry. I should have taken the road to Kashipur, which was 4 kilometres before Kakdwip. By 10.30 am. I was over the other-side of another ferry crossing, and a fellow passenger gave me tea at a place called Kachuberia, 32 km from Ganga Sagar.

Narrow bridges were being repainted, roads were being widened into two lanes where possible, and parts of the road was being resurfaced. I stopped for a picnic at 12 o'clock and headed for Kakdwip, where I took photos of a keel being laid for a new wooden boat. The next ferry to Ganga Sagar Island was a large one with a flat roof and standing room only, for about a hundred people. The wheel house was on the roof and it all looked very unstable to me!

On arrival at Ganga Sagar Island, I headed to the beach for 'arrival' photos, the culmination of about 3000 kilometres or 2000 miles of cycling. Twelve weeks with stops for my visit to the Lepra centre, and a couple of bouts of illness, not to mention my time exploring Calcutta and visiting the Chandak factory.

I left my bike with a couple of English-speaking men, and waded into the stream, and crossed the mud flats to the sea proper. When the water was up to my knees, the nephew of my bike minders had a photo session, of me in my Lepra tee-shirt, carefully preserved to be still white, and the bike. I gave them a polaroid photo as thanks.

The DM's chowkidar wouldn't let me stay as I had no letter. I ended up in the Youth Hostel for forty rupees. There was no tea or food. A new Tourist Lodge was being built and will open on the 8th of January. I went to a dhaba for tea but he had no food. A dhaba opposite him made me two omelettes with cold rice and dahl. He would have hot food at 8 o'clock. I ordered half a plate of rice, sabzi and fish with no chilli .and bought a Limca to take to the Youth Hostel. It was twilight at five thirty and the sun was setting

A huge area was being prepared for the Mela crowds – a bamboo framework, with split cane mats covering the roof and sides. Electric lights were being installed – they would be taken away after the Mela. A man I met on the way to Ganga Sagar told me that there was only one doctor in all the islands of the delta. A doctor comes to the Mela on the 13th of January and goes away afterward. The mela begins on the feast of Maha Sankranti, the 14th of January, and lasts for two weeks. King Bhagarithi's relations were turned to ashes by Vishnu's eyes here at Ganga Sagar. Kapil Muni was a sage of Vishnu, and the temple is named after him.

My earache and sore throat were back again. At least there was food and tea available here on Ganga Sagar Island. By 6 pm it was inky dark and I had two hours to kill before dinner. I get very lonely in the evenings and not being able to speak Bangla adds to the problem. Although several words are the same root, people say they can't speak Hindi. I have noticed that Indian people are fiercely

275

attached to their state. Is this provincial or nationalist? I couldn't decide.

A young lad came to tell me that the lights go out at 8.15 pm in the rooms. Corridor lights seem to link to the batteries under the staircase. There was supposed to be solar power for hot water and for when lights are not working. I had seen a man fiddling with the inverter batteries in the DM's Garden. I had my fish supper, but it had very fine bones, and there was hardly any fish, so I had mainly rice and vegetables with my Limca and went to bed.

Chapter 16

Whisky and Hot Milk

January 3, 1995

Ganga Sagar to Diamond Harbour 75 km/47 miles

I had a glass of hot milk, bought two bread buns and was on the road by 7.30 am. I was feeling rotten with a temperature, sore throat and earache, but I felt that I must reach Diamond Harbour, where at least there was food and drink.

Reaching the ferry by 930 am. I found out that the next ferry crossing was at 10 am. I felt too ill to cope with the bike and bike admirers, so I left the immediate ferry area, and went to buy some more bread and have a cup of tea.

I was queuing for the ferry ticket when my young friend of yesterday, who worked as a crew on the ferry, arrived and took charge of the bike. I was so thankful. I took a polaroid photo of him and he insisted on pushing the bike all the way to the main road on the other side of the creek. He then went into a shop and bought me a green coconut, and offered me biscuits. I said no but he bought two bananas which he tucked into my bar bag, and then slipped in a little green box, which I thought was probably a carton of fruit juice. When I came to drink it later, I discovered it was a box of glucose powder, a popular source of energy for invalids in India.

Before the buying episode I had given him my address, and he gave me his, getting a man to write it down for him. The scribe demanded one of my address labels 'because he was a government official.' If I'd felt better, I'd have loved to tell him that I didn't know him!

The forty plus miles to Diamond Harbour were a nightmare. My kidneys hurt, my legs hurt, I was running a temperature and there was a headwind too! I kept promising myself stops and treats every ten kilometres, to give me something to concentrate on. My rewards would be a banana, bread, a drink or two sweets. The last three kilometres were very long – I'm sure they measure to the outskirts of the towns, not the town centre, hence the 0 km sign one sometimes sees!

I made it to Diamond Harbour Tourist Hostel! I remember supporting myself on the counter, and being asked how long I wanted to stay, I said something like, "I'll tell you in the morning!"

I ordered a glass of hot milk, a whisky, a tray of tea and some dinner. I had to ring them again, from my room phone, as the order didn't come. I lay on the balcony of room eight, till the sun went off me, and then went to lie on the bed, and slept for an hour or two, after the whisky and hot milk.

When I woke, I went through my bags and found some Neurofen tablets. I had thought of going to a chemist shop but looking from my balcony I could see that the rickshaws and taxis had gone away. At 9 o'clock my chicken curry, rice and aloo gobi came. I had it with some of my tomatoes, after washing the cauliflower in the bathroom sink, because it was too spicy for me. I learnt this trick in Aurangabad in Bihar! There was a little mouse in my room, so I shut him in the bathroom – I will probably have a fit when I go to the toilet in the night!

My nose was running and my sinuses were blocked, my throat was sore and my eyes were weeping. I hoped I'd feel better in the morning.

I would leave at 8.30 or 9 am as I didn't want to hit the rush hour in Calcutta, I'd have to phone Mr. V. N. Chandak on the way.

January 4, 199

The Return to Calcutta and Bombay

The next morning, I discovered that there was a demonstration and no traffic was allowed on the road, apart from bikes! It would last for four or five hours, so it was a good thing that I had not taken a bus, or asked for a lift in a lorry. I had been tempted. At least there would be no heavy traffic to worry about, no speeding buses and blaring horns.

Not surprisingly, I don't remember much after leaving Diamond Harbour, on my way back to Calcutta. I remember stopping at a craft museum, I can picture the path up to the door but that is all. I didn't keep up my journal either.

I knew I was planning to contact Justice Basu again and visit the leprosy centre at Purulia. I intended to call on the Mother Theresa nuns and visit the Botanic Gardens, besides sorting out my flight to Bombay.

I had ten days until my flight to the UK.

My journal mentioned that, when I was changing my travel cheques, I made a provisional booking at the Calcutta YWCA. Mr Chandak had offered me the use of a flat of his, complete with a female servant, and meals at his house. However, I can't remember my return to the Chandaks, I can't remember anything except being in Bombay with Prem and Ramesh. Even today I have no idea when I left Calcutta

Epilogue

July 2025

It is now thirty years since my solo bike ride down the Ganges and the third time that I have tried to complete my account of the experience. I typed the first draft in 1995 using the diaries and journals I kept at the time, supplemented by hundreds of photographs taken along the route. The reels of film were numbered and each time I inserted a new reel of film in the camera I made a note in my journal. They were a good 'aide memoire'!

Mr Chandak and his family must have looked after me, and arranged for myself and the bike to fly to Bombay, for my next memory was being with Prem and Ramesh. I suppose I had a temperature and possibly a return of my pneumonia.

Through Ramesh's family connections, the local branch of the Lions Club International, invited me to give a talk about Leprosy Eradication, and the prestigious newspaper the Times of India interviewed me.

Prem made sure I was presentable for the talk. My hair was cut and dyed, and my ears pierced, so that I could borrow some of Prem's jewellery for the meeting. I wanted to wear the orange sari given to me by Mr Chandak's daughter, so Prem's dressmaker made the essential petticoat and blouse to wear with it. When the evening came,

I was adorned in Prem's diamond earrings and a ruby and pearl necklace.

Ramesh sat in the front row of the audience. Laksmi Singh was there too!

I spoke about the work Lepra was doing in Bhabua, conducting surveys to find people with leprosy, the treatment regime, and how it was possible to cure a leprosy sufferer at a cost of £21 per person. Of course, I was asked about my impressions of India, and what I liked and disliked. I was diplomatic with my answers, after all this branch of the Lions Club International was going to give me a donation for Lepra.

I spoke about the trek to Gangotri and mentioned the religious sites I had visited and the lovely people who had helped me. Bihar had the reputation of being the most backward and lawless State, so I purposely mentioned that the Bihari people I met were extremely friendly and helpful. Inviting me to take tea with them, giving me free teas, biscuits, and sometimes breakfasts!

The Times of India newspaper article found its way to Lepra in England, and I was invited to give a talk about 'My Cycle Yatra' at the Welcome Foundation Headquarters in London. This must have gone down well because I was asked to repeat it at the Lepra Annual General Meeting in Colchester later that year. That was a much more relaxed occasion and I told the story of the Allahabad waiter remarking that he would be my "special friend". One Cambridge paper published an article saying I had raised £10,000 for Lepra; I was described as 'super-Gran' by another!

Collecting the pledges, after I got home, took nine months. It had to be done in the evenings after work, and at weekends. Sponsors needed reminding about my "Granny down the Ganges" ride, as four months had passed since I first told them about my cycle ride for leprosy treatment. Many people were out, away, or doing weekend shopping. I often had to visit houses more than once.

281

My bike managed the Ganges pilgrimage perfectly! Not a single puncture! I was sorry that my bike computer stopped working and wished I had thought to bring a spare one. Healthwise, I was very grateful for the extra suspension through the seat as I had a history of spinal curvature that aggravated nerves in my neck and arms as they became compressed.

I had three or four bouts of illness, which were at one time diagnosed as pneumonia, but despite some painful bites, at least I didn't get malaria! I lost quite a lot of weight and my hair turned greyer. My diet was vegetarian, though it included eggs when available and occasionally fish, but was restricted by my dislike of red and green chillies. For my safety I ate only fruits that I could peel, like oranges and bananas. My 'go to' breakfast was an omelette without chillies, and lots of tea, without sugar.

Dhaba owners mix sugar with the milk when boiling it at the beginning of the day, and so I felt that if I ordered three cups of tea it would be worth the stall holder's effort to make me tea from scratch, without sugar. Tomatoes, once they were available at lower altitudes, were my main vegetable and I would wash them at night with my filtered water, ready for eating the next day. Bananas were my staple pick-me-up. I would count how many I had each day. Whenever I felt weak, I had a banana or two! After I discovered boiled eggs, they were my evening treat, whenever I could find an egg man. I bought them with the shells on, and would be given a pinch of salt wrapped in newspaper. This restricted diet helped me to avoid stomach upsets.

I collected more than £10,000 from UK donors and a further £5000 was donated by Indian supporters. At today's exchange rates this would be multiplied tenfold! News about me was reported in Indian National and State newspapers but I had usually moved on before seeing the publications. Unbeknown to me, a TV interview was planned for my homecoming but it had to be cancelled when, at the last minute, the airline changed my ticket, and I arrived at Heathrow a day later. The girls were disappointed about not being on TV and instead had to make do with a newspaper photo with me, in the rain, in Grantchester.

My office friends welcomed me back with a sign saying

"Fantastic achievement! 2000-year-old local government worker tackles 56 miles on a Mountain Bike!"

South Cambridgeshire District Council presented me with a £50 cheque for Lepra.

I intended to settle down, doing more short local charity rides at weekends, but the idea of doing another long ride, before my back and neck seized up completely, resulted in "Granny Goes Cycling again". This time my route included different Lepra projects in India.

I cycled from Calcutta down the east coast of India, over 3000-foot-high mountains, to a Lepra centre in western Orissa, to a tribal area, where there was a special unit performing reconstructive surgery, on hands and feet permanently deformed by leprosy. I then continued northwards finishing at Christmas 1996 with 'A Leprosy Conference' in Bhabua.

Lepra India asked me to consider cycling through the Kalahandi region, known as the 'drought, hunger. death district', but I was unable to save up my annual leave this time and only had five weeks to cover 1500 miles, so I couldn't fit it in.

My accommodation was of the 'concrete floor' variety rather than the 'bed with mosquito net' kind. There was a change of language too. Oriya is nothing like Hindi, and it is written in a different script. However, I carried pamphlets printed in Oriya, with details of the signs and symptoms of leprosy.

Back at work in Cambridge, I enrolled in an evening class to study A-level Human Biology, with the idea of taking early retirement at the age of 60, and going out to India to train as a physiotherapist, specialising in the prevention of deformity.

283

Somehow my exploits, both rides for Lepra, became known to the High Commissioner for India, and I was invited to a presentation at the Houses of Parliament. When I said I wanted to work in India, the High Commissioner offered me a five-year visa. This was later extended, and I worked in Bihar, Uttar Pradesh and Orissa States, in several Districts, until the Indian government took over Leprosy control in 2003.

I returned to England in 2003 and heard about the hundreds of children and adults dying of HIV/AIDs in many countries around the world.

Providing homes for, fundraising, and living with HIV/AIDs orphan children occupied my next twelve years. I spent six months in India, and six in the UK. I promoted Brighter Future International Trust, started by an Indian friend and his brother, which cared for the children of leprosy sufferers as well as their parents, mainly leprosy colony residents, in the state of Andhra Pradesh in South India.

Registering Brighter Future with the Charity Commission, I set about finding sponsors for the children and raising general funds for the organisation. I went to India again in February 2005, this time to open a permanent home for children of leprosy patients, donated by a gentleman friend of my daughter, so that they could go to school, and be treated like 'normal' children. Today there are 75 children in that home, 35 boys and 40 girls.

I suggested that Brighter Future's Director, and the government Leprosy officer, who was also HIV officer, make a survey of a village where there was a large trucking community, to confirm the hearsay evidence of hundreds of villagers dying of AIDS, and to identify HIV orphans. If there was a need, we would buy some property and convert it to provide a home for the children. Usually, their parents had died and they had been infected at birth. Generally, it was itinerant builders and transport workers who infected their wives.

Our survey of one small town, with a population of 53.032, revealed 500 HIV/AIDS infected families, with parents dying and 217 children, who may or may not be infected, but who will surely be orphaned. I made myself responsible for fundraising and publicity. My appeal for funding, asking for a bag of cement, a load of bricks etc enabled us to open our first home for seven HIV orphans in October 2005.

The children in our care had to be given clean water, clean food and living conditions to give them the best chance of surviving. They did not have chilli as sickness was a common side effect. There was no way to determine how long they would live or when they would die, and they were susceptible to additional morbidities like TB. Over the next five years we opened three homes in different districts of Andhra Pradesh and had almost 100 HIV children in our care. Initially there was no way to control or cure childhood HIV/AIDS. In 2012 the children in our home became the first to receive anti-HIV/AIDS treatment through the Clinton Foundation.

Several of these orphans are still in contact with me. They tell me about their work and their marriages. Some have children of their own, now that the mother and baby can be treated, to prevent the HIV passing to the baby. For a while I was the chairperson of Brighter Future International Trust besides fundraising, writing a monthly newsletter for sponsors, finding sponsors and spending 6 months every year as nurse, teacher and "aunty" to the children.

I was in contact with Ramesh, as he had sponsored a doctor for the HIV children. Ramesh had started a home for senior citizens, who for various reasons, could not live in the traditional joint family home. In 1917 he asked me to look at it and see if I could suggest any improvements for the residents. I took up the challenge, and spent six months at the home, painting the doors in colours of the residents' choice, adding pictures, starting an art class, making an English garden accessible for wheelchair users, and encouraging residents to write articles in a blog called in English 'The Voice of Awaas'.

There were some residents who could not afford the necessary rent increase, and I decided to try and raise a Hardship Fund to help them.

In 2019, on June 25th, I started "Granny Gets on her Bike Again" - a 1000-mile ride, around the English and French channel coasts. Time was no barrier; however, the expense of accommodation, was a restriction on my days of cycling. I included sightseeing with the 32 days of riding, and was blessed by meeting lovely people, having good weather, being sponsored by family and friends, and people I met en-route. I raised £3000 for the Hardship Fund for three senior citizens at Awaas Seva Sadan.

Then it was back to India to the old people to help, wherever I could, encouraging exercise, competitions and arranging the Christmas celebrations, including a party for the residents, and a sports day for the staff.

I left India just two weeks before Covid (coronavirus) closed the UK/international borders on March 23rd 2020. I was able to keep in touch with the spread and severity of Covid in India, a country with 1300 million people, through my ex-colleagues and friends. Our UK televisions showed the lack of oxygen for covid victims in India, the dearth of medicines and hospital places, and the horror of bodies unable to be properly cremated or buried.

My ex-physiotherapy colleague from Bhabua, Rajni, was now the Chief Leprosy Officer of Bihar State for Lepra, and his home village was near Bhabua. I asked Rajni about the situation in his village and the surrounding areas. He told me about the difficulties the poor, rural population had trying to get tested and treated. I decided to do another bike ride. However, being over 75, I was one of the groups who were to isolate, so as to not catch or spread Covid. I heard that the Prime Miniter had been cautioned for riding his bike more than 5 miles from his residence. I got out my Ordnance Survey map and drew a circle, in pencil, with a radius of 10 miles from my house, thinking that 10 miles distant, mainly among fields, would be the equivalent of 5 miles in the middle of London!

I knew from previous training runs that I would not be meeting many people. I would be above pedestrians in height, and could keep my distance if I had to stop and talk to anybody. I pencilled in my routes on the map, noted my bike computer readings and cycled around the villages of Suffolk from May to September 2021, until I has covered 2000 miles. This time the newspaper called me "Octogenarian Granny" I asked my faithful supporters of previous fundraising events to sponsor me again, and sent the money to Rajni in India.

I was able to work through Rajni and his staff to provide education about the disease, and treatment. Rajni selected five villages and three urban areas for me to help. I sent £200 to Rajni to get masks made, buy recommended medicines, and encourage the local village 'unqualified medical practitioners', (generally referred to in the West as 'quacks') to provide their services for free. We gave them blood pressure gauges, thermometers, and oximeters, while Rajni's staff started education about covid, its do's and don'ts.

As sponsorship came in, we were able to buy an oxygen making machine, more medicines, recommended by a chest specialist relation, and provide protein supplement foodstuffs' We paid the cost of going 12 miles to get tested for the poorest people, paid for wood for some cremations and were fortunate to avoid many deaths. Rajni told me recently that village people are now more aware about good nutrition and many grow their own vegetables and buy fish from local ponds.

I didn't think of my Ganga Yatra until 2025 when I made some sketches from a few of my photos and decided that at the age of 87 I

287

had better finish the job, try and get published and hopefully raise funds for Lepra.

The British Empire Leprosy Relief Association, renamed Lepra, was started in 1924. It returned to India in 1989 providing equipment and training, while the Indian government paid salaries and the Japanese government provided the drugs. Leprosy, TB, HIV/Aids, India is the world leader in most diseases but having a population of over 1300 million people such infection rates are not surprising. So far only Yellow Fever does not exist in India.

With their work in the field of leprosy and intimate contact with village populations, Lepra decided to take on yet another neglected tropical disease. Awareness about, and the treatment of Lymphatic Filaria, what we know as elephantiasis, is needed. There are 70 million cases in India. Essentially, they need special footwear, frequent washing and thorough drying, antifungal cream, and attention to every open wound. One of my friends provides antiseptic cream to the poorest sufferers in the districts covered by my dear friend, teacher and ex-colleague, Rajni. Another presentation of the disease enlarges the scrotum and is very debilitating socially, mentally, and physically.

Meanwhile 10,000 new leprosy cases were registered in Bihar last year, 100.000 in India!

Perhaps, God willing, and Coronavirus permitting, I may be able to do something to help assist the poorest people with filaria. Another Bike Ride?

My Indian friends want me to stay in India until I die,

My family ask me when I am going to stay at home!

GLOSSARY

allu paratha	fried flatbreads of flour, potato & spices,
ashram	a spiritual retreat, the dwelling of a sage
CH	Circuit House, for government guests
chai	tea, usually ready sweetened
chowkidar	watchman or gatekeeper
corrie	horseshoe shaped valley formed by ice
dhaba	small open sided stall or kiosk selling tea.
Divali	autumn festival of lights
Deepawali	autumn festival of lights
Dosa	a thin, savoury crepe of gram flour & rice
DM	District Magistrate,
Ganga	the river Ganges, Gangaji, or Ma Ganges,
ghat	steps on a riverbank or a range of mountains
joss sticks	type of incense
MOT	vehicle road worthiness test in UK
namkeen	savoury or salty snack
paddy	rice in husk, a field of rice
pan	a digestive of betel nut, & lime paste, and
puja	act of worship
PWD	Public Works Department
rhus	caster-oil plant or sumac tree
Shiva	one of the principal deities of Hinduism,
sindoor	red mark worn in the hair by married women
tilak	a mark of powder or paste on the forehead
tray-tea	tea served in a pot with separate milk
Vishnu	one of the three principal deities
eliche	cardamon

ADDENDA

AUTHORS NOTE

Born in London in 1937 and educated at St Joseph's Convent, before joining Hendon Grammar School Sixth Form, where she took A-levels in History, Geography and Economics. Manya graduated in 1958 with Honours in Geography and chose teaching as a career. Manya married Tony, a scientist, in 1959. Her teaching career dovetailed with marriage and bringing up twin daughters, born in 1960 and adopting two sons in 1972 and 1973.

Always keen to learn, Manya added DIY and gardening to her skills. After her husband's early death at the age of 50 Manya learned to type and found an office job in Cambridge that used her map-reading skills.

She took 'A' level Human Biology when she was 58, in preparation for volunteering in a medical field, after taking early retirement at 60.

Her retirement in 1997 became the springboard for raising funds for various charities, using the only skill left to her, the ability to cycle. Manya did four long cycle rides to raise funds for various charities.

Inspired by her visit to the Ganges valley, Manya went out to India to train as a physiotherapy technician, working with leprosy patients until 2003.

Living with, and fundraising for, HIV/AIDS orphans occupied the next twelve years. After another eight years helping in a home for senior citizens in India, Manya retired.

Now at 88 she has an electric bike, lives in Bury St Edmunds and counts her blessings.

pmanya.norris@gmail.com

If you would like to know more about Lepra
lepra@lepra.org.uk

If you have enjoyed this book, I would love to see your comments on Amazon

If you would like to follow my exploits, I have a blog on *http://pmanya.blogspot.com*

Printed in Dunstable, United Kingdom